THE WORLD OF SHAKESPEARE

THE WORLD
OF SHAKESPEARE

Love and Other Pastimes,

Animals and Monsters,

Plants and Flowers

Alan Dent

Taplinger Publishing Company
New York

First paperback edition, in one volume, published in 1979 by
TAPLINGER PUBLISHING CO., INC.
New York, New York

ISBN 0-8008-8597-X

Contents

PART ONE

Love and
Other Pastimes

CONTENTS

Contents

A-BED

This is a curious adverb of state or condition which Shakespeare uses half-a-dozen times and more, and in just as many different degrees of meaning.

When Duke Frederick misses his daughter Celia one morning, and asks what can have happened to her, an attendant Lord uses a phrase which can only mean that Celia went to bed, or was put to bed, in her normal way (*As You Like It,* II, ii, 5):

> The ladies, her attendants of her chamber,
> Saw her **a-bed**; and, in the morning early,
> They found the bed untreasured of their mistress.

She had risen early and run away with Rosalind to the Forest of Arden. Hence the whole comedy that follows.

When Sir Toby informs Sir Andrew that 'not to be **a-bed** after midnight is to be up betimes', he is being general rather than particular, though it takes some time for him to explain his breezy epigram to the foolish knight. Both sports and pastimes enter into the discussion (*Twelfth Night,* II, iii, 1).

When the King in his early-morning tirade before Agincourt has those two lines (*King Henry V,* IV, iii, 64):

> And gentlemen in England now **a-bed**
> Shall think themselves accurst they were not here; . . .

he never fails to thrill one by conjuring up a marvellous vision of a million citizens of England about to rise for the day, and still blearily unaware of what is happening in France that same morning. The two lines have in them quite as much imagination as the fifty-odd that Chorus has to speak at the beginning of the same Act.

When Guiderius and Arviragus, the two boys in the care

of old Belisarius, longingly discuss the civilization which only their supposed father has known, they come away with lovely images in a passage (*Cymbeline*, III, iii, 29) where only the word 'a-bed' is cryptic and gives us pause:

> GUIDERIUS: . . . Haply this life is best,
> If quiet life be best; sweeter to you
> That have a sharper known; well corresponding
> With your stiff age; but unto us it is
> A cell of ignorance; travelling **a-bed**; . . .
> ARVIRAGUS: . . . What should we speak of
> When we are old as you? when we shall hear
> The rain and wind beat dark December, how,
> In this our pinching cave, shall we discourse
> The freezing hours away? We have seen nothing . . .

But what 'travelling a-bed' means, no editor of Shakespeare, from George Steevens downwards, seems able to tell us.

Elsewhere and everywhere else one is 'a-bed' for the purposes of sleep and rest, tossing and turning, procreation or parturition, or simply in being ill and hoping to get well again – or failing in that hope.

ACTING

This art can of course be regarded as sport or pastime only when it is amateur as distinct from professional. Thus the strolling players in *Hamlet* are not considered here since they acted for a living; whereas the troupe in *A Midsummer Night's Dream* gain admittance since they were by profession weaver, carpenter, joiner, tinker, tailor, and bellows-mender respectively.

The same may be said of the rather shapeless and ill-directed little inset drama of The Nine Worthies in the fifth act of *Love's Labour's Lost*. This is a nice muddle from the very beginning when the King of Navarre announces the cast in an undecided mixture of prose and verse (v, ii, 529):

> Here is like to be a good presence of Worthies.
> He [Armado] presents Hector of Troy; the swain
> [Costard the clown], Pompey the Greek; the parish curate,
> Alexander; Armado's page, Hercules; the pedant,
> Judas Maccabaeus:
>> And if these four Worthies in their first show thrive,
>> These four will change habits, and present the other five.

Why does young Shakespeare in this little pageant-play give us only five Worthies instead of nine? The original nine are usually supposed to be three pagans, three Jews, and three Christians. The usual choice is Hector, Alexander, and Julius Caesar for the pagans; Joshua, David, and Judas Maccabaeus for the Jews; and King Arthur, Charlemagne, and Godfrey of Bouillon for the worthy Christians. But why has the dramatist – in this interlude in what is usually reckoned to be his first play – given us an incomplete list of five Worthies including Pompey and Hercules who are not on the traditional list? Doubtless young Shakespeare was deliberately wrong in the matter, just as John Dryden a century later was impeccably correct:

> Nine worthies were they called, of different rites,
> Three Jews, three pagans, and three Christian Knights.

Hamlet's speech to the players (III, ii, 1) is very well known, and most playgoers agree with his rounding upon the strolling troupe and telling them (not unlike a Granville-Barker of our own day) not to over-act, or over-shout, or over-gesticulate, and not to hold, as 'twere, a *distorting* mirror up to nature. But much less well-known – and well worth an occasional reading or even a performance – is W. S. Gilbert's satirical playlet, *Rosencrantz and Guildenstern* in which the First Player gives an indignant back-answer to Hamlet, putting him in his princely place:

Sir, we are beholden to you for your good counsels. But we would urge upon your consideration that we are accomplished players, who have spent many years in learning our profession; and we would venture to suggest that it would better befit your lordship to confine yourself to such matters as your lordship may be likely to understand. We, on our part, may have our own ideas as to the duties of heirs-apparent; but it would ill become us to air them before your lordship, who may be reasonably supposed to understand such matters more perfectly than your very humble servants.

Some may agree that this is a well-deserved rebuke, and a rebuke as just as it is eloquent.

ANGLING

Fishing with rod and line was one of the many games and sports which Cleopatra practised when Antony was away at his war-making. Quite early in the play she says to her handmaid Charmian (*Antony and Cleopatra*, II, v, 10):

> Give me mine **angle**,—we'll to the river: there,
> My music playing far off, I will betray
> Tawny-finn'd fishes; my bended hook shall pierce
> Their slimy jaws; and, as I draw them up,
> I'll think them every one an Antony,
> And say 'Ah, ha! y'are caught.'

Was this not love indeed?

Again, in *Much Ado About Nothing* (III, i, 26) when Beatrice is eavesdropping in 'the woodbine coverture', Ursula says to Hero:

> The pleasant'st **angling** is to see the fish
> Cut with her golden oars the silver stream,
> And greedily devour the treacherous bait:
> So **angle** we for Beatrice; ...

And Edgar, pretending madness to Lear, Gloster and Kent, has his insane and eerie exclamation (*King Lear*, III, vi, 6): 'Frateretto calls me, and tells me Nero is an **angler** in the lake of darkness.'

But there is very little else to suggest that the man Shakespeare often went fishing in the River Avon in youth or in age. Unlike his near-contemporary Izaak Walton he might, from any evidence in his plays, be termed an incompleat angler.

But it is Cleopatra, continuing her conversation with Charmian (*Antony and Cleopatra*, II, v, 16), who deserves the last word on this sport and proceeds upwards from it to a sport nearer and dearer to her spacious heart:

> CHARMIAN: 'Twas merry when
> You wager'd on your **angling**; when your diver
> Did hang a salt-fish on his hook, which he
> With fervency drew up.
> CLEOPATRA: That time,—O times!—
> I laugh'd him out of patience; and that night
> I laugh'd him into patience: and next morn,
> Ere the ninth hour, I drunk him to his bed;
> Then put my tires and mantles on him, whilst
> I wore his sword Philippan.

ARCHERY

Archery is a mode of attack in time of war, but only a sport in time of peace. The only reference to it in the latter form is in a little scene in *Titus Andronicus* (IV, iii, 2), where Titus and his brother Marcus and his young son Lucius bring in bows and arrows, and the father says to his son:

> Sir boy, now let me see your **archery**;
> Look ye draw home enough, and 'tis there straight.

This bout of archery happens in a public place in Rome. And the archers take aim with various gods in mind (IV, iii, 52):

> You are a good **archer**, Marcus;
> *Ad Jovem*, that's for you:—here, *Ad Apollinem*:—
> *Ad Martem*, that's for myself:—
> Here, boy, *To Pallas*:—here, *To Mercury*:—
> *To Saturn*, Caius, not to Saturnine;
> You were as good to shoot against the wind.—
> To it, boy!—Marcus, loose when I bid.—
> Of my word, I have written to effect;
> There's not a god left unsolicited.

But to Shakespeare himself, as poet and playwright, Cupid would appear to have been the bowman who gave him most pleasure and stirred his fancy most.

See also BOWLS AND BOWLING.

BANQUETING AND FEASTING

Whereas meals three or four times daily are ordinary things that keep one alive, banquets are – in the purest sense of that overworked word – extraordinary. They are, or should be, life at its uppermost level, so far as eating goes. They are feasting-in-style. They therefore qualify for entry into life's sports and pastimes.

In *King Henry V* the Archbishop of Canterbury deplores the irresponsible behaviour of Prince Hal (I, i, 55):

> His companies unletter'd, rude, and shallow;
> His hours fill'd up with riots, **banquets**, sports; . . .

We have scarcely met Antony and his Cleopatra for the first time when Enobarbus and the queen's attendants – including her two handmaids, her eunuch, and her soothsayer – appear

to be having a banquet on their own account (*Antony and Cleopatra*, I, ii, II).
Enobarbus speaks:

> Bring in the **banquet** quickly; wine enough
> Cleopatra's health to drink.

In *King Henry VI, Part One* (II, i, II), Talbot wants to storm the unprepared enemy:

> This happy night the Frenchmen are secure,
> Having all day coursed and **banqueted**:
> Embrace we, then, this opportunity, . . .

And Old Capulet in *Romeo and Juliet* uses that rare figure of speech, inverted irony, when he tries to coax some gate-crashing Montagues to stay on at his party (I, v, 123):

> Nay, gentlemen, prepare not to be gone;
> We have a trifling foolish **banquet** towards.

These and other banquets – whether in London or Alexandria, Orleans or Verona – were obviously a great success. But the best-known of all, the one given by the Macbeths at Forres, was doomed to failure, almost from the start, by the arrival of the bloody spectre of the newly-murdered Banquo, shaking his gory locks. This is not called a banquet by anyone who went to it, alive or dead. It is a banquet only in the stage-direction at the beginning of Act III Scene iv – '**Banquet** prepared.'

As for feasting, the little speech of the Herald in *Othello* (II, ii) – it is the whole scene and no one else has a word – might serve almost as a motto for this whole book. It is a proclamation which would also serve for any young actor to make his mark in, if he has a good proclaiming voice. Yet in the theatre it is stupidly and almost invariably cut:

It is Othello's pleasure, our noble and valiant general, that, upon certain tidings now arrived, importing the mere perdition of the

Turkish fleet, every man put himself into triumph; some to dance, some to make bonfires, each man to what sport and revels his addiction leads him: for, besides these beneficial news, it is the celebration of his nuptial:—so much was his pleasure should be proclaim'd. All offices are open; and there is full liberty of **feasting** from this present hour of five till the bell have told eleven. Heaven bless the isle of Cyprus and our noble general Othello!

BAWDRY

To talk bawdry, or even to live in it, cannot strictly be called either a sport or a pastime, since it simply signifies indulgence in lewd language or lewd practices. But Shakespeare uses the word only three times – as distinct from 'bawd' (which he uses unendingly) – and on each of these three occasions the malpractice could conceivably pass muster as a sport.

Thus, Touchstone says to Audrey, the country wench he proposes to marry (*As You Like It*, III, iii, 90):

> Come, sweet Audrey:
> We must be married, or we must live in **bawdry.**

Thus, Hamlet rebukes Polonius for his interruption of the First Player (*Hamlet*, II, ii, 507): 'Prithee, say on:—he's for a jig or a tale of **bawdry,** or he sleeps:—say on: come to Hecuba.'

And thus, in *The Winter's Tale*, the Clown's Servant, who is almost always severely cut when the play is acted. This unexplained character called 'Servant' is not even in the list of the dramatis personae. His function is to announce the arrival of Autolycus, and he does so in three patches of vigorous prose within the same little scene (IV, iii, 191). The second of these, a blue rather than a purple patch, runs thus:

He hath songs for man, or woman, of all sizes, no milliner can so fit his customers with gloves: he has the prettiest love-songs for maids; so without **bawdry**, which is strange; with such delicate budens [= delightful refrains] of 'dildos' and 'fadings', 'jump her and thump her'; and where some stretch-mouth'd rascal would, as it were, mean mischief, and break a foul jape into the matter, he makes the maid to answer, 'Whoop, do me no harm, good man'; puts him off, slights him, with 'Whoop, do me no harm, good man'.

Cuttable certainly, though the obvious references to old ballads must fascinate the folklorist.

BEAR-BAITING

The references in *The Merry Wives of Windsor* to dancing and performing bears – including Sackerson, which was a famous Elizabethan bear apparently called after its master, a bear-trainer – do not concern the so-called sport of setting dogs to attack a bear chained to a stake.

This savage form of fun is referred to only in *The Winter's Tale* and *Twelfth Night*. In the one the Clown says of Autolycus the peddling rogue (IV, ii, 101): 'He haunts wakes, fairs, and **bear-baitings**.' And in the other the foolish knight, Sir Andrew Aguecheek, remarks with a delicious melancholy (I, iii, 90): 'I would I had bestow'd that time in the tongues that I have in fencing, dancing and **bear-baiting**. O, had I but follow'd the arts!'

BETTING AND WAGERING

Osric in *Hamlet* goes on so about the betting and wagering that is to accompany Hamlet's duel with Laertes (v, ii, 146) that we are always glad that in the theatre his part is liberally slashed by his director:

OSRIC: The king, sir, hath **wager'd** with him six Barbary horses: against the which he has impawned, as I take it, six French rapiers and poniards, with their assigns, as girdle, hanger, and so: three of the carriages, in faith, are very dear to fancy, very responsive to the hilts, most delicate carriages, and of very liberal conceit.

HAMLET: What call you the carriages? . . .

OSRIC: The carriages, sir, are the hangers.

HAMLET: The phrase would be more germane to the matter, if we could carry a cannon by our sides: I would it might be hangers till then. But, on: six Barbary horses against six French swords, their assigns, and three liberal-conceited carriages; that's the French **bet** against the Danish . . .

And so the rigmarole goes on, both before and after, in the text if not in the theatre, where we know to expect very soon the comparatively significant speech to Horatio: 'We defy augury: . . . the readiness is all: . . .'

Nym with Pistol in *King Henry V* (II, i, 97) is at least brief about his bet when he says: 'You'll pay me the eight shillings I won of you at **betting**?' and gets the answer: 'Base is the slave that pays.' However, only ten lines later Nym repeats his demand, and receives from Pistol at least a promise: 'A noble shalt thou have, and present pay.'

Of countless other wagerers in the plays only Emilia and Iachimo need to be singled out. The first for her protestation to Othello about her mistress's innocence (IV, ii, 12):

I durst, my lord, to **wager** she is honest,
Lay down my soul at **stake**: if you think other,
Remove your thought,—it doth abuse your bosom.

20

And Iachimo in *Cymbeline* (1, vi, 15) utters this exquisitely phrased speech to himself while watching Imogen read the letter he has brought to her from her trusting husband:

> All of her that is out door most rich!
> If she be furnisht with a mind so rare,
> She is alone the Arabian bird; and I
> Have lost the **wager**. Boldness be my friend!
> Arm me, audacity, from head to foot!
> Or, like the Parthian, I shall flying fight;
> Rather, directly fly.

BILLIARDS

The only mention in the whole of Shakespeare is to an actual match that is never played, merely suggested. This is discussed by Cleopatra and her maids and her eunuch Mardian, while the Queen is trying to beguile the weary and aching time of Antony's absence in Rome (11, v, 3):

CLEOPATRA: Let it alone; let's to **billiards**:
                                    come, Charmian.
CHARMIAN: My arm is sore; best play with Mardian.
CLEOPATRA: As well a woman with an eunuch play'd,
  As with a woman.—Come, you'll play with me, sir?
MARDIAN: As well as I can, madam.
CLEOPATRA: And when good will is show'd, though't come too
    short,
  The actor may plead pardon. I'll none now:—
  Give me mine angle,—we'll to the river: ...

A delicately indelicate bit of by-play around a game of billiards that never even began.

BOAR-HUNTING

There are in Shakespeare enough references to the wild boar to convince us that this was at least as familiar a sight to the Elizabethan as the hare or the hedgehog are to us today.

Petruchio in *The Taming of the Shrew* (I, ii, 200) describes his own dauntless spirit:

> Have I not heard the sea, puff'd up with winds,
> Rage like an angry **boar** chafèd with sweat?

Aaron the Moor, in *Titus Andronicus* (IV, ii, 137) describes his own black rage in similar terms:

> ... but if you brave the Moor,
> The chafèd **boar,** the mountain lioness,
> The ocean swells not so as Aaron storms.

A Senator tells Timon in *Timon of Athens* (V, i, 164) of an invader who is boar-like, and as arrogant as his name:

> ... so soon we shall drive back
> Of Alcibiades th'approaches wild;
> Who, like a **boar** too savage, doth root up
> His country's peace.

In *As You Like It* (I, iii, 114) Rosalind, dressing up as the boy Ganymede to go into the Forest of Arden, is fully prepared for an encounter with a wild boar at least:

> A gallant curtle-axe upon my thigh,
> A **boar-spear** in my hand; ...

And it is in the Boar's-Head tavern in Eastcheap, at the rich human heart of *King Henry IV, Part Two* (II, iv, 228), that Doll Tearsheet has an ironic description of her old fondling fat knight:

Thou whoreson little tidy Bartholomew **boar-pig**, when wilt thou leave fighting o' days and foining o' nights, and begin to patch up thine old body for heaven?

But turning away from the plays to the poems, it is an actual and particular wild-boar that might be called the only other character over and above the eponymous pair in *Venus and Adonis*. This great, voluptuous, under-read and under-estimated poem is almost as much about the shepherd Adonis chasing the wild-boar as about the goddess Venus chasing young Adonis.

In its very beginning (lines 1–4) the theme is stated almost before 'sick-thoughted' Venus herself appears:

> Even as the sun with purple-colour'd face
> Has ta'en his last leave of the weeping morn,
> Rose-cheek'd Adonis hied him to the chase;
> Hunting he lov'd, but love he laugh'd to scorn: . . .

Venus tells the youth she will do all she can 'to make thee hate the hunting of the **boar**' (line 711). And it is Venus and not Adonis who describes the beast as 'this foul, grim, and urchin-snouted **boar**' (line 1105).

In the end – need one tell non-readers of this discursive epic? – it is the wild boar, and not Venus, that gets Adonis at the conclusion of the chase—which is the conclusion of the poem.

BOWLS AND BOWLING

In the Duke of York's garden at Langley, King Richard II's Queen declines a game of bowls (*King Richard II*, III, iv, I):

> QUEEN: What sport shall we devise here in this garden,
> To drive away the heavy thought of care?
> LADY: Madam, we'll play at **bowls**.

QUEEN: 'Twill make me think the world is full of rubs,
And that my fortune runs against the bias.

Menenius in *Coriolanus* (v, ii, 19), insisting to a Sentinel on his loyalty to his General, has a figurative reference to the same game:

> ... nay, sometimes,
> Like to a **bowl** upon a subtle ground,
> I have tumbled past the throw; and in his praise
> Have almost stampt the leasing: therefore, fellow,
> I must have leave to pass.

But throughout a whole scene of *Love's Labour's Lost* (iv, i,) a sport is in progress and it is never really clear whether the reference is to a game of bowls or a bout of archery. It is a scene in artificial language which strains the patience even of that patient scholar, Granville-Barker, who devotes one of his celebrated *Prefaces to Shakespeare* – the very first of them – to this play itself, and several pages to this particularly difficult scene. This is an analysis in which he more than once comes near to losing his critical temper. The scene – not a particularly short one either – is 'horribly stuffed' with archaic words and phrases, obscure topical jokes, maddening puns on 'suitors' and 'shooters'. It is a scene which achieves a non-archaic significance only in the very last line of all, when Costard suddenly hits upon the right modern word for Don Armado's page, Moth:

> And his page o' t'other side, that handful of wit!
> Ah, heavens, it is a most pathetical nit!

Dr Caroline Spurgeon, the supreme authority on Shakespearean images, has been able to count no fewer than nineteen images drawn from the game of bowls, and concludes – with something less than her usual caution – that it was the game that Shakespeare himself 'played and loved best'.

BROTHEL-HAUNTING

Laertes, brother of Ophelia and son of Polonius, was suspected of such a sport when he went back to Paris, and in a charmingly natural little scene in *Hamlet* (a scene which is too often cut in stage-performances) the old man sends his servant Reynaldo to find out how his son is behaving or misbehaving himself in that adventurous city (II, i, 19):

>   ... there put on him
> What forgeries you please; marry, none so rank
> As may dishonour him; take heed of that;
> But, sir, such wanton, wild, and usual slips
> As are companions noted and most known
> To youth and liberty.
> REYNALDO: As gaming, my lord.
> POLONIUS: Ay, or drinking, fencing, swearing,
>   Quarrelling, drabbing [= whoring]:—you may go
>   so far.

Reynaldo must bring all such reports back with him to Elsinore (II, i, 59):

>   ... or perchance,
> 'I saw him enter such a house of sale,'—
> Videlicet, a **brothel**, or so forth.

Marina in *Pericles* miraculously keeps her virgin virtue though immured for a time in exactly 'such a house of sale'. This strange wandering play has one pretty patch of dialogue (IV, ii 139) between a bawd, Boult (described as a 'Servant of a Pander' – which is surely the lowest of the low, in the matter of professions) and Marina herself, who emerges, somehow, uncontaminated:

BAWD: Boult, spend thou that in the town: report what a sojourner we have; you'll lose nothing by custom. When Nature framed this piece, she meant thee a good turn; therefore say what a paragon she is, and thou hast the harvest out of thine own report.

BOULT: I warrant you, mistress, thunder shall not so awake the beds of eels as my giving out her beauty stirs up the lewdly-inclined. I'll bring home some to-night.

BAWD: Come your ways, follow me.

MARINA: If fires be hot, knives sharp, or waters deep,
Untied I still my virgin knot will keep.
Diana, aid my purpose!

BAWD: What have we to do with Diana?

Edgar in *King Lear*, on the other hand, talks himself out of such resorts, though he sounds at times rather like a regular customer (III, iv, 95):

> Let not the creaking of shoes nor the rustling of silks
> betray thy poor heart to woman; keep thy foot out
> of **brothels**, thy hand out of plackets, . . .

Oddly enough the frequently-visited brothel in *Measure for Measure* is never called 'brothel' *tout court*, though the simple constable whose name is Elbow describes it (II, i, 65) as 'a hot-house, which, I think is, a very ill house too'. Moreover its manageress is called Mistress Overdone and her servant Pompey Bum, while Claudio and Lucio are among the establishment's many regular customers, its haunters. Disorderly, undoubtedly!

CARD-PLAYING AND PLAYING-CARDS

That major and senior drama-critic and superb Shakespearean scholar, Mr Ivor Brown, manifests his great interest in these notebooks by sending me a valuable note concerning Shakespeare and card-games. Where we refer to a 'pack' of cards, Shakespeare (he tells me) tends to use the much older word 'deck'; a usage which still survives in America. Thus Gloster at the end of the *Third Part of King Henry VI* has an intricate image which comes a shade clearer if we know this (v, i, 42–46):

> Alas, that Warwick had no more forecast,
> But, whiles he thought to steal the single ten,
> The king was slily fingered from the **deck**!
> You left poor Henry at the bishop's palace,
> And, ten to one, you'll meet him in the Tower.

Where Tranio in *The Taming of the Shrew* has a figurative reference to a card-game (II, I, 399–400):

> A vengeance on your crafty withered hide!
> Yet I have faced it with a **card of ten**
> 'Tis in my head to do my master good . . .

the New Penguin edition has a note that 'to outface with a card of ten' was a proverbial phrase for bluffing. But the reference may just possibly be to the half-forgotten card-game of one's childhood called Catch the Ten.

Then again, the French Dauphin in *King John* (v, ii, 105–108) has a figurative reference to playing-cards when he is seeking to win renown 'even in the jaws of danger and of death'. He says to the papal legate, Pandulph:

> Have I not here the best cards for the game
> To win this easy match, played for a crown?
> And shall I now give o'er the yielded set?
> No, no on my soul, it never shall be said.

Antony describes his Queen's seeming treachery to his faithful servant Eros in terms of cards (IV, xiv, 19–23):

> . . . She, Eros has
> Packed cards with Caesar, and false-play'd my glory
> Unto an enemy's triumph,
> Nay, weep not, gentle Eros, there is left us
> Ourselves to end ourselves.

And Aaron in *Titus Andronicus* (v, 1, 98–101) gloats over his own villainy and that of his two sons who have raped and mutilated Lavinia:

> Indeed, I was their tutor to instruct them;
> That codding (= eager) spirit had they from their mother,
> As sure a card as ever won the set;
> That bloody mind I think they learned of me . . .

Lysander has a footling pleasantry on the death of Pyramus in the play-scene in *The Dream* (v, 1, 298): – 'Less than an **ace**, man; for he is dead, he is nothing.' And Don Adriano de Armado bandies words drawn from playing-cards with Moth, his page in *Love's Labour's Lost* (1, ii, 49–53):

MOTH: I am sure you know how much the gross sum of **deuce ace** amounts to.
ARMADO: It doth amount to one more than two.
MOTH: Which the base vulgar do call three.
ARMADO: True.

That most sinister of all the playing-cards known as The Joker is not mentioned anywhere in Shakespeare, and indeed is not – according to the Oxford Dictionary – mentioned anywhere as a playing-card until as late as the year 1885. In play it 'counts usually as a trump, and sometimes the highest trump' but it would appear to be used only in certain gambling games, notably in the game of Poker (1848), the American variant of the English game of Brag (1734).

The Joker is depicted usually, but not always, as a jester with a diabolical grin, either squatting with knees wide apart or standing up, and usually with a bauble in one hand and an indeterminate ace-card in the other. 'The eye of childhood – or that of this compiler at least – feared him as a kind of painted devil (to adapt the phrase of Lady Macbeth).' And it is by no means irrelevant to recall, in one's Scottish infancy, that old women usually referred to playing-cards as Devil's Cards (and may do so still). One recalls also that in a first schoolroom reading of *Twelfth Night* – and indeed in every subsequent reading or viewing of that same play – one gets a curious sensation of a little jester turned evil, or of a little devil turned jester leaping uncannily through the lines whether Feste the clown sings or merely speaks them (IV, 2, 121):

> I am gone, sir, and anon, sir,
> I'll be with you again—
> In a trice, like to the old Vice,
> Your need to sustain.
> Who with dagger of lath, in his rage and his wrath,
> Cries Ah ha! to the devil;
> Like a mad lad – Pare thy nails, dad?
> Adieu, goodman devil!

It is by no means an outstanding lyric, its rhyme on 'devil' is no rhyme at all, not even an assonance, but a mere repetition. It is all undoubtedly inconsequent; but it is also faintly devilish.

The New Penguin edition of the play – meticulously edited by Professor M. M. Mahood – tells us that the Vice was a character who defied the devil in the early Tudor interludes which developed from the Morality plays, and that he was one ancestor of the Elizabethan stage fool. He also explains the curious 'Pare thy nails, dad?' with a reference to *Henry V* (IV, iv, 69–70) which suggests that the Vice in the old plays used to try to pare the Devil's long nails. This edition, which is particularly sound on the musical settings, declares that no early music has survived for 'I am gone, sir', this diabolical little ditty.

CHILDREN'S GAMES

Hide-and-seek, perhaps the earliest of children's games, does not seem to exist in Shakespeare, not at least under that apellation – which the *Oxford English Dictionary* declares to be no earlier than 1672. On the other hand, blindman's buff has the honour to be mentioned by Hamlet himself, under the title of 'hoodman-blind', and in the Closet Scene with his mother (*Hamlet*, III, iv, 77):

> What devil was't
> That thus hath cozen'd you at **hoodman-blind**? . . .
> O shame! where is thy blush?

A child's hoop, and the hoop-iron with which it is trundled, would seem to have been among the possessions of the little Prince Mamillius in *The Winter's Tale*; or so at least this writer thought until he looked for confirmation in the Mamillius scenes in the play. There is no mention whatever of any hoop or hoop-iron. Was there perhaps some picture of little Mamillius with this toy, the hoop in one hand, the hoop-iron in the other? Possibly, an early, long-lost photograph of Ellen Terry in the part?

But the recollection is as vague as a dream and, no less unconfirmable. It is much more certain that Ellen Terry played Mamillius in her infancy (with Mr and Mrs Charles Kean) and that in her old age she included the touching little part prominently in her lecture, 'The Children in Shakespeare's Plays'.

COCK-FIGHTING

This is a very ancient sport which used to be much practised in England (and which, though illegal, is practised still if we take note of hole-and-corner mentions in the public press). It is all the odder, therefore, that references to it are few and rare in Shakespeare, and usually oblique.

That vain and grotesque prince, Cloten, has a sidelong reference in *Cymbeline* (II, i, 18) when he says:

> I had rather not be so noble as I am; they dare not
> fight with me, because of the queen my mother: every
> Jack-slave hath his bellyful of fighting, and I
> must go up and down like a **cock** that nobody can match.

Also the Chorus in *King Henry V* (Prologue to Act I, lines 11–12) very obviously has in mind the little arena where cocks did – and do – their fighting when he refers to the inadequacy of the theatre to stage a human battle:

> . . . can this **cockpit** hold
> The vasty fields of France?

DALLYING AND ŒILLADES

In *Venus and Adonis* (lines 105–8) the goddess of love tells her wayward Adonis how his predecessor Mars, the god of war

> . . . for my sake hath learnt to sport and dance,
> To toy, to wanton, **dally**, smile, and jest;
> Scorning his churlish drum and ensign red,
> Making my arms his field, his tent my bed.

In *King Henry VI, Part One*, the king tells his uncle that he prefers to improve his mind rather than tempt his body (V, i, 22):

> And fitter is my study and my books
> Than wanton **dalliance** with a paramour. . . .

In *King Richard III* (III, vii, 74) Buckingham describes Gloucester with unconscious irony:

Not **dallying** with a brace of courtesans,
But meditating with two deep divines;
Not sleeping, to engross his idle body,
But praying, to enrich his watchful soul:
Happy were England, would this virtuous prince
Take on himself the sovereignty thereof;
But sure I fear we shall not win him to it.

Any other word for not-very-deep love-making is rare indeed in Shakespeare. Both 'flirt' and 'coquette' are eighteenth-century, whereas the silly 'spooning' is Edwardian and the coarse 'necking' belongs to the last decade or so. But 'flirt' is found in a compound form in *Romeo and Juliet* (II, iii, 156) when the Nurse says of Mercutio: 'Scurvy knave! I am none of his flirt-gills' and merely means 'fast girls'.

However, there is one strange word for a coquettish or calculating glance that is far from shallow, in fact as deep as it sounds. It is directly French in origin and it occurs twice in Shakespeare.

The first scene is between Falstaff and Pistol in *The Merry Wives of Windsor* (I, iii, 56), where the former says he has written a letter to Mrs Page,
> ... who even now gave me good eyes too,
examined my parts with most judicious **œillades**; sometimes
the beam of her view gilded my foot, sometimes my
portly belly.
PISTOL: Then did the sun on dunghill shine.

The second scene is in *King Lear* between Cornwall's widow, Regan, and the despicable Oswald who is Goneril's serving-man (and willing to serve anyone else who may come his way) (IV, v, 23):
REGAN: I know your lady does not love her husband;
I am sure of that: and at her late being here
She gave strange **œillades** and most speaking looks
To noble Edmund. I know you are of her bosom.
OSWALD: Ay, madam.

REGAN: I speak in understanding; you are, I know't:
    Therefore I do advise you, take this note:
    My lord is dead; Edmund and I have talk'd;
    And more convenient is he for my hand
    Than for your lady's:—you may gather more. . . .

Much virtue – and vice – in Oswald's laconic 'Ay, madam'.

But why one scene should make us laugh while the other scene makes us shudder is just part of the dramatic mystery of things.

DANCING

There is set-dancing in several of the plays – including Capulet's ball in *Romeo and Juliet*, the *bal masqué* in *Much Ado About Nothing*, and a rough dance of shepherds in *The Winter's Tale* described beforehand by the garrulous Second Clown (IV, iii, 326):

Master, there is three carters, three shepherds, three neat-herds, three swine-herds, that have made themselves all men of hair,—they call themselves Saltiers: and they have a **dance** which the wenches say is a gallimaufry of gambols, because they are not in't; but they themselves are o' the mind,—if it be not too rough for some that know little but bowling,— it will please plentifully.

There is, too, the incessant tripping of fairies in *A Midsummer Night's Dream* (not absolutely always to Mendelssohn, but sometimes to English folk-tunes—which makes a pleasant change).

Individual dances also get frequent mention. For example, in *King Henry V* (III, v, 32) the Duke of Bourbon echoes the Dauphin who has been chiding Frenchwomen for running after English soldiery:

    They bid us to the English dancing-schools,
    And teach **lavoltas** high and swift **corantos**;
    Saying our grace is only in our heels,
    And that we are most lofty runaways.

And Sir Toby teases Sir Andrew about his light-foot accomplishment and ends a scene by making him exit dancing like giddy goat, in *Twelfth Night* (I, iii, 116):

SIR TOBY: What is thy excellence in a **galliard**, knight?

SIR ANDREW: Faith, I can cut a caper. . . .

SIR TOBY: Wherefore are these things hid? wherefore have these gifts a curtain before 'em? . . . why dost thou not go to church in a **galliard**, and come home in a **coranto**?

But the obscurest reference of all – and it is in the same play – is to the **pavane**, a stately dance of the sixteenth century. This is in a passage where Sir Toby describes someone disparagingly (v, i 197): 'Then he's a rogue, and a *passy-measures pavin*'. It is a phrase which is even beyond the scholars, though Editor Ridley has a good, laboured try: 'The pavin (pavane) was a slow dance, one variety of which was "passy-measures" (passamezzo); and the "strains" of it were of eight bars each.' This seems to us the very ecstasy of pedantry.

DEVIATING

Post-Freudian scholarship has, rather surprisingly, been reticent in the matter of flashlighting certain excesses in friendship in the works of Shakespeare. For example, that between Rosalind and Celia in *As You Like It*, those heavenly cousins of whom the courtier, Monsieur Le Beau, says – for what it is worth – that their loves were 'dearer than the natural bond of sisters' (I, ii, 267). Or even that between Cassio and Iago in *Othello*, though the wicked fantasy and invention of the latter's story (about Cassio's sleep-talking) is a double-dyed device to torment Othello's rage at his wife and her imagined duplicity (III, iii, 413). It is perhaps the most diabolical lie in the whole of drama.

Yet again when Hero says of her cousin Beatrice in *Much Ado About Nothing* (III, i, 54):

> . . . she cannot love,
> Nor take no shape nor project of affection,
> She is so self-endear'd. . . .

she does not really imply that her merry cousin is self-sufficient to the point of eternal spinsterdom. And it would be a very daring and very young scholar who tried to maintain that Macbeth is revealing that onanism is among his many misdemeanours when he declares (III, iv, 142):

> . . . My strange and self-abuse
> Is the initiate fear, that wants hard use: . . .

What Macbeth really means here is quite beside the point. But it is not that! The play's most recent editor, Mr G. K. Hunter of the New Penguin Shakespeare, translates it thus: 'My strange self-deception (seeing Banquo's ghost) is only due to the terror of the beginner who lacks toughening experience.' The mutual passion between the Grecian captains, Achilles and Patrochus, is declared and explicit in *Troilus and Cressida*.

Reverting to Rosalind and Celia, we asked a young student of the play who had been deep in its study whether he found in it any reference to any kind of 'permissive' behaviour. He immediately quoted Celia's lines to her own father about her friendship with Rosalind (I, iii, 69):

> . . . if she be a traitor,
> Why, so am I; we still have slept together,
> Rose at an instant, learn'd, play'd, ate together;
> And wheresoe'er we went, like Juno's swans,
> Still we went coupled and inseparable.

Asked to explain, this modern student said, without a smirk or seeming smartness: 'Well, they slept together – she says so herself!'

This is the age we live in, and the way it thinks and reads. *C'est plus fort que moi!*

Deviating to my own childhood, let me recall here, across the many years, the English class-room in my Scottish school, and the consternation I once caused there by reading aloud a passage in *As You Like It* from my one-volume Shakespeare where the rest of the class used an edition for schools. The sensation – which took the form of giggling from the boys and gasps from the girls – came about when I had the luck to read part of the scene between Rosalind and Celia speculating on the identity of the poet – Orlando, of course – who had been hanging his verses on the trees of the Forest of Arden (III, 2, 191–198):

ROSALIND: I prithee tell me who is it quickly, and speak apace. I would thou couldst stammer, that thou mightst pour this concealed man out of thy mouth as wine comes out of a narrow-mouthed bottle: either too much at once, or none at all. I prithee take the cork out of thy mouth, that I may drink thy tidings.

CELIA: So you may put a man in your belly.

Our English master glared, seized my book to make quite certain I was reading what was printed, and thereafter sent a note to my poor father begging him to buy me the same 'school edition' used by the rest of the twelve-year-olds and thus to spare him the embarrassment of explanation. It was my first lesson in the dangers of non-conformity.

DICE, HAZARD, MAIN

Shakespeare's direct references to the actual game of dice are few, but two of them are most vivid and important. One is that of Edgar in *King Lear* (III, iv, 90) who in his self-derogation as the vagabond madman, Poor Tom, declares himself to have been

> ... one that slept in the contriving of lust,
> and waked to do it: wine loved I deeply,

> **dice** dearly; and in woman out-paramour'd
> the Turk: ...

The other is that of Chorus in *KingHenry V* (iv, Prologue,17):

> Proud of their numbers, and secure in soul,
> The confident and over-lusty French
> Do the low-rated English play at **dice**;
> And chide the cripple tardy-gaited night,
> Who, like a foul and ugly witch, doth limp
> So tediously away.

Shortly afterwards, when the Battle of Agincourt has turned
in favour of the English, the Dauphin of France has a reference
to this same sporting interlude (iv, v, 7):

> O pèrdurable shame!—let's stab ourselves.
> Be these the wretches that we played at **dice** for?

For this arresting piece of information – as for much else in
the English historical plays – Shakespeare went straight to the
old *Chronicles* of Raphael Holinshed.

> The Frenchmen in the meane while, as thoughe
> they had bin sure of victory, made great
> triumphe, for the captaines had determined before how
> to divide the spoile, and the souldiours the night
> before had plaid the englishemen at dice.

Was there ever so *obliged* a writer as Shakespeare?

Both 'hazard' and 'main' are words with a dozen different
meanings even as nouns. But the oldest significance of
'hazard' is 'a game at dice in which the chances are complicated by a number of arbitrary rules'; and in one of its
earliest uses (1575) a 'main' was in the game of hazard, 'a
number (from five to nine inclusive) called by the "caster"
before the dice are thrown'.

There is a reference to both, admittedly in the figurative
sense, in *King Henry IV, Part One* (iv, i, 45) where Hotspur says:

... were it good
To set the exact wealth of all our states
All at one cast? to set so rich a **main**
On the nice **hazard** of one doubtful hour?
It were not good; ...

DUELLING AND FENCING

There is a brief but loaded summary of the whole art of fencing in *Twelfth Night* (III, iv, 276) where Sir Toby teases Sir Andrew about the prowess of Sebastian who has challenged him to a duel:

Why, man, he's a very devil; I have not seen such
a firago. I had a pass with him, rapier, scabbard,
and all, and he gives me the stuck-in with such a
mortal motion, that it is inevitable; and on the answer,
he pays you as surely as your feet hit the ground
they step on: they say he has been **fencer** to the
Sophy [the Shah of Persia].

And Sir Andrew answers: 'Pox on't, I'll not meddle with him.'

There are some young men in the plays who seem to live entirely *for* fencing and duelling like Tybalt in *Romeo and Juliet*, or who live entirely *by* it like Osric in *Hamlet*. You might call them young blades rather than young men.

EATING AND DRINKING

Neither severally nor in combination do these two necessities of life constitute either a sport or a pastime. But there are at least two irresistible instances in the plays when they are considered together as the be-all and end-all of existence.

One is in *Twelfth Night* (II, iii, 9) where Sir Toby asks the

question: 'Does not our life consist of the four elements?' and
Sir Andrew supplies the characteristic answer: 'Faith, so they
say; but, I think, it rather consists of **eating and drinking.**'

The other is in *Measure for Measure* (III, ii, 102), where the
Duke, disguised as a friar, says to the unrepentant rake Lucio
that lechery is too general a vice, and gets the answer: 'Yes,
in good sooth, the vice is of a great kindred; it is well allied;
but it is impossible to extirp it quite, friar, till **eating and
drinking** be put down.'

FALCONRY

One has to know a little about falconry if one is fully to
understand some of the best-known plays. Indeed, the author
quite obviously presupposes much knowledge of this so-
called sport in his contemporary audiences.

Hamlet welcomes the Players to Elsinore warmly and even
excitedly (*Hamlet*, II, ii, 435):

HAMLET: Masters, you are all welcome. We'll e'en to't like French
falconers, fly at any thing we see: we'll have a speech straight:
come, give us a taste of your quality; come, a passionate speech.
FIRST PLAYER: What speech, my good lord?

This is clear and fine and urgent – all but that odd remark
about French falconers. And it is boring to have to learn, or
be told, that English falconers let some smaller bird fly into
the air before sending off the falcon in pursuit of it, whereas
the French falconers let off the falcon trusting it to aim at any
bird within its line, and who can blame them?

When Juliet on her balcony tries to recall Romeo (*Romeo
and Juliet*, II, i, 201):

Hist! Romeo, hist!—O, for a **falconer's** voice,
To lure this tassel-gentle back again!

she implies that she is already practised in the ancient art, 'the sport of kings', since at least four words in her last sentence of twelve has its special falconry sense – 'falconry', 'lure', 'tassel' (for 'tiercel'), and 'gentle'.

It is useful to have a glimmer of the meaning of these and a few other falconry words – that a 'tiercel' is a male falcon which is, surprisingly, only about a third of the size of the female falcon; that a 'haggard' is a wild female hawk caught when in her adult plumage; that a 'peregrine' hawk or falcon is a wandering bird of either sex; that a 'lure' is a bait to which a bird-wing or a tuft of feathers has been tied; that a 'jess' is a short strap of leather or silk fastened round each leg of a hawk used in falconry.

Facilities for *hawking* are among the pleasures offered by the Lord to poor bamboozled Christopher Sly in *The Taming of the Shrew* (Induction ii, 45–60):

> Dost thou love **hawking**? thou hast hawks will soar
> Above the morning lark.

GAMES IN GENERAL

It is true that Shakespeare mentions remarkably few games of any sort. But it would be wrong to conclude that he was no playboy, by which one means gamesman. The fact is that the greater part of the games we know are later in date than Elizabethan or Jacobean times. Chess, dice, and playing-cards are, of course, much older. But of the card-games still played – and some no longer played—nearly all are of later date than 1616, the year when Shakespeare died.

There is no record of solitaire (played with marbles on a special board) before 1746, or of any of the innumerable forms of patience, the solo card-game, before 1816. Accounts of whist are not traceable before 1663, and its predecessor which was spelt 'whisk' was only twenty years older and is therefore not found in Shakespeare. Neither, rather surprisingly, is backgammon. Still more surprising is the absence of skittles (which did not seem to exist under that name before 1634) and of its predecessor called 'ninepins' which is mentioned by other writers as early at 1580.

Cribbage does not appear to have existed before 1630, and ombre and loo (and the latter's predecessor 'lanterloo' and 'langtriloo') seem first to have been played by Restoration ladies – as we know from their stage-counterparts.

The easiest and apparently the most primitive of all the card-games, snap or snip-snap-snorum, goes no farther back than the middle of the eighteenth century.

Shakespeare's references to actual card-games are therefore few and indeterminate. When in *The Taming of the Shrew* (II, i 397) Tranio somewhat obscurely says to the departing Gremio:

> A vengeance on your crafty wither'd hide!
> Yet I have faced it with a card of ten. . . .

he may or may not be referring to some forerunner of the game of brag or poker in which a ten is more valuable than a court card. But other references are figurative or unspecific, like – in *King John* (v, ii, 105) – the Dauphin's phrase to Pandulph, the papal legate:

> Have I not here the best cards for the game,
> To win this easy match play'd for a crown? . . .

or like Antony to Eros in *Antony and Cleopatra* concerning the Queen who has been reported dead (IV, xiv, 15):

> I made these wars for Egypt; and the Queen,—
> Whose heart I thought I had, for she had mine;
> Which, whilst it was mine, had annext unto't
> A million moe, now lost,—she, Eros, has

41

Pack'd cards with Caesar, and false-play'd my glory
Unto an enemy's triumph.—
Nay, weep not, gentle Eros; there is left us
Ourselves to end ourselves.

Shakespeare has, on the other hand, some few references to games that have vanished utterly. There was, for example, 'cherry pit' inadequately described as a children's game in which cherry-stones were thrown into a pit. This is mentioned in *Twelfth Night* (III, iv, 116) where Sir Toby says to Malvolio, who is being treated like a lunatic: 'Ay, Biddy, come with me. What, man! 'tis not for gravity to play at **cherry-pit** with Satan: . . .' But it is not one of Sir Toby's more lucid observations.

Neither is Titania really lucid about the exact nature of the lost game or sport called 'nine-men's-morris' in *A Midsummer Night's Dream* (II, i, 94). When one first read it in the schoolroom in one's earliest teens, this long speech to Oberon, beginning 'These are the forgeries of jealousy', had all the magic of fairy-tale in its description of a mixed-up season:

> . . . the green corn
Hath rotted ere his youth attain'd a beard:
The fold stands empty in the drownèd field,
And crows are fatted with the murrion flock;
The **nine-men's morris** is fill'd up with mud;
And the quaint mazes in the wanton green,
For lack of tread, are undistinguishable: . . .

It would all seem to be a reference to the peculiarly nasty summer of the year 1594, which another Elizabethan poet, Charles Churchyard, specifically described:

> A colder time, in world was neuer seene
The skies do lowre, the sun and moone waxe dim
Sommer scarce knowne, but that the leues are greene
The winter's waste, driues water ore the brim. . . .

But Titania does it even better near the end of her same speech (lines 111–14):

> ... the spring, the summer,
> The childing [= fruitful] autumn, angry winter, change
> Their wonted liveries; and the mazèd world,
> By their increase, now knows not which is which.

Fifty years ago one fondly imagined that Titania in the beginning was referring to nine morris-dancers who exerted themselves in quaint mazes. But many a subsequent scholar has come along to assure us that the two items have no connection – that 'nine-men's-morris' was a plot of green turf cut into a sort of chessboard for youthful exercises, and that 'quaint mazes' were reserved for youthful play as distinct from youthful exercise. But the definition is too vague to be very satisfying.

Chess itself, incidentally, seems to have no mention whatsoever, though it is one of the most ancient of games. The stage-direction in the last act of *The Tempest* has a mention of chess being played by Ferdinand and Miranda. This raises a very interesting point. *The Tempest* did not reach publication until the First Folio, seven years after Shakespeare's death, and it is a generally accepted fact that the stage-directions, which are unusually detailed, were not Shakespeare's own. They also show remarkable variation. In some editions this particular stage-direction runs:

> *Here Prospero discovers Ferdinand and Miranda,*
> *playing at chess.*

But in another there is a by no means unimportant difference:

> *The entrance of the Cell opens, and discovers*
> *Ferdinand and Miranda playing at chess.*

Clearly these are notes made by two quite distinct producers for different productions of the play. Then again – if the query can be made at this time of day – was it a game of chess or a card game? Note the dialogue of the players carefully (v, i, 172):

MIRANDA: Sweet lord, you play me false.
FERDINAND: No, my dear'st love,
   I would not for the world.
MIRANDA: Yes, for a score of kingdoms you should wrangle,
   And I would call it fair play.

Whatever Prospero's daughter may mean by her second statement, she clearly means by her first that her opponent is cheating. And the point is, whether one can cheat or 'play false' at chess where the pieces are seen by both players.

Lucio in *Measure for Measure* (I, ii, 180) at the end of a conversation with Claudio on the latter's doubtful future has a recondite reference to tick-tack which was an earlier form of backgammon. He regrets that his friend's life should be 'foolishly lost at a game of **tick-tack**'.

A single reference to 'football' is hardly complimentary. It is in the passage-at-arms between Kent and the impudent steward, Oswald, in *King Lear* (I, iv, 82):

OSWALD: I'll not be struck, my lord.
KENT: Nor tripped neither, you base *football* player.
                              (*Trips him up.*)

HUNTING AND COURSING

Hunting was, of course, mankind's chief occupation and preoccupation (in times of peace particularly), and Dr Spurgeon, who could hunt images as intensively as the Elizabethans could hunt deer or other game, finds no fewer than thirteen figures of speech deriving directly from the sport.

She also dares to jump to a personal conclusion about the poet himself (though with the wariness of the born scholar): 'From his hunting images generally, we gather that he clearly had often seen a deer hunt, and had enjoyed the clamorous echo of hounds and horn, but that although he knew all about driving the deer into nets ("into a toil"), and shooting them with a crossbow, he had probably not much experience of hunting deer with hounds only. He had certainly seen the stag at bay, surrounded by the yelping dogs, stained with the blood of their prey, but he himself shows little enthusiasm for the sport ... by far the larger number of what may be grouped under his hunting and woodcraft similes are concerned with the habits and behaviour of the deer and the eager skill of the questing hounds, rather than with the actual chase.'

She is no less revealing, and no less cautious, on the subject of the pursuit of the hare: 'I should imagine from his images that he knew personally much more about the Cotswold sport of coursing and of hunting the hare generally than he did of deer hunting.' She then refers to an astonishing passage in *Venus and Adonis* without actually quoting (lines 673–708) – of the hunted hare doubling and crossing to put the hounds off his scent; 'but here again', says Dr Spurgeon, 'it is noticeable that the intensity of his feeling is for the victim, rather than for the fun of the chase'. The speaker is Venus in the course of one of her lengthy exhortations to Adonis to refrain from the chase of the boar, or of anything else but her sweet self alone:

> But if thou needs wilt **hunt**, be ruled by me;
> Uncouple at the timorous flying hare,
> Or at the fox which lives by subtlety,
> Or at the roe which no encounter dare:

Pursue these fearful creatures o'er the downs,
And on thy well-breathed horse keep with thy hounds.

And when thou hast on foot the purblind hare,
Mark the poor wretch, to overshoot his troubles
How he outruns the wind, and with what care
He cranks and crosses with a thousand doubles:
The many musets [= hedge-gaps] through the which he goes
Are like a labyrinth to amaze his foes.

Sometimes he runs among a flock of sheep,
To make the cunning hounds mistake their smell,
And sometimes where earth-delving conies keep,
To stop the loud pursuers in their yell;
And sometimes sorteth with a herd of deer:
Danger deviseth shifts, wit waits on fear:

For there his smell with others being mingled,
The hot scent-snuffing hounds are driven to doubt,
Ceasing their clamorous cry till they have singled
With much ado the cold fault cleanly out;
Then do they spend their mouths: Echo replies,
As if another chase were in the skies.

By this, poor Wat, far off upon a hill,
Stands on his hinder legs with list'ning ear,
To hearken if his foes pursue him still: ...

Yes, one would agree that the phrase 'poor Wat' for the poor
hare is far more likely to be the voice of the poet than that
of the yearning goddess.

See also BOAR-HUNTING.

LOVING AND LUSTING

Here, of course, the scope is infinite, just as the subject is inexhaustible. But by way of distraction or as a diversion for flagging readers one might offer here a questionnaire out of nine or ten plays in all.

Who then, made the following utterances, declarations, or avowals, and in what play? Each of them directly concerns the subject of love or mutual devotion.

1

I am no pilot; yet, wert thou as far
As that vast shore wash'd with the furthest sea,
I would adventure for such merchandise.

2

But trust me, gentleman, I'll prove more true
Than those that have more cunning to be strange.
I should have been more strange, I must confess,
But that thou overheard'st, ere I was ware,
My true love's passion: therefore pardon me;
And not impute this yielding to light love, . . .

3

What is't? a spirit?
Lord, how it looks about! Believe me, sir,
It carries a brave form:—but 'tis a spirit.
. . . I might call him
A thing divine; for nothing natural
I ever saw so noble.

4

I do love nothing in the world so well as you:
is not that strange?

5

How all the other passions fleet to air,—
As doubtful thoughts, and rash-embraced despair,
And shuddering fear, and green-eyed jealousy!
O love, be moderate; allay thy ecstasy;
In measure rain thy joy; scant this excess!
I feel too much thy blessing: make it less,
For fear I surfeit!

6

You are my true and honourable wife;
As dear to me as are the ruddy drops
That visit my sad heart.

7

I durst, my lord, to wager she is honest,
Lay down my soul at stake: if you think other,
Remove your thought,—it doth abuse your bosom.
If any wretch have put this in your head,
Let heaven requite it with the serpent's curse!
For, if she be not honest, chaste, and true,
There's no man happy; the purest of their wives
Is foul as slander.

8

What win I, if I gain the thing I seek?
A dream, a breath, a froth of fleeting joy.
Who buys a minute's worth to wail a week?
Or sells eternity to get a toy?
For one sweet grape who will the vine destroy?
   Or what fond beggar, but to touch the crown,
   Would with the sceptre straight be strucken down?

9

If it be love indeed, tell me how much.
There's beggary in the love that can be reckon'd.

10
I'll set a bourn how far to be beloved.
Then must thou needs find out new heaven, new earth.

1. It is Romeo making the least conventional and most imaginative of all his compliments to Juliet in the balcony scene (II, i, 124–6).
2. It is Juliet to Romeo (II, i, 142–7), twice using the stressed word 'strange' in its sense of 'distant' or 'reserved'. (The slightly unexpected 'gentleman' – though, of course, it occurs in the text – is a deliberate 'red herring' for the solver.)
3. It is Miranda's utterance when she first sets eyes on Ferdinand in *The Tempest* (I, ii, 410–20).
4. It is Bendick at last bursting into flame with Beatrice after three whole acts of sparks and smoke – *Much Ado About Nothing* (IV, i, 266).
5. It is Portia speaking to herself (though the passage is not marked as a soliloquy or an aside) while Bassanio is in process of choosing the right casket in *The Merchant of Venice* (III, ii, 108–14).
6. It is Brutus addressing the other Portia, Cato's daughter, in what may be called a spasm of wedded ecstasy – *Julius Caesar* (II, i, 288–90).
7. It is Emilia addressing Othello (IV, ii, 12–19) – with admirable frankness; though, as always, we note that with just a shade more of such frankness she might have obviated the whole tragedy.
8. It is Tarquin expressing a qualm at the pleasure, intense but brief, he may derive from the execution of his fell purpose. (From a poem not a play, it is true – *The Rape of Lucrece*, 211–17. But Tarquin's moment of compunction is almost as dramatic as anything in the tragedies.)
9. & 10. Both are snatches of dialogue – the opening dialogue – between Cleopatra and Antony, and in that order – in

Antony and Cleopatra (I, i, 14–17). Let the interchange be repeated here for absolute clarity's sake:

CLEOPATRA: If it be love indeed, tell me how much.
ANTONY: There's beggary in the love that can be reckon'd.
CLEOPATRA: I'll set a bourn how far to be belov'd.
ANTONY: Then must thou needs find out new heaven, new earth.

There is the whole essence of the play in this double inter-change, and the four lines have very seldom, in our experience, been given anything like their just deliberation. For in these four lines Antony and Cleopatra reveal to us that they are boundlessly and limitlessly in love for the rest of eternity.

These four lines do not absolutely open the great play, though they very nearly do so. In a manner that is utterly without precedent this interchange is preceded by a speech of thirteen lines uttered by a minor character called Philo to another minor character called Demetrius who has not a word to say in return. In the theatre, this opening speech is almost always handed to some minor actor who almost invariably fails to realize that he can here, if he knows how, set the whole mood of the play. It behoves this actor to give the tragedy its whole point, its *donnée*, in a matter of something around one hundred words, the very first of which is the negative particle which anyone – who had not *Antony and Cleopatra* in mind – would deny could possibly set off any play of any sort on its course. It is the particle 'Nay', and this is how it is breathtakingly done and proceeded with:

> Nay, but this dotage of our general's
> O'erflows the measure: those his goodly eyes,
> That o'er the files and musters of the war
> Have glow'd like plated Mars, now bend, now turn,
> The office and devotion of their view
> Upon a tawny front: his captain's heart,
> Which in the scuffles of great fights hath burst

> The buckles on his breast, reneges all temper,
> And is become the bellows and the fan
> To cool a gipsy's lust. Look where they come:
> Take but good note, and you shall see in him
> The triple pillar of the world transform'd
> Into a strumpet's fool: behold and see.

This prelude spoken, there is an annunciatory trumpet and then there enters our mighty duo with eternity already in their lips and eyes.

Only once, in the twelve revivals of this rarely-revived play that one has had to the luck to behold in a matter of twenty-five years – only once was Philo's prelude properly and more than adequately delivered. 'Nay' itself was loaded with protestation and resentment. The words 'tawny' and 'gipsy' and 'strumpet' were each given a sharp emphasis to reveal the common soldier's scorn at his general's thraldom. Almost all of the rest of the speech burned with pride at the valour of the great Triumvir – 'the triple pillar of the world' – and, at one and the same time, burned with indignation at the Queen who was manifestly reducing him to servitude and folly and eventual cowardice and shame.

This occasion was in an anonymous revival of the play by the Marlowe Society at Cambridge away back in the spring of 1946. It was Ivor Brown, of all good judges, who strongly recommended the present writer to cancel any other engagement for that week's end and see this play-production on the Saturday. One did, and the experience was unforgettable.

The direction was by George Rylands, the presiding genius of the Marlowe Society. It was in our experience the best of all his Shakespearean productions. Here was a director who seemed always far more at home with amateurs than with professionals. Untrained and malleable material always did bring out the best in him. He had a particular gift for ensuring that Shakespeare spoke for himself through his students. It is only another way of saying that he insisted on every word being clearly heard and with its proper emphasis down to the smallest syllable of the smallest word in the smallest part.

In this great particular play characters like Agrippa, the Soothsayer, Scarus and even Pompey are usually so subordinated by the almost over-rich substance of the writing as to go almost unnoticed. But all such characters were on this occasion at Cambridge clearly individualized. One had never heard Enobarbus' line: 'He will to his Egyptian dish again!' better or more scathingly pointed. 'O, rare for Antony!' – as Agrippa exclaims. But the whole thing was revelationary from the very start – from Philo's thirteen lines of prelude. (Philo has an unremarkable three or four lines at the end of the scene, and nothing else at all to say in the whole play, such was Shakespeare's largesse when writing in the high Roman fashion.)

For Cleopatra herself George Rylands happily discovered a young woman, neither professional nor in the least beautiful to watch or gaze upon, who had that attribute to which the Shakespearean scholar in him attached a far greater importance – a warm, variable, and expressive voice which she had enough art to use intelligently and obediently. Between them the player and her director conveyed an astonishing amount of that Eternal Womanliness – that *mélange* of vanity, allurement, spite, adorableness, cruelty, tenderness, witchery, ardour, guile, and won't-take-No-for-an-answer-hood – which has been the despair of many of our very best professional actresses.

It is a significant fact that the best English actresses of the last two centuries have not even attempted the formidable part of Shakespeare's Cleopatra – not Siddons nor Ellen Terry nor Mrs Campbell; just as among the supreme actors of the same period, neither Kean nor Kemble nor Henry

Irving nor Forbes-Robertson ever attempted her counterpart Antony. It is true that Kemble wanted to revive the play with himself as Antony and his sister, the great Mrs Siddons, as Cleopatra. The latter would not risk failing in the part and refrained from even trying with her brother or anyone else. She gave the superb reason that she thought the representation might be too much for her public. And it is on record that when she declined the part of Cleopatra she said to Kemble that 'she should hate herself if she should play the part as it ought to be played'.

In consequence of its being neglected, or at least resisted, by all our supreme acting couples in the last 150 years, this great play has inspired no major dramatic criticism between Hazlitt and Ivor Brown himself. Hazlitt, who saw only Charles Mayne Young and Helen Faucit as the mighty duo in 1813, was nevertheless a great dramatic critic and could write of the play in his study as though he had seen it greatly done in the mind's eye; he concludes his general essay on the play itself: 'Shakespeare's genius has spread over the whole play a richness like the overflowing of the Nile.'

This is an example of the grand manner; and Ivor Brown himself attains to the same over and over again when he comes to deal with this, his first favourite among all the plays, in his *magnum opus*, the book simply and sufficiently entitled *Shakespeare*. This work first appeared in the year 1949, the fruit of a lifetime of study, and it should be made compulsive study – indeed, it probably is so – in all schools and theatres where Shakespeare is loved and read and acted.

* * *

Mr Ivor Brown in the middle of his great book – no less a judge than Bernard Shaw described it quite categorically as 'the best book about Shakespeare yet written' – has two consecutive chapters entitled 'Woman Colour'd Ill' and 'Lass

Unparallel'd'. These are the heart of his study, and the heart-beat is almost audible as one reads.

The chapters form a closely-sustained argument to the effect that the mysterious Dark Lady was as important in Shakespeare's life as the character of Cleopatra was pre-eminent in his life-work. The scholar-critic thinks – and makes us think with him – that the Dark Lady (whosoever she was) dominated and devastated Shakespeare far more profoundly than did his wife, his best friend, or his troops of friends. The scholar-critic similarly thinks – and makes us think with him – that Cleopatra is by far the most complex character who ever beguiled his brain and challenged his creative powers to limn her satisfactorily and consistently.

He is careful not to identify these two great influences, one of them upon Shakespeare's life, and the other upon Shakespeare's life-work. But then comes a paragraph when he has just mentioned the death or vanishing from his life of the Dark Lady, and when the two seem almost to merge and become one:

She was dead: or she had moved altogether away from the humble sphere of a player-poet. That would have meant that she had left London, for the English capital of Shakespeare's day – no longer than Oxford in our time – was no easy place in which to miss or to avoid people of note or notoriety. Had she moved onwards and upwards in her conquering progress the player-poet would hardly have forgiven her: and *Antony and Cleopatra* is essentially a hymn of forgiveness. By the time that Shakespeare had finished with the Dark Lady in this tremendous tragedy, she had declared her immortal longings and made Death proud to take her. Almost one might say that the 'daughter of the game' was now a royal spirit, soaring, on the wings of her own beauty, into an empyrean; the whitely wanton, and at other times gipsy wanton, had, through sheer integrity of wantonness and complete concentration upon passion, somehow become in tune with the infinite.

He continues no less superbly:

The last two acts of *Antony and Cleopatra*, acts which contain the most heart-searching poetry that Shakespeare ever wrote, cannot be interpreted in any other way than as a salute to love which tolerates no mitigation, to a lavishness and a luxury which count the world well lost if love be satisfied. They are also a farewell. The Dark Lady may or may not have been dead. But something snapped. The ecstasy and the agony were over.

Elsewhere, within the same two chapters, Mr Brown divagates with the serene impartiality of Goethe himself:

His [Antony's] first speech of any length is a disclaimer of political ambition, since the summit of life is to be discovered in the map of love and not in any chart of earthly kingdoms.

> Let Rome in Tiber melt, and the wide arch
> Of the ranged empire fall! Here is my space.
> Kingdoms are clay: our dungy earth alike
> Feeds beast as man: the nobleness of life
> Is to do thus: when such a mutual pair,
> And such a twain can do't, in which I bind,
> On pain of punishment, the world to weet
> We stand up peerless.

'The nobleness of life'. To that ideal of love-over-all Antony is true: he tosses away his universe for a woman: and the very size of that sacrifice, the strength of the decision, seem to fire Shakespeare's keenest admiration. It is impossible to read or see this play without conviction as to where the playwright's sympathy is placed. He no longer rails at the tyranny of passion; he accepts it, even reveres it, so it be tyrannical enough. It has been well said that gambling is only contemptible if carried on within your means. For Shakespeare, in the mood of this play, this view holds of wenching as well as of wagering. Sexual surrender can lose its shabbiness by loyalty to its own excess.

Time and again Shakespeare, in Sonnet and in play, had cried out against this excess, the expense of spirit in a waste of shame [Sonnet

129]. But now he has lost that careful temper: the lurking Puritan within him has been ousted for a season by the forthright hedonist. So the play moves through its early and not easily staged acts with their abundance of classical history, vexatious to a modern audience, and their manifold changes of scene, as it were a film unfolding. For these reasons and because it needs almost superhuman performance and is lost without the best in casts and direction, *Antony and Cleopatra* will rarely, if ever, be 'good box-office'. The action scrambles forward until it reaches the peaks of the last two acts, peaks not only of the play's own composition but of the Shakespearean workmanship which gives to every word a higher power. It is in the closing passages of this tragedy that we come, in my opinion, closer to Shakespeare's heart than anywhere else, even in *Hamlet*. The temper and opinion there revealed are certainly not characteristic: Shakespeare was, on the whole, a temperate man, careful of his money, nervous that his sensibility might betray him, afraid of his passions. But upon this occasion, he stripped moderation from his mind and paid salutation to a man who would keep nothing.

> His legs bestrid the ocean: his rear'd arm
> Crested the world; his voice was propertied
> As all the tunèd spheres, and that to friends;
> But when he meant to quail and shake the orb,
> He was as rattling thunder. For his bounty,
> There was no winter in't; an autumn 'twas
> That grew the more by reaping: his delights
> Were dolphin-like; they show'd his back above
> The element they lived in: in his livery
> Walked crowns and crownets; realms and islands were
> As plates dropt from his pocket.

He paid salutation no less to the woman who would take all. Half-measures, prudent courses, on the part of either of them would have lost their creator's enraptured obeisance. To find nobleness in such squanderings of property and power was not his enduring philosophy; far from it. But when the vision of such bounty did blaze upon his eyes, he wrote with an intensity, even with a sublimity, not elsewhere equalled in the canon. Cleopatra has the phrase 'less unparallel'd' dropped upon her dying body: it is this concept of supremacy, of uniqueness ('we stand up peerless') and of absolute dedication to love which upon this occasion evoked from him those breath-taking achievements, the death-scenes of Antony and Cleopatra: self-slaughtered both, they die in the high Roman way and make death their proud partners on the last of all the Orient's soft beds.

Mr Ivor Brown continues in this 'high Roman fashion' anent the great play's ending:

For my part, I read the great finale of *Antony and Cleopatra* as a valediction. Something had ended in Shakespeare's life. His health was better, his grip upon himself far more assured than when he was pouring out – one might almost say retching up – the lazar-house cursings of *Timon*. My submission is that because the Dark Lady would neither entrance nor madden him again, he could look back and withhold the stinging phrase with which he had encouraged the ebon hair and eyes, the white and blue-veined skin of that exquisite but 'jigging' wantonness. He would do more than spare, since now, being released, he was free to praise and, because she would not hurt him again, he would forgive, he would adore. For certainly both Antony and Cleopatra died enobled and esteemed. The world first bidden to 'weet' that they stand up peerless sees them lie down no less supreme in their own reckless, lavish, superbly improvident kind,

> Now boast thee, death, in thy possession lies
> A lass unparallel'd.

The brief, affectionate 'lass', the weighty rolling 'unparallel'd' – they are typical Shakespearean magic. They are also a proclamation of pardon, a statement of forgiveness as well as of farewell – to the wanton Cleopatra certainly, and, as I think, to another also, the poet's own love of ecstasy and despair. This, at least, is beyond dispute: that if we owe some of the Sonnets and all of *Antony and Cleopatra* to a Lady Anon, Tudor-Jacobean beauty of her day, then our debt to the unnamed, elusive creature outranges calculation.

MUSIC, HO!

The best-known things about music are too familiar, but they cannot be ignored. Things like Lorenzo's lines to young Jessica in the moonlit garden of Belmont in *The Merchant of Venice* (v, i, 83).

> The man that hath no **music** in himself,
> Nor is not moved with concord of sweet sounds,
> Is fit for treasons, stratagems, and spoils;
> The motions of his spirit are dull as night,
> And his affections dark as Erebus:
> Let no such man be trusted.—Mark the **music.**

(It could readily be argued that this is not strictly true, though it is divinely phrased.)

We like the three last words particularly since they imply that Lorenzo has run out of platitudes on the subject.

We may also note that in the theatre the part of Lorenzo, usually given to some young actor unable to disguise his liking for the sound of his own voice, has been docked by the director of some much better lines in the same long speech (v, i, 70), uttered when Jessica has said that music makes her melancholy:

> The reason is, your spirits are attentive:
> For do but note a wild and wanton herd,
> Or race of youthful and unhandled colts,
> Fetching mad bounds, bellowing, and neighing loud,
> Which is the hot condition of their blood;
> If they but hear perchance a trumpet sound,
> Or any air of **music** touch their ears,
> You shall perceive them make a mutual stand,
> Their savage eyes turn'd to a modest gaze,
> By the sweet power of **music**: . . .

Still better known is the opening of *Twelfth Night* (i, i, 1) where the love-sick Orsino demands a dose of music as though it were a dose of medicine, however exquisite his phrases:

> If **music** be the food of love, play on;
> Give me excess of it, that, surfeiting,
> The appetite may sicken, and so die.—
> That strain again!—it had a dying fall:
> O, it came o'er my ear like the sweet sough,
> That breathes upon a bank of violets,
> Stealing and giving odour!—Enough; no more;
> 'Tis not so sweet now as it was before.

Parenthetically let it be noted that we use the New Cambridge edition's 'sough' instead of 'sound' or 'south' (which was Pope's suggestion). 'Sough' was the expressive word used by William Hazlitt for the tender voice used by Edmund Kean's Othello towards his Desdemona, 'like the soughing of the wind through cedars'.

It is Othello himself, by the way, who reminds us that Shakespeare can say as much, on a subject like music, in an aside of a single line as in a set piece of many lines. In the throes of Othello's jealous rage at Desdemona (and at the height of Iago's evil provocation) he has this of his wife's singing (iv, i, 189): '. . . an admirable **musician**! O, she will sing the savageness out of a bear! . . .'

Almost with his last breath old John of Gaunt in *King Richard II* (ii, i, 12) has a beautiful line that deserves isolation: 'The setting sun, and **music** at the close.'

Cleopatra, with her Antony absent in Rome, begins a scene (*Antony and Cleopatra*, ii, v, 1) with a demand for the solace of sound: 'Give me some **music**,—**music**, moody food Of us that trade in love' (whereupon an Attendant crying: 'The **music**, ho!' provided the late Constant Lambert with the title for his capital book of musical criticism).

59

Pericles falls asleep in the arms of his restored daughter Marina, in *Pericles, Prince of Tyre* (v, i, 232):

> ... I hear
> Most heavenly **music**!
> It nips me unto listening, and thick slumber
> Hangs upon mine eyes: let me rest.

And even in that inconsiderable play, *The Two Gentlemen of Verona*, Proteus makes preparation for his serenade to Silvia in language of a lovely simplicity (IV, ii, 16):

> But here comes Thurio: now must we to her window,
> And give some evening **music** to her ear.

Other references to music are, of course, beyond number, and we can cite only a few. But in *Antony and Cleopatra* itself we must not overlook – as the play's directors so often do in the theatre – this magical little scene. It is but thirty lines in all; it happens on the ramparts of Cleopatra's palace at Alexandria; and music is an integral part of it (IV, iii, 1):

Enter two Soldiers to their guard

1.S. Brother, good night: to-morrow is the day.
2.S. It will determine one way: fare you well.
    Heard you of nothing strange about the streets?
1.S. Nothing. What news?
2.S. Belike 'tis but a rumour. Good night to you.
1.S. Well, sir, good night.

Enter other Soldiers

2.S. Soldiers, have careful watch.
3.S. And you. Good night, good night.

They place themselves in every corner of the stage

4.S. Here we: and if to-morrow
    Our navy thrive, I have an absolute hope
    Our landmen will stand up.

3.S.   'Tis a brave army,
  And full of purpose.
     Music of the hautboys as under the stage
4.S.   Peace! what noise?
1.S.   List, list!
2.S. Hark!
1.S.   **Music** i'the air.
3.S.   Under the earth.
4.S. It signs [= bodes] well, does it not?
3.S.   No.
1.S.   Peace, I say!
  What should this mean?
2.S. 'Tis the god Hercules, whom Antony loved,
  Now leaves him.
1.S.   Walk; let's see if other watchmen
  Do hear what we do?
2.S.   How now, masters!
All (*speaking together*) How now!
  How now! Do you hear this?
1.S.   Ay; is't not strange?
3.S. Do you hear, masters? do you hear?
1.S. Follow the noise so far as we have quarter;
  Let's see how it will give off.
All. Content. 'Tis strange.

The opportunities here for a musical composer of genius are immense, and they do not seem – in our time at least – to have been grasped. The dramatic intensity of the little scene is also very remarkable (and would seem to have been insufficiently remarked – even by Granville-Barker who at least commends the notable economy of the dialogue). The line about Hercules is sheer inspiration, and those who meekly assume that the whole thing derives from Plutarch may like to read the corresponding Plutarch passage and to note that Hercules gets no particular mention, also that instead of this magical and mystical surmise there is a long image of a corybantic procession which Shakespeare wisely disregarded as an irrelevant episode:

Furthermore, the self same night within little of midnight, when all the city was quiet, full of fear and sorrow, thinking what would be the issue and end of this war, it is said that suddenly they heard a marvellous sweet harmony of sundry sorts of instruments of music, with the cry of a multitude of people, as they had been dancing and had sung as they used in Bacchus' feasts, with movings and turnings after the manner of the Satyrs. And it seemed that this dance went through the city unto the gate that opened to the enemies, and that all the troupe who made the noise they heard went out of the city at that gate. Now such as in reason sought the depth of the interpretation of this wonder, thought that it was the god to whom Antonius bore singular devotion to counterfeit and resemble him, that did forsake them.

No mention, be it noted, of Shakespeare's six sentries, or of their inarticulate speech, or of the subterranean *source* of the music they suddenly hear, or of its being played by hautboys, nor any mention of the god Hercules by name.

It is not contested that Shakespeare could take his good where he found it, or knew where it was to be found; and how much of it to take, and how little, for his own poetic purpose.

MUSIC-MAKING

There are so many ways of music-making that it seems best to arrange the instruments in alphabetical order.

See also under SONGS AND SINGING.

BAGPIPES. Salarino in *The Merchant of Venice* has a picturesque phrase about men who are easily amused and 'laugh, like parrots, at a **bag-piper**' (I, i, 53). Shylock in the same play talks of some other men who, 'when the **bag-pipe** sings i'th' nose, Cannot contain their urine' (IV, i, 49). And a few lines later this same Jew refers to the same instrument, semi-contemptuously, as a 'woollen **bag-pipe**'.

At the Sheep Fair in *The Winter's Tale* a Servant tells the Clown of the arrival of Autolycus (IV, iii, 181): 'O master, if you did but hear the pedlar at the door, you would never dance again after a tabor and pipe; no, the **bagpipe** could not move you; he sings several tunes faster than you'll tell money; he utters them as he had eaten ballads, and all men's ears grew to his tunes.'

Falstaff describes himself to Prince Hal as being as melancholy as 'the drone of a Lincolnshire **bagpipe**' in *King Henry IV, Part One* (I, ii, 75).

These are Shakespeare's only mentions of this instrument (of both torture and delight). It exists nowhere in *Macbeth*. It is not (in truth and *pace* Scotland) a particularly Scottish instrument. One has heard it played in Lombardy and northern Greece and (or something very like it) even in the heart of Turkey.

*   *   *

CYMBALS. In the build-up for the very last entrance of Coriolanus, a mere Second Messenger (V, iv, 50) has a finely sonorous little speech containing Shakespeare's only mention of the cymbals:

> Why, hark you!
> The trumpets, sackbuts, psaltries, and fifes,
> Tabors, and **cymbals**, and the shouting Romans,
> Make the sun dance. Hark you!

*   *   *

DRUMS. There are drums innumerable, and one must be eclectic. Another splendid line for an important character's entrance is the Third Witch's 'A **drum**, a **drum**! Macbeth doth come.' (*Macbeth*, I, iii, 30). (And see under TRUMPETS.)

Philip of France is warned by his ambassador Chatillon of

the approach of the English king and his wife, niece, and retinue – in *King John* (II, i, 76):

> CHATILLON: The interruption of their churlish **drums**
> Cuts off more circumstances: they are at hand,
> To parley or to fight; therefore prepare.
> KING PHILIP: How much unlook'd for is this expedition!

A warm French welcome!

Alternately purring like a peaceful tom-cat and roaring like a martial lion, Bolingbroke in *King Richard II* (III, iii, 40) returns from banishment in a mixed-up state, but speaking in splendid style:

> Provided that my banishment repeal'd
> And lands restor'd again be freely granted:
> If not, I'll use th' advantage of my power,
> And lay the summer's dust with showers of blood
> Rain'd from the wounds of slaughter'd Englishmen:
> The which, how far off from the mind of Bolingbroke
> It is, such crimson tempest should bedrench
> The fresh green lap of fair King Richard's land,
> My stooping duty tenderly shall show.
> Go, signify as much, while here we march
> Upon the grassy carpet of this plain.
> Let's march without the noise of threatening **drum**, . . .

It is given to a Third Senator to announce Alcibiades and his 'terrible approach' in *Timon of Athens* (V, ii, 15):

> The enemies' **drum** is heard, and fearful scouring
> Doth choke the air with dust: in, and prepare:
> Ours is the fall, I fear; our foes the snare.

And there is in *All's Well That Ends Well* some distinctly tiresome word-play on 'drum', and 'drums', and 'John Drum' (to whom Parolles is compared repeatedly in III, vi). If one is obliged to study this scene it may be helpful to know that Shakespeare's contemporary, John Marston, wrote a play called *Jack Drum's Entertainment* which is reputed to be a satire on Ben Jonson; also that to this day 'drummed out' is military slang for a soldier ejected from his regiment for insubordination (or from a party for drunkenness).

* * *

FIFES (See under CYMBALS).

FLUTES. These are played in Shakespeare only in *Antony and Cleopatra*, and on two different occasions. One is in Enobarbus' justly celebrated description of the royal barge (II, ii, 198):

> ... the oars were silver,
> Which to the tune of **flutes** kept stroke, and made
> The water which they beat to follow faster,
> As amorous of their strokes. ...

The other is at the end of quite a party in Pompey's galley when only Enobarbus and Menas are left aboard. And if Enobarbus is not, so to speak, half-seas-over and Menas the other half-seas-over then their author cannot communicate the fact in likely dialogue (II, vii, 130):

ENOBARBUS (*to the departing Pompey*): Take heed you fall not.
Menas, I'll not on shore.
MENAS: No, to my cabin.—
These drums!—these trumpets, **flutes**! what!
Let Neptune hear we bid a loud farewell
To these great fellows: sound and be hang'd, and sound out!
                    [*a flourish with drums*
ENOBARBUS: Hoo! says a'.—There's my cap.
MENAS: Hoo!—Noble captain, come. [*exeunt*

'Hoo!' is a notable interjection occurring nowhere else in the works of Shakespeare. One must take it to be something between a scream and a roar.

* * *

HARPS. These are few and far between, but always interestingly and sometimes surprisingly introduced.

First a clash of temper and taste between the hot English Hotspur and the blunt Welsh Glendower in *King Henry IV, Part One* (III, i, 115):

HOTSPUR: I'll have it so: a little charge will do it.
GLENDOWER: I'll not have it alter'd.
HOTSPUR: Will not you?
GLENDOWER: No, nor you shall not.
HOTSPUR: Who shall say me nay?
GLENDOWER: Why, that will I.
HOTSPUR: Let me not understand you, then; speak it in Welsh.
GLENDOWER: I can speak English, lord, as well as you;
    For I was train'd up in the English court;
    Where, being but young, I fram**è**d to the **harp**
    Many an English ditty lovely well,
    And gave the tongue a helpful ornament,—
    A virtue that was never seen in you.
HOTSPUR: Marry, And I am glad of it with all my heart:
    I had rather be a kitten, and cry mew,
    Than one of these same metre ballet-mongers; . . .

Next, Mowbray of Norfolk to his king, who has just banished him to live abroad for ever – *King Richard II* (I, iii, 159):

    The language I have learn'd these forty years,
    My native English, now I must forgo:
    And now my tongue's use is to me no more
    Than an unstringed viol or a **harp**;
    Or like a cunning instrument cased up,
    Or, being open, put into his hands
    That knows no touch to tune the harmony: . . .

Then, a piece of blazing obscurity in *The Tempest* (II, i, 84) from that cipher of a character, Prospero's usurping brother, Antonio. In the very middle of a yawn-making argument between these shipwrecked nobleman and their retinue – an ineffably tedious and witless discussion as to whether or not Dido could be called the Widow Dido after Aeneas left her, and whether it was Tunis she inhabited or Carthage – then Antonio suddenly says of the elderly Gonzalo (who thought 'twas Carthage): 'His word is more than the miraculous **harp**.'

Scholar Henry Hudson here excels himself by telling us that this 'miraculous harp' or lyre belonged to Amphion, king of Thebes; that it was given to him by the god Mercury for his great love of music, and that the walls of Thebes miraculously rose up in answer to his playing. This scholar goes on to quote William Wordsworth: 'The gift to King Amphion, that wall'd a city with its melody', and finally surpasses himself by confuting the non-stop noblemen in their prattle: 'Tunis is in fact supposed to be on or near the site of ancient Carthage.'

Finally we may note with a chuckle Theseus' prompt response in *A Midsummer Night's Dream* (v, i, 44) when offered as part of his wedding-entertainment something called 'The battle with the Centaurs, to be sung By an Athenian eunuch to the **harp**'. Theseus said: 'We'll none of that.'

*   *   *

HAUTBOYS. The word is an earlier form of 'oboe', and it occurs only in a long and capital speech of Falstaff at the end of Act III of *King Henry IV, Part Two*. He is describing the almost repellent leanness of Justice Shallow, young or old. Shallow appears to have been what Ayrshire children of my young days would call a 'skinnymalink'; and Sir John gobbles him up in soliloquy (III, ii, 336):

'. . . for you might have thrust him and all his apparel into an eel-skin; the case of a treble **hautboy** was a mansion for him, a court:—and now has he land and beefs. Well, I'll be acquainted with him, if I return; ... if the young dace be a bait for the old pike, I see no reason, in the law of nature, but I may snap at him. Let time shape, and there an end.'

But hautboys are mentioned also in a stage-direction as providing subterranean music in a most strange little scene in *Antony and Cleopatra* (see under MUSIC HO !).

★   ★   ★

LUTES. The simple beauty of this little word 'lute' – it signifies an obsolete form of harp with a kind of fiddleback to it – inspires many a lovely line here and there throughout the plays.

'For Orpheus' **lute** was strung with poets' sinews', says Proteus in *Two Gentlemen of Verona* (III, ii, 78).

'As bright Apollo's **lute**, strung with his hair', says Berowne in *Love's Labour's Lost* (IV, iii, 340).

'To the lascivious pleasing of a **lute**', says Gloster in *King Richard III* (I, i, 13).

'Take thy **lute**, wench: my soul grows sad with troubles', says Queen Katharine in *King Henry VIII* (III, i, 1), and the Wench immediately complies with the ravishing song that begins:

> Orpheus with his **lute** made trees,
> And the mountain-tops that freeze,
>   Bow themselves, when he did sing:
> To his music plants and flowers
> Ever sprung; as sun and showers
>   There had made a lasting spring.

And old Gower the Chorus, at the beginning of Act IV (Prologue, 25) of *Pericles, Prince of Tyre*, talks of the lost daughter Marina

>   ... when to the **lute**
> She sung, and made the night-bird mute,
> That still records with moan; ...

Other Elizabethans preceded and followed Shakespeare with lute-song. The courtier and poet, Sir Thomas Wyatt, concluded a ditty of his with the line: 'My lute, be still, for I have done', and Wyatt died twelve years before Shakespeare was born. And Thomas Campion, poet and musician who sang his own songs to his own accompaniment, has one beginning: 'When to her lute Corinna sings'. Campion was to die in 1620, four years after Shakespeare's death.

*   *   *

ORGAN. The two references to the noblest of musical instruments are both figurative and indirect but also very fine.

One is in *The Tempest* where Alonso, King of Naples, has almost his only solemn speech (III, iii, 95), imagining the death of his son Ferdinand:

> O, it is monstrous, monstrous!
> Methought the billows spoke, and told me of it;
> The winds did sing it to me; and the thunder,
> That deep and dreadful **organ**-pipe, pronounced
> The name of Prosper: it did bass my trespass.
> Therefore my son i'the ooze is bedded; and
> I'll seek him deeper than e'er plummet sounded,
> And with him there lie mudded.

The other moving and solemn passage is spoken by Prince Henry in *King John* (v, vii, 20) just before the king, poisoned and dying, is borne into the orchard at Swinstead Abbey:

> 'Tis strange that death should sing.—
> I am the cygnet to this pale faint swan,
> Who chants a doleful hymn to his own death,
> And from the **organ**-pipe of frailty sings
> His soul and body to their lasting rest.

*   *   *

PIPES. The shepherd's pipe, usually accompanied by the tabor or the drum, provided peaceful music as distinct from the martial sort. Thus Benedick in *Much Ado About Nothing* (II, iii, 12) describes Claudio as having turned from being a soldier into a man of peace: 'I have known when there was no music with him but the drum and the fife; and now had he rather hear the tabor and the **pipe**.' The same two instruments are coupled again by the Servant in *The Winter's Tale* on the arrival of Autolycus the pedlar (see above under BAGPIPES).

Again it is pipes, of a sort unspecified, which provide in *Much Ado About Nothing* (v, iv, 128) the dance with which that comedy gaily concludes, with Benedick having the very last word: 'Strike up, **pipers**.' And 'shepherds **pipe** on oaten straws' in the Song of Spring near the end of *Love's Labour's Lost* (v, ii, 896).

★   ★   ★

PSALTERIES. The only mention of these ancient instruments – a kind of dulcimer but with strings plucked with a plectrum – is in *Coriolanus* (see above under CYMBALS).

★   ★   ★

REBECK. This ancient instrument again has only one mention, and that is not as an instrument but as the surname of a musician in *Romeo and Juliet*. He is one of the small band which presumably plays at old Capulet's party and certainly plays at Juliet's funeral ceremony. He is 'Hugh Rebeck', and his fellow players – or the only two who play or speak (IV, v, 96) – are 'Simon Catling' and 'James Soundpost'.

The rebeck was a three-stringed instrument played with a bow. A catling was a small-sized lute-string made of catgut. A soundpost – still very much in existence – is a peg between the back and the belly of any stringed instrument, used as an essential support.

These provide goodly names for musicians. It is, none the less, a system of nomenclature which Shakespeare does not greatly or regularly favour, though he did well with 'Mistress Overdone' for the brothel-keeper in *Measure for Measure* and with 'Doll Tearsheet' for the witty slut in *King Henry IV, Part Two*.

*   *   *

RECORDERS. 'Come, some music! come, the recorders!' (*Hamlet*, III, ii, 309). The speaker is, of course, Hamlet, and the 'Recorders Scene' is said to be one of the highlights of the distracted Prince's role. Is it, really and truly?

Hamlet calls for one or two of these instruments – a wooden whistle not unlike a tin-whistle – and there is some delay in the actors' bringing them. One perfectly understands the delay. The actors are presumed to have accompanied their little play, *The Murder of Gonzago*, with recorders and some other instrument; and may therefore be supposed to have had these instruments ready to hand. But why should the Players immediately oblige, or oblige at all?

They have been reasonably well welcomed on arrival. But they are hardly settled down for a night or two at the Danish Court before the Prince of Denmark has given them an exceptionally severe and critical lecture on the art of play-acting (see under ACTING), and they have also been asked to absorb a speech, which is part of the Prince's own purpose and which eventually ensures their little play having a reception which is not so much 'mixed' as disastrously broken off before its conclusion (whatever that conclusion may have been).

Admittedly the third act of *Hamlet* is the most dramatic single act in the whole of the literature of the theatre. But at least one of its fervid admirers questions the 'Recorders Scene'. Every Hamlet in one's own experience (and in one's reading of the part's histrionic history) must have wondered why it exists at all. Shakespeare, for once in a way, is entirely to blame. The little scene has no dramatic validity. It sets out to prove that to play a recorder is 'as easy as lying' and it fails to prove this. It proves nothing whatever except that Guildenstern cannot begin to play a recorder, and that Hamlet apparently can! But to what purpose?

Hippolyta in *A Midsummer Night's Dream* (v, i, 122) mentions the same instrument in her criticism of the Prologue to Pyramus and Thisbe. 'Indeed he hath play'd on this prologue like a child on a **recorder**; a sound, but not in government.' Here again it is implied that to play a recorder at all is certainly not 'as easy as lying'. 'In government' means simply 'in tune'.)

* * *

SACKBUTS. These also are obsolete instruments, mentioned only once in the whole of Shakespeare (see under CYMBALS). The sackbut was a wind instrument, a kind of bass instrument with a slide, like that of a trombone, for altering the pitch.

* * *

TABORS AND TABORINES (see also under PIPES). These are forms of drum (quite distinct from the tambour and the tambourine). The tabor was a small drum used chiefly as an accompaniment to the pipe or trumpet.

A tabor is carried by Feste in *Twelfth Night* (III, i, 1) when he exchanges some not very witty chop-logic with Viola:

VIOLA: Save thee, friend, and thy music! dost thou live by thy **tabor**?
FESTE: No, sir, I live by the church.
VIOLA: Art thou a churchman?
FESTE: No such matter, sir: I do live by the church; for I do live at my house, and my house doth stand by the church.
VIOLA: So thou mayst say, the king lies by a beggar, if a beggar dwell near him; or, the church stands by thy tabor, if thy tabor stand by the church.
FESTE: You have said, sir.

It is not perhaps the worthiest scene in this delicious play.

It is with a tabor, too, that Ariel in *The Tempest* (IV, i, 175) lures and beguiles the shipwrecked Italians – 'Then I beat my **tabor**' – till they are all standing up to the neck in the waters of a stagnant pool. Perhaps the sprite had been overhearing too much of their laboured persiflage?

Tabourines rattle at the very end of a superb scene in which Antony and Cleopatra do honour to the warrior Scarus for his valour in that day's battle (IV, viii, 22):

ANTONY: Behold this man;
   Commend unto his lips thy favouring hand:—
   Kiss it, my warrior:—he hath fought to-day
   As if a god, in hate of mankind, had
   Destroy'd in such a shape.
CLEOPATRA: I'll give thee, friend,
   An armour all of gold; it was a king's.
ANTONY: He hath deserved it, were it carbuncled
   Like holy Phoebus' car.—Give me thy hand:—
   Through Alexandria make a jolly march;
   Bear our hack'd targets like the men that owe them:
   Had our great palace the capacity
   To camp this host, we all would sup together,
   And drink carouses to the next day's fate,
   Which promises royal peril.—Trumpeters,
   With brazen din blast you the city's ear;
   Make mingle with our rattling **tabourines**;
   That heaven and earth may strike their sounds together,
   Applauding our approach.

                    ★   ★   ★

TRUMPETS (see under CYMBALS and TABORS in this section).
   Trumpets snarl innumerably in the plays:
   'There roar'd the sea, and **trumpet**-clangour sounds.' –
Pistol in *King Henry IV, Part Two*, (V, v, 41).
   'The Moor! I know his **trumpet**.' – Iago in *Othello* (II, i, 179).

'What **trumpet's** that?' 'I know't, my sister's.' – Regan in *King Lear* (II, iv, 184).

'**Trumpet**, blow loud. Send thy brass voice through all these lazy tents.' – Aeneas in *Troilus and Cressida* (I, iii, 256).

'Now,—when the angry **trumpet** sounds alarum, and dead men's cries do fill the empty air.' – Warwick at Saint Albans in *King Henry VI, Part Two* (v, ii, 3)—a play which no one, not even the dramatic critics, pretends to know well.

'The **trumpet** sounds retreat; the days is ours.' – Prince Hal in *King Henry IV, Part One* (v, iv, 162).

'By Chrish, la, tish ill done; the work ish given over, the **trumpet** sound the retreat.' – Macmorris in *King Henry V* (III, ii, 89).

'Sound drums and **trumpets**, boldly and cheerfully; God and Saint George!' – Richmond in *King Richard III* (v, iii, 270).

'Sound drums and **trumpets**, and the king will fly.' – Richard Plantagenet in *King Henry VI, Part Three* (I, i, 118).

'Sound drums and **trumpets**;—and to London all.' – Warwick in *King Henry VI, Part Two* (v, iii, 32).

These are ten of the many examples. And after all this 'brazen din' (in Mark Antony's phrase) it says much for John Dryden that there is no kind of anti-climax in his poem in honour of St Cecilia's Day in the year 1687, nearly seventy years after Shakespeare's heyday:

> The trumpet's loud clangor
> Excites us to arms,
> With shrill notes of anger
> And mortal alarms.
> The double double double beat
> Of the thundering drum
> Cries, Hark! the foes come;
> Charge, charge, 'tis too late to retreat.

VIOLS AND VIOL-DE-GAMBOYS. The viol – which is the violin's predecessor – is mentioned by Mowbray, Duke of Norfolk, in *King Richard II* in the course of his noble speech on his own banishment from England for evermore. The king has just expressed his fate more characteristically (I, iii, 150).

> The sly slow hours shall not determinate
> The dateless limit of thy dear exile;—
> The hopeless word of 'never to return'
> Breathe I against thee, upon pain of life.

And Mowbray has his eloquent and much less affected reply including the lines (I, iii, 160–62):

> My native English, now I must forgo:
> And now my tongue's use is to me no more
> Than an unstrangéd **viol** or a harp; . . .

The viol is again mentioned in *Pericles, Prince of Tyre* (III, ii, 88) as part of the music that brought back to life Queen Thaisa who had been long tossing in the waves in a kind of floating coffin:

> The rough and woeful music that we have,
> Cause it to sound, beseech you.
> The **viol** once more: . . .

And one may still live to see the day when, in a production of *Twelfth Night*, Sir Andrew Aguecheek is seen to take his early violoncello (the viola de gamba) between his knees and play it. For we have Sir Toby Belch's authority (I, iii, 25), expressed to Maria, that the foolish knight 'plays o' th' **viol-de-gamboys**, and speaks three or four languages word for word without book, and hath all the good gifts of nature.'

VIRGINALS. The first English stringed keyboard instrument. When there were two keyboards it was called 'the virginals'. It is known that Queen Elizabeth herself played it, and played it well. It had no legs and when wanted it was placed on a table or a suitable stand.

Shakespeare's sole reference is oblique and curious. This occurs in *The Winter's Tale* (I, ii, 125), where the insanely jealous Leontes is speculating on the possible bastardy of his little son by Hermione, the prince Mamillius. He fumes because Hermione is persuading his friend Polixenes, by means of hand-clasps, to extend his stay. Leontes mutters to himself: 'Still **virginalling** upon his palm?', then turns to the little boy and says aloud: 'How now, you wanton calf! *Art* thou my calf?'

See also under SONGS AND SINGING

SCRAPPING AND WRESTLING

It is odd to find that a 'scrap', in the sense of a fight or tussle between two, is only as old as the year 1874 when it had a slang origin. Shakespeare uses the now-archaic word 'foin' in this sense, especially concerning a fight or scrimmage with pointed weapons. (See also under DUELLING AND FENCING).

Thus in *Part Two* of *King Henry IV* Mistress Quickly says of Falstaff to the sheriff's officers, Fang and Snare (II, 1, 12–14): 'Alas the day, take heed of him, he stabbed me in mine own house, most beastly in good faith, 'a cares not what mischief he does, if his weapon be out, he will **foin** like any devil, he will spare neither man, woman, nor child'.

And again, in the same act of the same play, Doll Tearsheet reminds Falstaff of his mortality (II, 4, 222–25): 'Thou whoreson little tidy Bartholomew boar-pig, when wilt thou leave fighting o' days and **foining** o' nights, and begin to patch up thine old body for heaven?' And Doll receives her immortal answer from the old knight: 'Peace, good Doll, do not speak like a death's-head, do not bid me remember mine end.'

There would seem to be no reference to boxing, or fighting

with gloves, anywhere in Shakespeare. Half-a-dozen times
at least a 'box on the ear' is given or taken. Thus Portia
discussing her suitors with her maid Nerissa (in *The Merchant
of Venice*) said of the Scottish lord that he 'borrowed a box
of the ear of the Englishman, and swore he would pay him
back when he was able'. (Editor Ridley in the New Temple
edition drily comments here: 'This would not do for performance before King James.')

Again, in the innermost heart of the unfamiliar trilogy
about the Wars of the Roses, *Part Two* of *King Henry VI*,
we may like to note a colloquy between Lord Say (who is
just about to be beheaded off-stage) and that bloodthirsty
rebel Jack Cade. The rebel has just expressed himself in
admirably clear prose on the subject of his distrust of
education (IV vii 22):

> Well, he shall be beheaded for it ten times. Ah,
> thou say, thou serge, nay, thou buckram lord! now art thou
> within point-blank of our jurisdiction regal ... I am the besom
> that must sweep the court clean of such filth as
> thou art. Thou has most traitorously corrupted the
> youth of the realm in erecting a grammar school:
> and whereas before, our forefathers had no other books
> but the score and the tally, thou hast caused printing
> to be used, and contrary to the king, his crown and
> dignity, thou hast built a paper-mill. It will be
> proved to thy face thou hast men about thee that usually
> talk of a noun and a verb, and such abominable words
> as no Christian ear can endure to hear ...

Then Lord Say and Jack Cade have their relevant interchange (IV, vii, 81–82):

SAY: These cheeks are pale for watching for your good.
CADE: Give him a box o' the ear, and that will make them red again.

The word 'boxing' – in the sense of that sport or pastime

in which two men wearing boxing-gloves exchange blows and parries and feints in accordance with the set rules and for the delectation of onlookers – does not seem to have been in use before the very beginning of the eighteenth century (and therefore a full century after Shakespeare's death).

In Shakespeare this ancient sport of wrestling is almost entirely in the hands (and arms, and legs) of Charles the Wrestler in *As You Like It*. This is the character with whom Orlando tries a fall, and, very surprisingly, wins it to the deep and lasting admiration of Rosalind who is a spectator at the match. The part of Charles is one which depends much more upon physical stamina than upon eloquence, and yet – such is the incalculable nature of the playwright – he is given perhaps the most beautiful little prose-speech (under fifty words) of any minor character in all the works. Usually this is beyond the vocal and expressive powers of the brawny young actor chosen for Charles. But this is what he has to say (I, I, 115):

OLIVER: Where will the old duke live?
CHARLES: They say he is already in the forest of Arden, and a many merry men with him; and there they live like the old Robin Hood of England; they say many young gentlemen flock to him every day, and fleet the time carelessly as they did in the golden world.

Charles has altogether some 350 words of such good prose to speak, at the end of which he is thrown by Orlando, and borne away. He does not reappear in the play, though doubtless he might be recognized as the heftiest of the banished Duke's supporters in the Forest of Arden. No Charles that one can trace ever developed into a celebrated actor, though this is a nice subject for theatrical research through the ages.

A certain celebrated actor, still very much alive, strikingly failed to make a success as Orlando in his youth. The truth is that he very nearly lost the wrestling-match at the beginning of the play. Vividly across the years one remembers him being 'thrown' by an over-enthusiastic Charles the Wrestler, so that he smacked the stage with his shoulders and had some considerable difficulty in getting to his feet again without help.

SHOVEL-BOARD

With a marvellous mixture of sheer good luck and some little skill in plodding research, one can follow an obscure hint in Shakespeare to something like the humble and ubiquitous modern tavern-game of 'shove-ha'penny'. It occurs in a passage-at-arms in the Boar's-Head Tavern in Eastcheap when Falstaff and Pistol seem bent on quarrelling and Doll Tearsheet and Bardolph are at least trying to keep the peace – *King Henry IV*, *Part Two* (II, iv, 182):

FALSTAFF: Pistol, I would be quiet.

PISTOL: Sweet knight, I kiss thy neif: what! we have seen the seven stars.

DOLL: For God's sake, thrust him down stairs: I cannot endure such a fustian rascal.

PISTOL: Thrust him down stairs! know we not
Galloway nags?

FALSTAFF: Quoit him down, Bardolph, like a **shove-groat shilling**: nay, an a' do nothing but speak nothing, a' shall be nothing here.

BARDOLPH: Come, get you down stairs.

PISTOL: What! shall we have incision? shall we imbrue?—
[*he snatches up his sword*
Then death rock me asleep, abridge my doleful days!
Why, then, let grievous, ghastly, gaping wounds
Untwine the Sisters Three! Come, Atropos, I say!
[*he offers to fight*

HOSTESS: Here's goodly stuff toward!

Goodly stuff indeed, but far from easy with its many allusions to old plays and forgotten ballads!

We know that 'neif' or 'nieve' means 'hand' or 'fist', that it is also used by Bottom the Weaver and Robert Burns in that sense, and that it is still current in Scottish dialect where it nowadays means a *clenched* fist. We know too that 'Galloway nags' are the little horses peculiar to south-west Scotland.

But Falstaff's 'Quoit him down, Bardolph, like a shove-groat shilling' is the exciting line that gives us pause. 'Quoit' here means simply 'strike' or 'pitch', and 'shove-groat shilling' clearly implies the shoving of a coin of sorts, hence shovel-board. Editor Hudson tells us that *shove-groat shillings* were broad shillings of King Edward VI. In *The Merry Wives of Windsor* they are spoken of as *Edward shovel-boards.*' We turn the pages and find there (I, i, 144):

FALSTAFF: Pistol, did you pick Master Slender's purse?
SLENDER: Ay, by these gloves, did he ... of seven groats in mill-sixpences, and two Edward **shovel-boards**, that cost me two shilling and two pence a-piece of Yead Miller, by these gloves.

And in his note to the passage Editor Hudson is again most helpful: '*Milled*, or *stamped*, sixpences were used as *counters*; said to have been first coined in 1561.—Edward *shovel-boards* were the broad shillings of Edward VI, used for playing the game of *shuffle-board*; the shilling being placed on the edge of the table, and driven at the mark by a stroke of the hand.'

And my old Fleet Street colleague, Mr Vernon Bartlett, is more helpful still in his recent book, *The Past of Pastimes*: ' "Shovel-board" was a large-scale variety of that splendid public house game, shove ha'penny, ... [It] is played on a small board of hardwood or slate on a pub table, and its antiquity is indicated by the fact that it was formerly known as "shove groat" or "slyp groat". . . . Say what you will, there is a certain beauty about the gentleness with which some farm labourer with a fist like a sledge-hammer will nudge his coin into the proper "bed" with the palm of his hand.'

It may round off this little exercise if we finally point out that the boy-king Edward VI died in 1553, eleven years before Shakespeare was born.

SONGS AND SINGING

AIRS. 'Now, divine **air**! now is his soul ravish'd!' Thus Benedick, while the musicians play the air Balthazar is about to sing in *Much Ado About Nothing* (II, iii, 60). And he goes on: 'Is it not strange that sheeps' guts should hale souls out of men's bodies?' Across the years – nearly fifty of them now – one remembers the hum of appreciation, a kind of audible smile, that went through the audience when the Benedick of Henry Ainley uttered this whimsey. The song that follows is 'Sigh no more, ladies'.

The oafish Cloten, with that occasional lyrical tone to his rough tongue, has a very similar remark in *Cymbeline* (II, iii, 19). This concerns that abstruse play's beautiful song, 'Hark, hark! the lark', which he preludes with the line: 'A wonderful sweet **air**, with admirable rich words to it.' He follows the song's performance with some further words to the musicians (II, iii, 30): 'So, get you gone. If this penetrate [to Imogen], I will consider your music the better: if it do not, it is a vice in her ears, which horse-hairs and calves'-guts, nor the voice of unpaved eunuch to boot, can never amend.'

★   ★   ★

ANTHEMS. One of the Two Gentlemen of Verona (Valentine) asks the other one (Proteus) for a word of comfort in his sorrows – 'as ending **anthem** of my endless dolour' (III, i, 240).

And Falstaff, in *King Henry IV, Part Two* (I, ii, 194), protests to the Lord Chief Justice that he is not nearly so old as he looks and sounds: 'For my voice,—I have lost it with hallooing, and singing of **anthems.**'

BALLADS. Shakespeare is bounteous with mention of actual ballads (existing or lost), most especially in *The Winter's Tale*, where Autolycus sells them among his knick-knacks. But none of these has anything like the suggestive allurement of the story begun by little Prince Mamillius in the same play, a tale 'of sprites and goblins' of which, maddeningly, we possess nothing but the very first line: 'There was a man, dwelt by a churchyard' (II, i, 29).

There is one mention of ballad-makers in a remarkable colloquy between the serving-men of Aufidius in *Coriolanus*. The lines are seldom heard in the theatre because they are usually cut from any performance. But the colloquy is worth studying if only for its unusual pro-war trend. It concludes thus (IV, v, 202), and the discussion, of course, concerns Coriolanus himself:

THIRD SERV.: ... he has as many friends as enemies: which friends, sir, as it were, durst not, look you, sir, show themselves, as we term it, his friends whilst he's in directitude.

FIRST SERV.: Directitude! what's that?

THIRD SERV.: But when they shall see, sir, his crest up again, and the man in blood, they will out of their burrows, like conies after rain, and revel all with him.

FIRST SERV.: But when goes this forward?

THIRD SERV.: To-morrow; to-day; presently; you shall have the drum struck up this afternoon: 'tis, as it were, a parcel of their feast, and to be executed ere they wipe their lips.

SECOND SERV.: Why, then we shall have a stirring world again. This peace is nothing, but to rust iron, increase tailors, and breed **ballad-makers.**

FIRST SERV.: Let me have war, say I; it exceeds peace as far as day does night; it's spritely, waking, audible, and full of vent [= pluck and courage]. Peace is a very apoplexy, lethargy; mull'd, deaf, sleepy, insensible; a getter of more bastard children than war's a destroyer of men.

SECOND SERV.: 'Tis so: and as war, in some sort, may be said to be a ravisher, so it cannot be denied but peace is a great maker of cuckolds.

FIRST SERV.: Ay, and it makes men hate one another.

THIRD SERV.: Reason; because they then less need one another. The wars for my money. I hope to see Romans as cheap as Volscians.— They are rising, they are rising.

ALL THREE: In, in, in, in!

They have points of view, and express them racily. It is stupid as well as snobbish to cut them entirely.

★　　★　　★

CATCHES. A catch, or round in which each singer echoes the one before, producing light-hearted or comical effects, is a word which would seem to have been brand-new when Shakespeare introduced it in his *Twelfth Night* around the year 1600.

Feste has just delivered himself of the song 'O mistress mine', when Sir Toby says: 'But shall we make the welkin dance indeed? shall we rouse the night-owl in a **catch** that will draw three souls out of one weaver? shall we do that?' And Sir Andrew agrees: 'An you love me, let's do't: I am dog at a **catch**. . . . Let our **catch** be, "Thou knave."' (II, iii, 56). They set about it. Then Malvolio comes in to quieten the roysterers: 'My masters, are you mad? or what are you? Have you no wit, manners, nor honesty, but to gabble like tinkers at this time of night? Do you make an ale-house of my lady's house, that ye squeak out your coziers' **catches** without any mitigation or remorse of voice?' And Sir Toby rudely answers the pompous Puritan: 'We did keep time, sir, in our **catches**. Sneck-up!' (II, iii, 84). It is as though the players could not utter the new word often enough. The catch was the catch-word of the season.

Some other quite elemental characters – Caliban and his new friends, Trinculo and Stephano – also prove themselves dogs at a catch – in *The Tempest* (III, ii, 118):

CALIBAN: Thou makest me merry; I am full of pleasure:
   Let us be jocund: will you troll the **catch**
   You taught me but while-ere?
STEPHANO: At thy request, monster, I will do reason, any reason.—
   Come on, Trinculo, let us sing.
   'Flout 'em and scout 'em,' etc.
CALIBAN: That's not the tune.

There follows the stage-direction: '*Ariel plays a tune on a tabor and pipe*', and the scene goes on magically to its celebrated climax:

STEPHANO: What is this same?
TRINCULO: This is the tune of our **catch**, played by the picture of
   Nobody.
STEPHANO: If thou be'st a man, show thyself in thy likeness: if thou
   be'st a devil, take't as thou list.
TRINCULO: O, forgive me my sins!
STEPHANO: He that dies pays all debts: I defy thee.—
   Mercy upon us!
CALIBAN: Art thou afeard?
STEPHANO: No, monster, not I.
CALIBAN: Be not afeard; the isle is full of noises,
   Sounds, and sweet airs, that give delight, and hurt not.
   Sometimes a thousand twangling instruments
   Will hum about mine ears; and sometimes voices,
   That, if I then had waked after long sleep,
   Will make me sleep again: and then, in dreaming,
   The clouds methought would open, and show riches
   Ready to drop upon me; that, when I waked,
   I cried to dream again. . . .

*   *   *

DITTIES. It is a carefree-sounding word. But an odd majority of those mentioned or quoted by Shakespeare are melancholy. 'It was a lover and his lass' in *As You Like It* is sung in good cheer by two Pages, but it meets with a jarring note in Touchstone's criticism (v, iii, 33):

TOUCHSTONE: Truly, young gentlemen, though there was no great matter in the **ditty**, yet the note was very untuneable.

FIRST PAGE: You are deceived, sir: we kept time, we lost not our time.

TOUCHSTONE: By my troth, yes; I count it but time lost to hear such a foolish song. God b'wi'you; and God mend your voices!— Come, Audrey.

One rejoices to see that the performers answered the self-appointed music-critic – with right and justice, apart from a not unimportant misunderstanding between 'keeping time' and 'keeping in tune'.

In *Much Ado About Nothing* (II, iii, 73) the famous song which begins 'Sigh no more, ladies' goes on to ask them further:

> Sing no more **ditties**, sing no moe
> Of dumps so dull and heavy. . . .

In *King Henry IV, Part One* (III, i, 120) that consummate Welshman, Owen Glendower, tells Hotspur:

> I can speak English, lord, as well as you;
> For I was train'd up in the English court;
> Where, being but young, I framed to the harp
> Many an English **ditty** lovely well, . . .

And later in the same scene Mortimer, Earl of March, says to his own Welsh-speaking lady (III, i, 202):

> I understand thy kisses, and thou mine,
> And that's a feeling disputation:
> But I will never be a truant, love,
> Till I have learn'd thy langyage; for thy tongue
> Makes Welsh as sweet as **ditties** newly penn'd,
> Sung by a fair queen in a summer's bower,
> With ravishing division, to her lute.

And twenty lines or so later Hotspur has an interchange with his own Welsh-speaking wife which Eric Partridge in his immensely suggestive book, *Shakespeare's Bawdy*, convinces us to be very sexual indeed in its double-meanings:

HOTSPUR: Come, Kate, thou art perfect in lying down: come, quick, quick, quick, that I may lay my head in thy lap.
LADY PERCY: Go, ye giddy goose.   [*The music plays*
HOTSPUR: Now I perceive the devil understands Welsh;
And 'tis no marvel he is so humorous.
By'r lady, he is a good musician.
LADY PERCY: Then should you be nothing but musical; for you are altogether govern'd by humours. Lie still, ye thief, and hear the lady **sing** in Welsh.

One well remembers the grace and beauty – positively Welsh in its intensity and fun – of Margaret Leighton as Lady Percy. She had that prince of Hotspurs, Olivier, very much with her. It was the great season when the Old Vic was at the New Theatre; and Ralph Richardson was the glorious Falstaff in this same play; and the war was ended, and it seemed that civilization had begun all over again.

*   *   *

HYMNS. A hymn is, according to the dictionary, a solemn song to God or some lesser deity. (It can therefore be both ancient and modern.) All of Shakespeare's references are intensely poetical.

Capulet on Juliet's death ordains (*Romeo and Juliet*, IV, v, 88): 'Our solemn **hymns** to sullen dirges change.'

Lorenzo at Belmont orders a hymn to be sung for the return of Portia (*The Merchant of Venice*, v, i, 66): 'Come, ho, and wake Diana with a **hymn**!' and Jessica, a shade unnecessarily replies, that she is never merry when she hears such sweet music.

In *A Midsummer Night's Dream* (I, i, 73) Theseus tells Hermia that, if she chooses not to marry, she may for the rest of her life have to be 'chanting faint **hymns** to the cold fruitless moon' (observe the loaded meaning of the word 'fruitless'). And in the same play Titania, in the course of a lovely forty-lines-long speech on the disorders in Nature caused by her quarrel with Oberon has the line (II, i, 102): 'No night is now with **hymn** or carol blest.'

Claudio in *Much Ado About Nothing* (v, iii, 11) has the effrontery to give an order to the chorus at Hero's mock-funeral: 'Now, music, sound, and sing your solemn **hymn**.'

And Shakespeare himself, presumably, in the Sonnets (No. 29, lines 10–12) describes how he can soar out of unhappiness:

> Haply I think on thee,—and then my state,
> Like to the lark at break of day arising
> From sullen earth, sings **hymns** at heaven's gate; . . .

★   ★   ★

TUNES. Of all the kings in Shakespeare the least satisfactory and most inconsequent is surely Cymbelina, whose only two virtues are (1) that he gave his name to one of Shakespeare's least satisfactory and most inconsistent plays and (2) that at least he was the father of that most satisfactory and consistent of heroines, the princess Imogen.

And of the whole part of Cymbeline himself, only a single line – which is only half a line – is glowing with poetry. It is in the scene (*Cymbeline*, v, v, 236) in which Imogen confronts Pisanio whom she suspects of having tried to poison her, and accuses him in the presence of the king himself with the words:

> O, get thee from my sight;
> Thou gavest me poison: dangerous fellow, hence!
> Breathe not where princes are.

It is a proud and flashing utterance (to which Ellen Terry's famous Imogen must have done justice). And Cymbeline's half-line of comment is a sudden ecstatic appreciation of his radiant daughter. It is of six syllables only, but they are a little poem in purest music. They are the words: 'The **tune** of Imogen!'

SWIMMING

There is far more swimming done in *The Tempest* than in any other of the plays. Ariel can obviously swim like a fish as well as fly like a bat or a swallow, and he says so in an entreaty to Prospero to command him anything (I, ii, 189):

> All hail, great master! grave sir, hail! I come
> To answer thy best pleasure; be't to fly,
> To **swim**, to dive into the fire, to ride
> On the curl'd clouds,—to thy strong bidding task
> Ariel and all his quality.

And both Stephano and Trinculo in the same play tell us that they swim like ducks and better than geese.

Every schoolboy remembers how Cassius was challenged by Julius Caesar to swim in the Tiber (I, ii, 100) and how he describes the incident to Brutus long afterwards:

> For once, upon a raw and gusty day,
> The troubled Tiber chasing with her shores,
> Caesar said to me, 'Dare'st thou, Cassius, now
> Leap in with me into this angry flood,
> And **swim** to yonder point?' Upon the word,
> Accoutred as I was, I plungèd in,
> And bade him follow: so, indeed, he did.
> The torrent roar'd; and we did buffet it
> With lusty sinews, throwing it aside
> And stemming it with hearts of controversy;
> But ere we could arrive the point proposed,
> Caesar cried, 'Help me, Cassius, or I sink!' ...

And the Fool says expressively to King Lear, when the latter tears off his clothes in the storm (*King Lear*, III, iv, 113): 'Prithee, nuncle, be contented; 'tis a naughty night to **swim** in.'

TENNIS

Shakespeare's references to the game of bowls are much **more** frequent and detailed than those to tennis, and it is probably rightly argued that the former was what he greatly preferred above all other ball-games.

But the allusion to tennis-balls in *King Henry V* (I, ii, 235–99) must give us particular pause, especially as neither Dr Caroline Spurgeon (1935) nor Mr Eric Partridge in *Shakespeare's Bawdy* (1947) makes any mention of them. A chestful of tennis-balls is sent as a present from the Dauphin of France to the King of England, and it is not possible at this time of day. They arrive as **balls**, *tout court* and unqualified, and that they were meant as a direct insult is perfectly clear from the text. One gives here the Olivier film-text, but though transposed it is unaltered:

Enter Ambassadors of France

KING HENRY: Now are we well prepared to know the pleasure
  Of our fair cousin Dauphin; for we hear
  Your greeting is from him, not from the king.
AMBASSADOR: May't please your majesty to give us leave
  Freely to render what we have in charge;
  Or shall we sparingly show you far off
  The Dauphin's meaning and our embassy?
KING HENRY: We are no tyrant, but a Christian king; ...
  Therefore with frank and with uncurbed plainness
  Tell us the Dauphin's mind.
AMBASSADOR: Thus, then, in few.
  Your highness, lately sending into France,
  Did claim some certain dukedoms, in the right
  Of your great predecessor, King Edward the Third.
  In answer of which claim, the prince our master
  Says, that you savour too much of your youth; ...
  He therefore sends you, meeter for your spirit,

This tun of treasure; and, in lieu of this,
Desires you let the kingdoms that you claim
Hear no more of you. This the Dauphin speaks.
KING HENRY: What treasure, uncle?
DUKE OF EXETER: **Tennis-balls**, my liege.
KING HENRY: We are glad the Dauphin is so pleasant with us;
His present and your pains, we thank you for:
When we have match'd our **rackets** to these **balls**,
We will, in France, by God's grace, play a **set**
Shall strike his father's crown into the hazard. ...
And tell the pleasant prince, this mock of his
Hath turn'd his **balls** to gun-stones, and his soul
Shall stand sore charged for the wasteful vengeance
That shall fly with them: for many a thousand widows
Shall this his mock mock out of their dear husbands;
Mock mothers from their sons, mock castles down;
And, some are yet ungotten and unborn
That shall have cause to curse the Dauphin's scorn. ...
So, get you hence in peace; and tell the Dauphin,
His jest will savour but of shallow wit,
When thousands weep, more than did laugh at it.
Convey them with safe conduct.—Fare you well.
                              [*Exeunt Ambassadors*

All who saw the film must well remember the long pause
immediately after Exeter's 'Tennis-balls, my liege', and then
the mounting rage and speed of the Olivier Henry thereafter
– with, all the while, a chest full of offensive white tennis-balls
in full view of everybody throughout the episode.

Later on in the play Exeter has a colloquy with the Dauphin
and the French King, when the subject is raised again (II, 3,
127–140):
DAUPHIN: Say, if my father render fair return,
It is against my will; for I desire
Nothing but odds with England: to that end
As matching to his youth and vanity,
I did present him with the Paris **balls**.

EXETER: He'll make your Paris Louvre shake for it
 Were it the mistress Court of mighty Europe:
 And be assured you'll find a difference,
 As we his subjects have in wonder found
 Between the promise of his greener days
 And there he masters now: now he weighs time,
 Even to the utmost grain: that you shall read
 In your own losses if he stay in France.
FRENCH KING: To-morrow shall you know our mind at full.

It is all very mettlesome and eloquent. But it is also an example of periphrasis – i.e. saying in many words what a single short word (familiar in to-day's colloquial English) would express. Shakespeare's historical authority the chronicler Holinshed, is no less periphrastic in his way and in his quaint old spelling:

Whilest in the Lent season the king laie at Killingworth, there came to him from Charles Dolphin of France certeine ambassadors, that brought with them a barrell of Paris *balles* [the italics are Holinshed's]; which from their meister they presented to him for a token that was taken in verie ill part, as sent in scorne, to signifie, that it was more meet for the king to passe the time with such childish exercise, than to attempt any worthie exploit.

WALKING

Walking for no other purpose than exercise is fairly infrequent in the plays. Gloucester in *King Henry VI, Part Two* (I, iii, 150) deliberately walks himself into a good temper:

  Now, lords, my choler being over-blown
  With **walking** once about the quadrangle,
  I come to talk of commonwealth affairs. . . .

There is an extremely odd little scene in *Macbeth* (III, vi) of some fifty lines in all, which has two references to Banquo's habit of 'walking too late', and so much else beside of mysterious interest and power that one has no hesitation whatever in giving it here in its inexplicable entirety. The scene tells us a little, though not enough, about the baffling character called Lennox, and it tells us just as little about the only other character in the scene, who is a Lord without even a name. The scene, set in the king's palace at Forres, is oddly placed between two meetings of the Witches – the rarely played Hecate scene and the Cauldron scene (both sometimes attributed, at least in part, to Middleton rather than Shakespeare).

Let us quote it complete, before asking further about its significance, and let us note while reading it that almost every line of it gives us pause for wonderment at the sincerity of the speaker, whether it be Lennox or the Lord:

LENNOX: My former speeches have but hit your thoughts,
    Which can interpret further: only, I say,
    Things have been strangely borne. The gracious Duncan
    Was pitied of Macbeth:—marry, he was dead:—
    And the right-valiant Banquo **walk'd** too late;
    Whom, you may say, if't please you, Fleance kill'd,
    For Fleance fled: men must not **walk** too late.
    Who cannot want the thought, how monstrous
    It was for Malcolm and for Donalbain
    To kill their gracious father? damned fact!
    How it did grieve Macbeth! did he not straight,
    In pious rage, the two delinquents **tear,**
    That were the slaves of drink and thralls of sleep?
    Was not that nobly done? Ay, and wisely too;
    For 'twould have anger'd any heart alive
    To hear the men deny't. So that, I say,
    He has borne all things well: and I do think
    That, had he Duncan's sons under his key,—
    As, an't please heaven, he shall not,—they should find
    What 'twere to kill a father; so should Fleance.

But, peace!—for from broad words, and 'cause he fail'd
His presence at the tyrant's feast, I hear,
Macduff lives in disgrace: sir, can you tell
Where he bestows himself?
LORD: The son of Duncan,
From whom this tyrant holds the due of birth,
Lives in the English court; and is received
Of the most pious Edward with such grace,
That the malevolence of fortune nothing
Takes from his high respect: thither Macduff
Is gone to pray the holy king, upon his aid
To wake Northumberland and warlike Siward:
That, by the help of these—with Him above
To ratify the work—we may again
Give to our tables meat, sleep to our nights;
Free from our feasts and banquets bloody knives;
Do faithful homage, and receive free honours;—
All which we pine for now: and this report
Hath so exasperate the king, that he
Prepares for some attempt of war.
LENNOX: Sent he to Macduff?
LORD: He did: and with an absolute 'Sir, not I',
The cloudy messenger turns me his back,
And hums; as who should say, 'You'll rue the time
That clogs me with this answer.'
LENNOX: And that well might
Advise him to a caution, to hold what distance
His wisdom can provide. Some holy angel
Fly to the court of England, and unfold
His message ere he come; that a swift blessing
May soon return to this our suffering country
Under a hand accurst!
LORD: I'll send my prayers with him.

This may be called Lennox's single scene. He has only a
line or two more to utter – though they are usually lines well
worth uttering. At his very first appearance in the play he

has to speak about that no less cryptic character, Ross, the quite astonishing two lines (I, ii, 47–8):

> What a haste looks through his eyes! So should he look
> That seems to speak things strange.

Later (IV, i, 139) Lennox has a brief colloquy with Macbeth himself just after the latter has again interviewed the Witches:

MACBETH: I did hear
  The galloping of horse: who was't came by?
LENNOX: 'Tis two or three, my lord, that bring you word
  Macduff is fled to England.
MACBETH: Fled to England!
LENNOX: Ay, my good lord.

John Masefield, finely imaginative as a critic as well as a poet, says of this: 'An echo of the galloping stays in the brain, as though the hoofs of some horse rode the night, carrying away Macbeth's luck for ever.' No less superbly and in the same essay he answers the current cliché question as to what *Macbeth* is all *about*: – '[it] is about the desecration of the holiness of human life.'

If all this should seem to be taking us very far away from the pastime of walking, whether by day or by night, and whether for exercise or for relaxation, let us easily revert to it by way of Prospero in *The Tempest*. This old or ageing magician – in whom it is possible, without any great stretch of imagination, to recognize the great creative poet himself nearing the end of his enterprise – proposes to take a walk up and down in order to still his 'beating mind' (IV, i, 161).

He might well. Not only has he been conjuring visions and masques to entertain his daughter Miranda and her chosen Ferdinand. But he has also recollected a conspiracy being waged against him, just before delivering himself of twelve lines of farewell, unsurpassed for ache and quiet beauty. These done – and they have to be breathed as Gielgud breathes them – old Prospero descends from the superhuman to the human again, and sends the young people in to rest, and says he must walk a little in order to recover and refresh himself. To still his 'beating mind'!

Rosalind in *As You Like It* and Imogen in *Cymbeline* are perhaps the most practised walkers in the whole of Shakespeare. They are both not at all unlike the strapping heroines of George Meredith nearly three centuries later – Lucy and Clare in *Feverel*, Rhoda and Dahlia Fleming, Diana and Carinthia. These Meredithian ladies were, in their turn, affectionately parodied by Max Beerbohm in the hefty Euphemia Clashthought (a piece of nomenclature which is in itself an inspired piece of parody or literary caricature).

In order to send the reader back to the joys of Max's *Christmas Garland*, one should only have to quote the last paragraph in the last parody of that ineffable collection. Euphemia, on a Sunday morning in the snowbound countryside, gazes upon her fiancé Sir Rebus, somnolent beside a decanter of old port. She suddenly decides to leave him there and go for a solitary long walk – perhaps because it seems the Meredithian thing to do:

'Mother Earth, white-mantled, called to her. Casting eye of caution at recumbence, she paddled across the carpet and anon swam out over the snow. Pagan young womanhood, six foot of it, spanned eight miles before luncheon.'

WAR-MAKING

There is certainly as much of war as there is of peace in the entire output of Shakespeare – as much about discord as there is about concord. It does not follow, by any manner of means, that Shakespeare was a bloody-minded man, simply because he makes Othello speak nobly of war (III, iii, 355) in the volcanic outburst when he tells us that jealousy makes him leave behind his tranquillity and contentment:

> Farewell the plumèd troop, and the big **wars**
> That make ambition virtue! O, farewell,
> Farewell the neighing steed, th' ear-piercing fife,
> The royal banner, and all quality,
> Pride, pomp, and circumstance of glorious **war**!

Shakespeare in himself is no more Othello – or Coriolanus or Hotspur or Achilles, or Mark Antony – than he is that boy-soldier without a name in *King Henry V* who gets battle-scared before Harfleur, and says straight from the heart (III, I, 43): – 'Would I were in an alehouse in London! I would give all my fame for a pot of ale and safety.'

Shakespeare is just as interested in this common soldier as he is in his uncommon heroes, and we may quote more of the Boy here since he is usually cut to ribbons in the theatre (III, I, 60–75):

As young as I am, I have observed these three swashers, I am boy to them all three; but all they three, although they would serve me, could not be man to me; for, indeed, three such antics do not amount to a man. For Bardolph, he is white-liver'd and red-fac'd; by the means whereof he faces it out, but fights not. For Pistol, he hath a killing tongue and a quiet sword: by the means whereof he breaks words, and keeps whole weapons. For Nym, he hath heard that men of few words are the best [= bravest] men; and therefore he scorns to say his prayers, lest he should be thought a coward; but his few bad words are match'd with as few good deeds; for he never broke any man's head but his own, and that was against a post when he was drunk. They will steal any thing, and call it purchase. Bardolph stole a lute-case, bore it twelve leagues, and sold it for three-halfpence. Nym and Bardolph are sworn brothers in filching; and in Calais they stole a fire-shovel: I knew by that piece of service the men would carry coals [= *do the basest things*]. They would have me as familiar with men's pockets as their gloves or their handkerchers: which makes much against my manhood, if I should take from another's pocket to put into mine; for it is plain pocketing-up of wrongs, I must leave them, and seek some better service: their villany goes against my weak stomach, and therefore I must cast it up.

It might be possible to grade the plays of Shakespeare in descending order of the amount of war-making they contain. First, undoubtedly, would come the three parts of *King Henry VI*. Even more than the other histories these are – in Iago's phrase – 'horribly stuffed with epithets of war'. (The three parts have been ingeniously welded into a single viable play by the director John Barton and with the title *The Wars of the Roses*).

Our first illustrating passage is from Part One (II, 4, 107–134):

PLANTAGENET: Now, by my soul, this pale and angry rose,
   As cognizance of my blood-drinking hate,
   Will I for ever, and my faction, wear,
   Until it wither with me to my grave,
   Or flourish to the height of my degree.
SUFFOLK: Go forward, and be choked with thy ambition!
   And so, farewell, until I meet thee next.
SOMERSET: Have with thee, Pole.—Farewell, ambitious Richard.
PLANTAGENET: How am I braved, and must perforce endure it!
WARWICK: This blot that they object against our house,
   Shall be wiped out in the next Parliament,
   Call'd for the truce of Winchester and Gloster:
   And if thou be not then created York,
   I will not live to be accounted Warwick.
   Meantime, in signal of my love to thee,
   Against proud Somerset and William Pole,
   Will I upon thy party wear this rose:
   And here I prophesy,—this brawl to-day,
   Grown to this faction, in the Temple Garden,
   Shall send between the red rose and the white,
   A thousand souls to death and deadly night.

PLANTAGENET: Good Master Vernon, I am bound to you,
  That you on my behalf would pluck a flower.
VERNON: On your behalf still will I wear the same.
LAUYER: And so will I.
PLANTAGENET: Thanks, gentle sir,
  Come, let us four to dinner. I dare say
  This quarrel will drink blood another day.

From Part Two of *King Henry VI* (III, 2, 160) comes this bloody scene:
  (*The folding-doors of an inner chamber are thrown open, and Gloster is discovered dead in his bed; Warwick and others standing by it.*) . . .

WARWICK: See how the blood is settled in his face!
  Oft have I seen a timely-parted ghost,
  Of ashy semblance, meagre, pale and bloodless,
  Being all descended to the labouring heart;
  Who, in the conflict that it holds with death,
  Attracts the same for aidance 'gainst the enemy;
  Which with the heart there cools, and ne'er returneth
  To blush and beautify the cheek again.
  But see, his faces is black and full of blood
  His eyeballs further out than when he lived,
  Staring full ghastly like a strangled man;
  His hair uprear'd, his nostrils stretch'd with struggling,
  His hands abroad display'd, as one that grasp'd
  And tugg'd for life, and was by strength subdued;
  Look, on the sheets his hair, you see, is sticking;
  His well-proportioned beard made rough and rugged,
  Like to the summer's corn by tempest lodged.
  It cannot be but he was murder'd here;
  The least of all these signs were probable.

And barely thirty lines later, we have this no less sanguinary interchange (III, 2, 210):
SUFFOLK: Blunt-witted lord, ignoble in demeanour!
  If ever lady wrong'd her lord so much,

98

Thy mother took unto her blameful bed
Some stern untutor'd churl, and noble stock
Was graft with crab-tree slip; whose fruit thou art,
And never of the Nevilles' noble race.
WARWICK: But that the guilt of murder bucklers thee,
And I should rob the deathsman of his foe,
Quitting thee thereby of ten thousand shames,
And that my sovereign's presence makes me mild,
I would, false murderous coward, on thy knee
Make thee beg pardon for thy passèd speech,
And say it was thy mother that thou meant'st,—
That thou thyself wast born in bastardy,
And, after all this fearful homage done,
Give thee thy hire, and send thy soul to hell,
Pernicious blood-sucker of sleeping men!

In Part Three of *King Henry VI* (II, 3, 14) we have this from RICHARD DUKE OF YORK (father of Gloucester later to become King Richard III):

Ah, Warwick, why hast thou withdrawn thyself?
Thy brother's blood the thirsty earth hath drunk,
Broach'd with the steely point of Clifford's lance;
And, in the very pangs of death, he cried
Like to a dismal clangor heard from far,
'Warwick, revenge! brother, revenge my death!'
So, underneath the belly of their steeds,
That stain'd their fetlocks in his smoking blood,
The noble gentleman gave up the ghost.

And Warwick's reply which is no less bloodthirsty (II, 3, 23):

Then let the earth be drunken with our blood:
I'll kill my horse because I will not fly.
Why stand we like soft-hearted women here,
Wailing our losses, whiles the foe doth rage,
And look upon, as if the tragedy
Were play'd in jest, by counterfeiting actors?

Here on my knee I vow to God above,
I'll never pause again, never stand still,
Till either death hath closed these eyes of mine,
Or fortune given me measure of revenge.

Professor Edward Dowden, doing his best work one hundred years ago and at one time frequently quoted, is now much out of fashion. But like many another Shakespearean scholar he is likely to emerge from his temporary eclipse. He is particularly good and suggestive on the three parts of *King Henry VI* which so many of the pundits have tended to ignore as being merely Shakespeare's prentice-work:

Among his 'wolfish Earls' Henry is in constant terror, not of himself being torn to pieces, but of their flying at one another's throats. Violent scenes, disturbing the cloistral peace which it would please him to see reign throughout the universe, are hateful and terrible to Henry. He rides out hawking with his Queen and Suffolk, the Cardinal and Gloster; some of the riders hardly able for an hour to conceal their emulation and their hate. Henry takes a languid interest in the sport, but all occasions supply food for his contemplative piety; he suffers from a certain incontinence of devout feeling, and now the falcons set him moralising. A moment after, and the peers, with Margaret among them, are bandying furious words. Henry's anguish is extreme, but he hopes that something may be done by a few moral reflections suitable to the occasion.

In *King Richard III* (v, 3, 328) Richard's himself again, especially before Bosworth Field:

Let's whip these stragglers o'er the seas again;
Lash hence these overweening rags of France,
These famish'd beggars, weary of their lives;
Who, but for dreaming on this fond exploit,
For want of means, poor rats, had hang'd themselves.
If we be conquered, let man conquer us,
And not these bastard Bretons; whom our fathers
Have in their own land beaten, bobb'd, and thump'd,

And, on record, left them the heirs of shame.
Shall these enjoy our lands? lie with our wives?
Ravish our daughters? Hark! I hear their drum—
Fight, gentlemen of England! Fight, bold yeomen!
Draw archers, draw your arrows to the head!
Spur your proud horses hard, and ride in blood;
Amaze the welkin with your broken staves.

In *King Richard II* – and especially in the character of Bolingbroke (III, 3, 31–48) – the tempest in the blood is again high:

BOLINGBROKE: ... Noble lords,
(*To Northumberland*): Go to the rude ribs of that ancient castle;
  Through brazen trumpet send the breath of parley,
  Into his ruin'd ears, and thus deliver:
  Henry Bolingbroke
  On both his knees doth kiss King Richard's hand,
  And sends allegiance and truth faith of heart
  To his most royal person; hither come
  Even at his feet to lay my arms and power,
  Provided that, my banishment repeal'd,
  And lands restored again, be freely granted:
  If not, I'll use the advantage of my power
  And lay the summer's dust with showers of blood
  Rain'd from the wounds of slaughter'd Englishmen;
  The which, how far off from the mind of Bolingbroke
  It is, such crimson tempest should bedrench
  The fresh green lap of fair King Richard's land,
  My stooping duty tenderly shall show ...

In *King John* the subject of war is handled with a kind of
sinister gusto, and nowhere more than in this speech of
Falconbridge (II, 1, 456–467), which is only one of many such:

PHILIP FALCONBRIDGE,
  THE BASTARD: Here's a flaw [= gust]
  That shakes the rotten carcass of old Death,
  Out of his rags. Here's a large mouth, indeed,

101

That spits forth death and mountains, rocks and seas;
Talks as familiarly of roaring lions
As maids of thirteen do of puppy-dogs!
What cannoneer begot this lusty blood?
He speaks plain cannon fire, and smoke, and bounce;
He gives the bastinado with his tongue;
Our ears are cudgell'd; not a word of his
But buffets better than a fist of France:
Zounds, I was never so bethump'd with words
Since I first called my brother's father dad.

Those of us who saw *King Henry IV Part One* and *Part
Two* playing alternately in the 1945 Old Vic production at
the New Theatre will never forget them; and will indeed
regard them as the supreme theatrical experience of the middle
of this century. They first began at the end of September and
the beginning of October of that year which brought the end
of the Second World War.

England was staggered with relief at the lifted burden of
the war. And here was Shakespeare's supreme double-play
of war and peace. Here was Richardson, superlative as the
Falstaff of both Parts. Here was Olivier as Hotspur in Part
One, and as Justice Shallow in Part Two – a marvellously
contrasted double of fiery youth and crabbed age. Here were
Nicholas Hannen's ageing King and Sybil Thorndike's
ageless Mistress Quickly. Here were Joyce Redman's frank
Doll Tearsheet, and Margaret Leighton's beautifully tolerant
and tender Lady Percy. No circumstances can ever again arise
to make the double play seem more right, more Shakespearean; and though it is now nearly thirty years since Roger
Furse's royal-blue drop-curtain, emblemed with swans, first
rose upon the play so richly presented we have often – in the
mind's eye – seen it rise again to disclose such majesty and riot.

In *Part One* we need only quote Hotspur at his most
martial (v, 2, 92–100):

> Let each man do his best: and here draw I
> A sword, whose temper I intend to stain
> With the best blood that I can meet withal
> In the adventure of this perilous day.
> Now, Esperance! Percy! and set on,
> Sound all the lofty instruments of **war**,
> And by the music let us all embrace;
> For, heaven to earth, some of us never shall
> A second time to such a courtesy.
>   (*The trumpets sound*)

In *Part Two* we need only give Doll Tearsheet's farewell
to Falstaff (II, 4, 60–62):

> Come, I'll be friends with thee, Jack:
> thou art going to the **wars**; and whether
> I shall ever see thee again or no, there
> is nobody cares.

But if we seek peace rather than war in this great double
play, there is peace in plenty at Gadshill in the First Part, in
Gloucestershire in the Second, and in the Boar's Head in
Eastcheap in both.

A colloquy between Falstaff and the jealous Ford (disguising
himself as Master Brook) comes nearer to strife than anything
else in *The Merry Wives of Windsor* (II, 2, 204):

FORD: Now, Sir John, here is the heart of my purpose. You are a
gentleman of excellent breeding, admirable discourse, of great
admittance, authentic in your place and person, generally allow'd
for your many **war-like**, court-like, and learnèd preparations,—
FALSTAFF: O, sir!
FORD: Believe it, for you know it. There is money; spend it, spend
it; spend more; spend all I have; only give me so much of your
time in exchange for it, as to lay an amiable siege to the honesty
of this Ford's wife; use your art of wooing; win her to consent to
you; if any man may, you may as soon as any.
FALSTAFF: Would it apply well to the vehemency of your affection,

that I should win what you would enjoy? Methinks you prescribe to yourself very preposterously.

FORD: O, understand my drift. She dwells so securely on the excellency of her honour, that the folly of my soul dares not present itself; she is too bright to be look'd against. How could I come to her with any detection in my hand, my desires had instance and argument to commend themselves. I could drive her then from the ward of her purity, her reputation, her marriage-vow, and a thousand other her defences, which now are too-too strongly embattled against me.

What say you to 't, Sir John?

FALSTAFF: Master Brook, I will first make bold with your money; next give me your hand, at last, as I am a gentleman, you shall, if you will, enjoy Ford's wife.

The King himself spouts blood and fire in *King Henry V* (III, iii, 10–18):

> The gates of mercy shall be all shut up;
> And the flesh'd soldier – rough and hard of heart—
> In liberty of bloody hand shall range
> With conscience wide as Hell: mowing like grass
> Your fresh-fair virgins and your flowing infants;
> What is it then to me, if impious **war**,—
> Array'd in flames, like to the prince of fiends—
> Do, with his smirch'd complexion all fell feats
> Enlink'd to waste and desolation?

In *King Henry VIII* it is Cardinal Wolsey who gives phrase to the dire effects of total war (III, ii, 367–373):

> . . . Oh, how wretched,
> Is that poor man that hangs on princes' favours!
> There is, betwixt that smile we would aspire to,
> That sweet aspect of princes, and their ruin,
> More pangs and fears than **wars** or women have:
> And when he falls, he falls like Lucifer,
> Never to hope again.

In *Julius Caesar* it is Mark Antony who best describes the havoc of war in a speech which, though every schoolboy may know it, cannot be evaded (III, I, 263):

> A curse shall light upon the limbs of men;
> Domestic fury and fierce civil strife
> Shall cumber all the parts of Italy;
> Blood and destruction shall be so in use,
> And dreadful objects so familiar,
> That mothers shall but smile when they behold
> Their infants quarter'd with the hands of **war**;
> All pity chok'd with custom of fell deeds;
> And Caesar's spirit, ranging for revenge,
> With Atê by his side come hot from Hell,
> Shall in these confines with a monarch's voice
> Cry *Havoc*! and let slip the dogs of **war**;
> That this foul deed shall smell above the earth
> With carrion men, groaning for burial.

Much less well-known is a speech of Octavius Caesar in *Antony and Cleopatra* (IV, I, 10–16), which concludes with a curious expression of sympathy for Mark Antony himself:

> —Let our best heads
> Know, that to-morrow the last of many battles
> We mean to fight. Within our files there are,
> Of those that served Mark Antony but late,
> Enough to fetch him in. See it be done:
> And feast the army; we have store to do't,
> And they have earn'd the waste. Poor Antony!

More tortuous still is the misanthropic hero of *Timon of Athens* (V, I, 166–174) saying in good set terms what he thinks of the mad world's favourite pastime:

> If Alcibiades kill my countrymen
> Let Alcibiades know this of Timon,
> That Timon cares not. But, if he sack fair Athens,
> And take our goodly agèd men by th' beards,

Giving our holy virgins to the stain
Of contumelious, beastly, mad-brained **war**,
Then let him know – and tell him Timon speaks it
In pity of our agèd and our youth, –
I cannot choose but tell him that I care not,
And let him take't at worst; for their knives care not,
While you have throats to answer ...

The unfortunate hero of *Titus Andronicus* buries two of his sons (I, I, 89–95) who have been slain in the course of war:

Make way to lay them by their brethren –
                    [*the tomb is opened*]
There greet in silence as the dead are wont,
And sleep in peace, slain in your country's **wars**!
O sacred receptacle of my joys,
Sweet cells of virtue and nobility,
How many sons of mine hast thou in store,
That thou wilt never render to me more!

Two of the dire ladies in *Troilus and Cressida* have dreams of the 'bloody turbulence' of war (v, iii, 8–13):

CASSANDRA: Where is my brother Hector?
ANDROMACHE: Here, sister, arm'd and bloody in intent.
Consort with me in loud and due petition,
Pursue we him on knees; for I have dream'd
Of bloody turbulence, and this whole night
Hath nothing seen but shapes and forms of slaughter.
CASSANDRA: O, it is true.

In *The Merchant of Venice*, that popular drama written around the subject of race-hatred, there is no actual bloodshed though much talk of it in connection with the payment of a bond. And perhaps the whole play's most ominous phrase, 'fit for treasons, stratagems, and spoils' (v, 1, 85) is uttered by the moonstruck Lorenzo as applicable to the sort of man who has no time for music in his soul.

Nothing in the whole of *Macbeth*, that blood-boltered tragedy of ambition, is more frightening than this colloquy – eight words in all – between the tyrant and the first of his hired assassins (III, 4, 11–12):

MACBETH: There's blood upon thy face
FIRST MURDERER: 'Tis Banquo's then.

Othello, giving instructions to his lieutenant Iago after the brawl, also generalizes about peace and war in *Othello* (II, 3, 240–243) before going back to bed:

Iago, look with care about the town,
And silence those whom this vile brawl distracted—
Come, Desdemona: 'tis the soldier's life
To have their balmy slumbers waked with strife.

Edgar in the heart-aching tragedy of *King Lear* (III, 4, 76–78) has a snatch of a sinister song with the odour of blood in it:

Child Roland to the dark tower came;
His word was still, Fie, foh and fum,
I smell the blood of a British man.

Fortinbras at the very end of *Hamlet* orders a ceremonial funeral for the play's dead hero (V, 2, 388–393):

Let four captains
Bear Hamlet, like a soldier, to the stage;
For he was likely, had he been put on,
T'have proved most royally; and, for his passage,
The soldiers' music and the rites of **war**
Speak loudly for him.—

Twenty lines of what is perhaps the oddest of all the comedies, *All's Well That Ends Well* (II, 3, 273) may be said to contain the whole play in its quiddity – the praise of war, of subtlety, and of infidelity and lack of faith:

PAROLLES: – To the **wars**, my boy, to the **wars**!
He wears his honour in a box unseen,
That hugs his kicky-wicky here at home,
Spending his manly marrow in his arms,
Which should sustain the bound and high curvet
Of Mars's fiery steed. To other regions
France is a stable, we that dwell in't jades.
Therefore to the **war**.
BERTRAM: It shall be so. I'll send her to my house,
Acquaint my mother with my hate to her,
And wherefore I am fled . . . **war** is no strife
To the dark house and the deserted wife
PAROLLES: Will this capriccio hold in thee, art sure?
BERTRAM: Go with me to my chamber, and advise me,
I'll send her straight away; to-morrow
I'll to the **wars**, she to her single sorrow.
PAROLLES: Why, these balls bound, there's noise in it. 'Tis hard:
A young man married is a man that's marred:
Therefore away, and leave her bravely: go . . .

In *Pericles, Prince of Tyre* the character called Boult whose lowest of professions is that of Servant to a Pander in a brothel, thinks he might be even worse off as a soldier in a war (IV, 5, 160–164):

> What would you have me do? go to the **wars**,
> would you? where a man may serve seven years
> for the loss of a leg, and have not money enough
> in the end to buy him a wooden one?

In another very odd play, *Measure for Measure*, another brothel-keeper argues that war is very bad for her business (I, 2, 75–77):

MISTRESS
OVERDONE: Thus, what with the **war**, what with the sweat, what with the gallows, and what with poverty, I am custom-shrunk.

Among the sweeter comedies, *As You Like It* has no note

of war at all, but only a contrasting note of peace from a peace-loving shepherd (III, 2, 67–71):

CORIN: Sir, I am a true labourer: I earn what I eat, get that I wear; owe no man hate, envy no man's happiness; glad of other men's good, content with my harm; and the greatest of my pride is to see my ewes graze and my lambs suck.

In *Twelfth Night* the only mention of war is a vague incidental rumble in the background (V, 1, 47–57):

VIOLA: Here comes the man, sir that did rescue me.
    [*Enter Officers with Antonio*]
DUKE: That face of his I do remember well.
    Yet when I saw it last, it was besmear'd
    As black as Vulcan in the smoke of **war**:
    A baubling vessel was he captain of,
    For shallow draught and bulk unprizable,
    With which such scathful grapple did he make
    With the most noble bottom of our fleet,
    That very envy and the tongue of loss
    Cried fame and honour on him . . .

In *Much Ado About Nothing* the witty young men are soldiers by profession, but soldiers on leave in sunny Sicily (I, 1, 43–54):

BEATRICE: I pray you, how many hath he kill'd and eaten in these **wars**? But how many hath he kill'd?
    For indeed, I promised to eat all of his killing.
LEONATA: Faith, niece, you tax Signor Benedick too much, but he'll be meet with you I doubt it not.
MESSENGER: He hath done good service, lady, in these **wars**.
BEATRICE: You had musty victual, and he hath help to eat it; he's a very valiant trencher-man; he hath an excellent stomach.
MESSENGER: And a good soldier too, lady.
BEATRICE: And a good soldier to a lady; but what is he to a lord?
MESSENGER: A lord to a lord, a man to a man; stuff'd with all honourable virtues.

BEATRICE: It is so, indeed; he is no less than a stuff'd man; but for the stuffing, – well, we are all mortal.
LEONATO: You must not, sir, mistake my niece. There is a kind of merry **war** betwixt Signor Benedick and her: they never meet but there's a skirmish of wit between them.

In the early farce, *The Two Gentlemen of Verona*, there is but a single and a flying reference to things martial (v, 2, 15–16):

THURIO: How likes she my discourse?
PROTEUS: Ill, when you talk of **war**.
THURIO: But well, when I discourse of love and peace?
JULIA [aside]: But, indeed, better when you hold your peace.

In the other early farce, *The Comedy of Errors*, the allusion is again a hind-sight reference (v, 1, 189–193):
Antipholus of Ephesus to the Duke thereof:

> Justice, most gracious Duke, O grant me justice!
> Even for the service that long since I did thee,
> When I bestrid thee in the **wars** and took
> Deep scars to save thy life; even for the blood
> That then I lost for thee, now grant me justice.

In *Love's Labour's Lost* (v, 2, 653) the fantastical Spaniard called Don Adriano has a comment on Hector the Trojan whose part he has to play in a masque at the end of the comedy itself (v, 2, 653). These striking words were very memorably spoken at Stratford-on-Avon by Paul Scofield in his early twenties:

> The sweet **war-man** is dead and rotten; sweet chuck, beat not the bones of the buried: when he breathed, he was a man.

Prospero in *The Tempest* sets the very elements at war with one another v, 1, 41–50):

- I have bedimm'd
The noontide sun, call'd forth the mutinous winds,
And 'twixt the green sea and the azure'd vault
Set roaring **war**: to the dread-rattling thunder
Have I given fire, and rifted Jove's stout oak
With his own bolt: the strong-based promontory
Have I make shake, and by the spurs pluck'd up
The pine and cedar: graves at my command
Have waked their sleepers, oped, and let 'em forth
By my so potent art.

The fantasy, *A Midsummer Night's Dream*, comes no nearer to war than a fairy wrangle between Oberon and Titania as to which should possess a little Indian boy. All the rest is misunderstanding and moonshine and magic, a ducal wedding and some bungled play-acting by artisans.

Mankind – whether making war or trying to maintain peace – is pleasantly rebuked by the sprite Puck (III, 2, 115) in the single line, 'Lord, what fools these mortals be.'

That necromancer among stage-directors, Mr Peter Brook, has recently and sensationally given the world – the whole world – a production of this play which is said to make it look like a supernatural circus. One shall hope to catch up with this at Omsk, or Ormskirk, or Oklahoma City.

PART TWO

Animals
and Monsters

CONTENTS

Contents

AGENTS AND FAMILIARS

It is, very justly, through the mouth of Macbeth that Shakespeare deploys his most sinister use of a casual-seeming word like 'agent' to connote all the powers of evil; and it is done in two lines in the speech Macbeth makes after completing his plan for the murder of Banquo (III, ii, 51):

> Good things of day begin to droop and drowse,
> Whiles night's black **agents** to their preys do rouse.

A Familiar, also in its more sinister sense and used as a noun, was the companion or common attendant of a witch, and usually an evil spirit disguised as a cat, dog or other animal. La Pucelle, Shakespeare's version of Joan of Arc in *King Henry VI, Part One*, is little better than a witch, though a very courageous one; and Talbot asks the Duke of Burgundy about her and mentions her usual companion without specifying its nature (III, ii, 121):

> Thanks, gentle Duke. But where is Pucelle now?
> I think her old **familiar** is asleep.

In a later scene in the same play La Pucelle uses the same word, though adjectivally, to a group of Fiends (not Angels) whom she conjures up in a clap of thunder, appealing to them for help which they refuse (v, iii, 8):

> This speedy and quick appearance argues proof
> Of your accustom'd diligence to me.
> Now, ye **familiar** spirits that are cull'd
> Out of the powerful legions under earth,
> Help me this once, that France may get the field.
> O, hold me not with silence over-long!
> Where I was wont to feed you with my blood, ...

But the Fiends 'walk, and speak not, and hang their heads';
and then vanish without helping. It is all very *fürchtenmachend*,
as Germans would say – chilling rather than warming.

ALLIGATOR AND CROCODILE

The Alligator is agreeably called 'an allegory on the banks of
the Nile' by Sheridan's Mrs Malaprop. But the *Oxford English
Dictionary* calls it, much less agreeably, 'a genus of Saurians of
the crocodile family', and goes on to say that in popular usage
alligators are 'all large American Saurians, some of which are
true crocodiles'. With relief one turns from the biological
muddle to Shakespeare's world. And there we find that the
alligator exists only as a stuffed corpse in the apothecary's shop
to which Romeo goes to purchase poison (*Romeo and Juliet*, v,
i, 37):

> I do remember an apothecary,
> And hereabouts he dwells, which late I noted . . .
> And in his needy shop a tortoise hung,
> An **alligator** stuff'd, and other skins
> Of ill-shap'd fishes; . . .

Away back in 1935 the needy apothecary in this little scene
was vividly played by a new young actor called Alec Guinness;
and this commentator concluded his very first review in the
Manchester Guardian (as it then was) with the query and the
comment: 'Why does Shakespeare make him fuss so much at
being paid by Romeo? Perhaps in Mantua the chemists were
not cash?'

The Crocodile itself has familiar mention in *Hamlet*,
Othello and *Antony and Cleopatra*. But one would rather note
the unfamiliar passage in which Queen Margaret says the

King must be wary of Gloster (*King Henry VI, Part Two*, III, i, 224):

> Henry, my lord, is cold in great affairs,
> Too full of foolish pity; and Gloster's show
> Beguiles him as the mournful **crocodile**
> With sorrow snares relenting passengers; ...

The reference is to the hideous old legend that when a crocodile swallowed a man it could leave his head unswallowed out of pity, hence the phrase 'crocodile tears'. One would rather think the monster leaves it uneaten out of distaste, as a thing unpalatable, very much as a man repudiates the head of a fish or a rabbit or a chicken.

ANCHOVIES AND HERRINGS

These are bracketed together because both belong to the same fishy family. Anchovies occur only in Falstaff's bill for supper at the end of the great Eastcheap Tavern scene in the heart of *King Henry IV, Part One* (II, iv, 520):

> Item, **anchovies** and sack after supper ... *2s. 6d.*

Herrings occur much oftener, but usually only in metaphor. Feste, describing his position in the Lady Olivia's household, says to Viola, 'I am indeed not her fool, but her corrupter of words', and says also, 'She will keep no fool, sir, till she be married; and fools are as like husbands as pilchers are to **herrings** – the husband's the bigger.' (*Twelfth Night*, III, i, 31). In the same play (I, v, 114) the same fish cause Sir Toby's **one** and only belch, 'A plague o' these pickle-**herring**!'

ANIMALS IN GENERAL

In perhaps the loftiest of all his prose speeches Hamlet rates mankind as 'the beauty of the world! the paragon of **animals**!' (*Hamlet*, II, ii, 306) only to go on characteristically, 'And yet, to me, what is this quintessence of dust?'

Jaques, in *As You Like It*, has a humane dislike of hunting as a sport, and is described to the Banished Duke as 'commenting upon the sobbing deer' and as inveighing against the practice of hunting throughout the land (II, i, 58):

> Thus most invectively he pierceth through
> The body of the country, city, court,
> Yea, and of this our life; swearing that we
> Are mere usurpers, tyrants, and what's worse,
> To fright the **animals**, and to kill them up
> In their assign'd and native dwelling-place.

A little earlier in the same speech Jaques is described as 'weeping into the needless stream'. The adjective is so printed in the First Folio (when the play first appeared) and 'needless' appears with slavish conformity in every subsequent edition one has ever seen. Yet surely 'heedless' makes far better sense. Can this be an example of what may be called 'perpetual misprint'?

The synonymous and slightly more pejorative word 'beasts' occurs even more frequently – nowhere perhaps more strikingly than in Prospero's threat to punish his reluctant slave, Caliban (*The Tempest*, I, ii, 366):

> Hag-seed, hence!
> Fetch us in fuel. And be quick, thou'rt best,
> To answer other business. Shrug'st thou, malice?
> If thou neglect'st, or dost unwillingly

What I command, I'll rack thee with old cramps,
Fill all thy bones with aches, make thee roar,
That **beasts** shall tremble at thy din.

In *The Comedy of Errors* (ii, i, 15) Luciana, who is the spinster sister of Mrs Antipholus of Ephesus, has a by-no-means uninteresting homily on the subject of marriage:

Why, headstrong liberty is lash'd with woe.
There's nothing situate under heaven's eye
But hath his bound, in earth, in sea, in sky.
The **beasts**, the fishes, and the winged fowls,
Are their males' subjects, and at their controls.
Man more divine, the master of all these,
Lord of the wide world and wild wat'ry seas,
Indu'd with intellectual sense and souls,
Of more pre-eminence than fish and fowls,
Are masters to their females, and their lords;
Then let your will attend on their accords.

To which the married Adriana has the tart reply of a single line – 'This servitude makes you to keep unwed.'

ASPS, ADDERS, VIPERS

The Asp, oddly enough, is not mentioned by that name in the text of *Antony and Cleopatra*. It is three times given its old poetic form of 'aspic' in the last act. 'Have I the **aspic** in my lips?' (v, ii, 291) says Cleopatra when her maid Iras falls dead. And after Cleopatra's own death her guardsman attendant, taking up the fig basket, has a line of explanation of which – Heaven knows why! – he is usually deprived (v, ii, 358):

This is an **aspic's** trail, and these fig-leaves
Have slime upon them, such as th' **aspic** leaves
Upon the caves of Nile.

On several other occasions in the same place – it is the culmination of what is surely the greatest of great plays – the creature is insistently referred to as the 'worm' by both Cleopatra and the Clown who brings it. Thus Cleopatra says to this 'rural fellow' who bring her figs (v, ii, 141):

> Hast thou the pretty **worm** of Nilus there
> That kills and pains not?

The bearer says to her, 'I wish you all joy of the worm.' Cleopatra addresses the same slayer as 'thou mortal wretch' and 'poor venomous fool', and then – most thrillingly and movingly – refers to it as her 'baby' in her death speech addressed to Charmian:

> Peace, peace!
> Dost thou not see my baby at my breast
> That sucks the nurse asleep?

The Asp appears too – though again in the form of 'aspic' – in one of Othello's direst eruptions of jealous rage, spoken in Iago's presence (*Othello*, III, iii, 444):

> Arise, black vengeance, from thy hollow cell.
> Yield up, O love, thy crown and hearted throne
> To tyrannous hate! Swell, bosom, with thy fraught,
> For 'tis of **aspics'** tongues.

The Aspic, as Shakespeare calls it, is principally from 'the caves of Nile'. It is a small, venomous, hooded serpent and it is still found in Egypt and Libya.

The Adder or Viper – pretty much the same thing, the non-herpetologist imagines – sidles often and often into the plays, and then slithers out again after no more than a line or two.

'**Adder's** fork and blind-worm's sting' are among the ingredients of the hell-broth prepared by the Witches in their cauldron in *Macbeth* (IV, i, 16). Timon of Athens, that noble misanthrope and highly articulate ass, finds in the play of the same name (IV, iii, 180) that the earth, while he is digging it,

> Engenders the black toad and **adder** blue,
> The gilded newt and eyeless venom'd worm,
> With all th' abhorred births below crisp heaven,
> Whereon Hyperion's quick'ning fire doth shine.

And there are several other reptilian glimpses in the plays.

There are references also, less familiar but no less striking, in the poems. Thus Venus in a myrtle grove is alarmed by the baying of dogs which suggests that her Adonis is engaged on a boar-hunt (lines 877–882):

> By this, she hears the hounds are at a bay;
> Whereat she starts, like one that spies an **adder**
> Wreath'd up in fatal folds just in his way,
> The fear whereof doth make him shake and shudder; . . .

And Lucrece, soliloquizing in her distress, has a meditation on the theme that 'no perfection is so absolute That some impurity doth not pollute', and phrases it thus (lines 869–872):

> Unruly blasts wait on the tender spring;
> Unwholesome weeds take root with precious flow'rs;
> The **adder** hisses where the sweet birds sing;
> What virtue breeds iniquity devours. . . .

The word 'viper' itself is usually in Shakespeare a mere term of abuse, as when Pistol in his vilification of Corporal Nym says, 'O **viper** vile!' in *King Henry V* (II, i, 44). But the adjectival form of the same word, qualifying 'worm' for double emphasis, is used by Henry VI in his derogation of civil war (*King Henry VI, Part One*, III, i, 72):

> Civil dissension is a **viperous** worm
> That gnaws the bowels of the commonwealth.

ASSES

'What are we, Apemantus? says Timon (*Timon of Athens*, II, ii, 64), and Apemantus gives him the answer 'Asses'. He uses the word figuratively, as is usual throughout the plays, to signify something no better than a fool.

We may pick out a phrase fitting Troilus from the bitter railing of Thersites (*Troilus and Cressida*, v, iv, 5): 'That same young Trojan **ass**, that loves the whore there'. And the jealous Mr Ford has twelve loaded words about the un-jealous Mr Page in *The Merry Wives of Windsor* (II, ii, 301): 'Page is an **ass**, a secure **ass**: he will trust his wife; . . .', which flashlights the characters of both these husbands. Dogberry too repeatedly insists on being 'writ down an **ass**' in *Much Ado About Nothing* (IV, ii, 73).

Much of the fun of Bully Bottom lies in the fact that, when he is 'translated' from man to beast, he keeps calling himself an ass without realizing that he has temporarily become one, not only in his head but in his appetites. Thus Puck, in his longish speech to Oberon who wants to know what has been happening in 'this haunted grove' (*A Midsummer Night's Dream*, III, ii, 5), begins his explanation: 'My mistress with a monster is in love,' and concludes:

> I led them on in this distracted fear,
> And left sweet Pyramus translated there;
> When in that moment, so it came to pass,
> Titania wak'd, and straightway lov'd an **ass**.

The most controversial ass of all is Hamlet's when (II, ii, 388) the Strolling Players are at hand and the Prince has this very odd little colloquy with Polonius:

> POLONIUS: The actors are come hither, my lord.
> HAMLET: Buz, buz!

POLONIUS: Upon my honour –
HAMLET: Then came each actor on his **ass** –
POLONIUS: The best actors in the world, etc.

This may be interpreted in a variety of ways. The very latest thing in Hamlets – young Ian McKellen – makes a mad buzzing of bees out of his first comment, and out of his second distinctly and plainly says, 'Then came each actor on his arse', clearly meaning the human fundament or backside. This is underlined by the players making their entry as tumblers, one after the other, as has often been done before. The present age is so permissive that no criticism of this well-travelled production drew any particular attention to this reading.

The only editor of old who spent any ingenuity on the episode is Hudson: 'Hamlet affects to discredit the news: all a mere buzzing or rumour. Polonius then assures him, "On my honour"; which starts the poor joke, "If they are come on your honour, 'then came each actor on his *ass*'"; (so punctuated) these latter words being probably a quotation from some ballad.'

All this is laboured, and surely disingenuous rather than ingenious. Quotes within quotes within quotes!

BABOONS, APES, MARMOSETS

The simians (or *Simiadae*) are almost as frequent as the snakes and reptiles. The oddest of the references to Apes is in that oddest of all the plays, *Love's Labour's Lost* (III, i, 89), where Moth says:

The fox, the **ape**, and the humble-bee,
Were still at odds, being but three.
Until the goose came out of door,
Staying the odds by adding four.

This is twice repeated, between Moth and Don Adriano de Armado, his master. M. R. Ridley in the New Temple Shakespeare has this note: 'The emphasis laid by repetition on this doggerel indicates clearly enough that it had some piquant topical flavour which, for us, it has wholly lost.' But why 'clearly enough'?

Apemantus in *Timon of Athens* sneers at the time-serving guests who cluster round Timon who is still at the peak of his prosperity (I, i, 251):

> That there should be small love 'mongst these sweet knaves,
> And all this courtesy! The strain of man's bred out
> Into **baboon** and monkey.

The Baboon likewise proves as useful as arrowroot to the Witches in their cooking of hell-broth (*Macbeth*, IV, i, 37):

> Cool it with a **baboon's** blood,
> Then the charm is firm and good.

And the same word is used by Falstaff as a mere term of abuse in *King Henry IV, Part Two* (II, iv, 229):

> DOLL: They say Poins has a good wit.
> FALSTAFF: He a good wit! hang him, **baboon**!
> His wit's as thick as Tewksbury mustard; ...

A smaller sort of Monkey was one of the wild things of Prospero's island which Caliban proposed to find for his new master Trinculo in *The Tempest* (II, ii, 157):

> I prithee let me bring thee where crabs grow;
> And I with my long nails will dig thee pig-nuts;
> Show thee a jay's nest, and instruct thee how
> To snare the nimble **marmoset**; ...

Oberon envisages what may happen to his queen Titania after the love-philtre is applied to her sleeping eyes (*M.N.D.*, II, i, 179):

The next thing then she waking looks upon,
Be it on lion, bear, or wolf, or bull,
On meddling **monkey**, or on busy **ape**,
She shall pursue it with the soul of love.

Instead of which she falls in love with an Athenian weaver wearing an ass's head (temporarily).

Falstaff, soliloquizing in prose, recalls Justice Shallow in the old days (*King Henry IV, Part Two*, III, ii, 324) when he was 'lecherous as a **monkey**, and the whores call'd him mandrake'. And Othello, even while welcoming Lodovico to Cyprus, lets fall his terrible phrase in condemnation of disloyalty (IV, i, 262): 'Goats and **monkeys**!' like a splash of boiling water. Vividly one recollects Laurence Olivier here.

BASILISK AND COCKATRICE

By definition the Basilisk is a fabulous monster 'hatched by a serpent from a cock's egg' – though the ability of a cock to lay an egg is a circumstance beyond my ken. Its breath and even its look was said to be fatal. In *King Henry V* (v, ii, 17) the Queen of France has a difficult line in her speech to the King of England, when she tells him how glad she is to see him smiling at last and no longer glaring with 'the fatal balls of murdering **basilisks**'.

Gloster, in the middle of *King Henry VI, Part Three*, has a long soliloquy so much in the vein of the opening of *King Richard III* that Olivier interpolated much of it into the opening soliloquy of his own film version of the latter play. (Years earlier the American actor, John Barrymore, made a gramophone recording of this speech from the older play which is still well worth hearing. It begins, 'Ay, Edward will use women honourably!')

The same intensely Glosterian speech has the lines (III, ii, 182):

> Why, I can smile, and murder whiles I smile;
> And cry 'Content' to that which grieves my heart;
> And wet my cheeks with artificial tears,
> And frame my face to all occasions:
> I'll drown more sailors than the mermaid shall;
> I'll slay more gazers than the **basilisk**; . . .

In *King Richard III*, again, Gloster has a pretty exchange with the Lady Anne, who has just spat upon him (I, ii, 144):

GLOSTER: Why dost thou spit at me?
LADY ANNE: Would it were mortal poison, for thy sake!
GLOSTER: Never came poison from so sweet a place.
LADY ANNE: Never hung poison on a fouler toad.
Out of my sight! thou dost infect mine eyes.
GLOSTER: Thine eyes, sweet lady, have infected mine.
LADY ANNE: Would they were **basilisks,** to strike thee dead!

It must be guessed that 'Cockatrice' is another name for the same dubious and deadly monster. Sir Toby Belch in *Twelfth Night* tells us of the device whereby he makes both Viola and Sir Andrew too scared to engage one another in a duel (III, iv, 185): 'This will so fright them both, that they will kill one another by the look, like **cockatrices**.' Juliet says of the cockatrice that it has a 'death-darting eye' (*Romeo and Juliet*, III, ii, 47). The old Duchess of York in *King Richard III* says of the same horror that its 'unavoided eye is murderous' (IV, i, 55). And the ravisher of Lucrece has 'a **cockatrice**' dead-killing eye' (*The Rape of Lucrece*, 540).

BATS AND LEECHES

These be blood-suckers. 'Wool of **bat** and tongue of dog' are among the dire things that boil and bubble in the Witches' cauldron (*Macbeth*, IV, i, 15); and Macbeth himself, telling his lady that Banquo and Fleance still live and breathe, has a speech that is among the most cold-blooded in the whole play (III, ii, 39):

> There's comfort yet; they are assailable;
> Then be thou jocund: ere the **bat** hath flown
> His cloister'd flight . . . there shall be done
> A deed of dreadful note.

In *The Tempest* Caliban curses Prospero with 'all the charms of Sycorax, toads, beetles, **bats**' (I, ii, 339). But to Ariel in the most aerial of his songs the bat is merely a flying machine (v, i, 91):

> On the **bat's** back I do fly
> After summer merrily.

It is somewhat odd that the incubus, the succubus, and the vampire bat, all occurring in Elizabethan and earlier literature, are nowhere mentioned by Shakespeare. The only mention of the leech is figurative and is to be found at the very end of *Timon of Athens*. Alcibiades, advancing to self-promotion in Athens, utters these, the very last, lines in the play (v, iv, 79):

> Dead
> Is noble Timon: of whose memory
> Hereafter more. Bring me into your city,
> And I will use the olive with my sword:
> Make war breed peace; make peace stint war; make each
> Prescribe to other, as each other's **leech**.
> Let our drums strike.

> [*Exeunt*

129

There is also Pistol's resonant line or two in *King Henry V* (II, iii, 56):

> Yoke-fellows in arms,
> Let us to France, like **horse-leeches**, my boys,
> To suck, to suck, the very blood to suck!

This wrings a remark from the Boy who is not bloody-minded, 'And that's but unwholesome food, they say.'

BEARS

The Bear to Shakespeare was a familiar creature, and he usually writes vividly and imaginatively about it. Thus Prospero tells Ariel of the torments from which his master released him (*The Tempest*, I, ii, 287):

> ... thy groans
> Did make wolves howl, and penetrate the breasts
> Of ever-angry **bears**: ...

Falstaff describes himself to Prince Hal as being 'as melancholy as a gib-cat or a lugg'd [i.e. baited] **bear**' (*King Henry IV, Part One*, I, ii, 72). The Duke of Orleans describes English mastiffs as 'foolish curs, that run winking into the mouth of a Russian **bear**, and have their heads crusht like rotten apples' (*King Henry V*, III, vii, 137). Ajax is thus described to Cressida, 'He is as valiant as the lion, churlish as the **bear**, slow as the elephant' (*Troilus and Cressida*, I, ii, 20). 'Chain me with roaring **bears**,' says Juliet to Friar Laurence as an alternative to being married to Paris (*Romeo and Juliet*, IV, i, 80). Decius Brutus (in *Julius Caesar*, II, i, 203) tells us how Caesar

> loves to hear
> That unicorns may be betray'd with trees,
> And **bears** with glasses, ...

Macbeth says fearfully to the Ghost of Banquo (*Macbeth*, III, iv, 100):

> Approach thou like the rugged Russian **bear**,
> The arm'd rhinoceros, or the Hyrcan tiger;
> Take any shape but that, . . .

Lear describes himself to his daughter Goneril (*King Lear*, IV, ii, 41) as

> A father, and a gracious aged man,
> Whose reverence even the head-lugg'd **bear** would lick, . . .

Othello calls his wife 'an admirable musician! O, she will sing the savageness out of a **bear**!' (*Othello*, IV, i, 185).

All these things, and many other such, are high images suggested by the bear. But we may sense the bear itself, the actual animal harried and worried and teased by dogs to make an Elizabethan holiday, in the poet's only comedy of the workaday life around him as he wrote.

All this is contained in a snatch of conversation in *The Merry Wives of Windsor* between Slender and Anne Page (I, i, 262), a snatch which is rich in actual information as well as in grounds for surmise:

SLENDER: Why do your dogs bark so? Be there **bears** i' th' town?

ANNE: I think there are, sir; I heard them talk'd of.

SLENDER: I love the sport well; but I shall as soon quarrel at it as any man in England. You are afraid, if you see the **bear** loose, are you not?

ANNE: Ay, indeed, sir.

SLENDER: That's meat and drink to me, now. I have seen Sackerson loose twenty times, and have taken him by the chain; but, I warrant you, the women have so cried and shriek'd at it, that it pass'd; but women, indeed, cannot abide 'em; they are very ill-favour'd rough things.

BEETLES AND BUGS

There is something diabolical about the Beetle, whether in Shakespeare or out of it. Not for nothing is it one of the familiars of witches, like the bat, the toad, and the owl. In this direct sense it is mentioned in *The Tempest* as one of the associates of the foul witch who was Caliban's mother. Thus Caliban snarls against Prospero (I, ii, 339):

> All the charms
> Of Sycorax, toads, **beetles**, bats, light on you!

In *Measure for Measure* it is the subject of a metaphysical aphorism, made by Isabella, which might be defined as more emotional than intellectual (III, i, 75):

> The sense of death is most in apprehension;
> And the poor **beetle** that we tread upon,
> In corporal sufferance finds a pang as great
> As when a giant dies.

But in the three really sinister mentions of this coleopterate creature it is always 'shard-borne', and neither the English dictionaries nor the Shakespearean scholars can tell us what this adjective means. Does it mean 'born out of dung' like the so-called dung beetle or dor (*Geotrupes Stercorarius*), which is declared by the *Oxford English Dictionary* to fly after sunset? Or does it mean 'carried along by shards', which are scaly cases that conceal the wings proper?

Jean-Henri Fabre, the Belgian entomologist, said in his *The Glow-Worm and Other Beetles* that *Stercorarius*, 'black in all parts exposed to the light of day, displays a ventral surface of a glorious amethyst violet'. This aged scientist studied beetles so closely and for so many years that he ended up looking rather like one.

In *Antony and Cleopatra* we have Agrippa and Enobarbus discussing Lepidus and his affection for Octavius and Antony (III, ii, 19):

> AGRIPPA: Both he loves.
> ENOBARBUS: They are his shards, and he their **beetle**.

In *Cymbeline* old Belisarius says to his two boys (III, iii, 19):

> ... often, to our comfort, shall we find
> The sharded **beetle** in a safer hold
> Than is the full-wing'd eagle.

And Macbeth, much more familiarly, hints darkly to his wife concerning the imminent murder of Banquo and his son (*Macbeth*, III, ii, 39):

> Then be thou jocund: ere the bat hath flown
> His cloister'd flight; ere, to black Hecate's summons,
> The shard-borne **beetle** with his drowsy hums
> Hath rung night's yawning peal, there shall be done
> A deed of dreadful note.

Dover Wilson in his Cambridge Shakespeare (1947) at least allows that 'the meaning is disputed in all three instances'. He also quotes Professor Grierson's translation of what it is that the shard-borne beetle has done 'with his drowsy hums'; he 'hath tolled night's slumbrous curfew'. But surely this is professorial non-poetry!

One would rather say that this – like some half-dozen other passages in *Macbeth* – is one of those phrases too highly poetical to be truly meaningful. And one would repeat that the beetle in Shakespeare, whether shard-borne or otherwise, is diabolical.

BIRDS IN GENERAL

These sing, or are silent, throughout the plays and the poems. The references are simply too many to choose amongst. So one concentrates on a single sonnet, and gives four lines of it without any comment whatsoever. It is the opening of Sonnet 73:

> That time of year thou mayst in me behold
> When yellow leaves, or none, or few, do hang
> Upon those boughs which shake against the cold,
> Bare ruin'd choirs, where late the sweet **birds** sang.

BLACKBIRD AND OUSEL

The Blackbird (*Tardus merula*), one of our best-loved songsters with the liquid throat, is referred to very rarely and only by its old name of 'ousel'.

This is used figuratively and as a term of mild disparagement in an interchange in Gloucestershire, early one morning, between Justice Shallow and Justice Silence (*King Henry IV, Part Two*, III, ii, 1):

SHALLOW: Come on, come on, come on, sir; give me your hand, sir, give me your hand, sir: an early stirrer, by the rood! And how doth my good cousin Silence?
SILENCE: Good morrow, good cousin Shallow.
SHALLOW: And how doth my good cousin, your bedfellow? and your fairest daughter and mine, my god-daughter Ellen?
SILENCE: Alas, a black **ousel**, cousin Shallow!

We hear, and know, no more about Ellen.
But the bird itself appears vividly in Bottom the Weaver's

little ditty about birds in general (*A Midsummer Night's Dream*, III, i, 124), the song that begins:

> The **ousel**-cock so black of hue,
> With orange-tawny bill, ...

This, by the way, in the First Folio agreeably appears as follows:

> The Woosell cocke, so blacke of hew,
> With Orenge-tawny bill ...

As Mark Twain might say, their spelling in those early days left much to be desired. Or as an earlier American, Artemus Ward, said of an earlier poet, 'It is a pity that Chawcer, who had geneyus, was so unedicated. He's the wuss speller I know of.'

BULLS AND OXEN

Theseus in *A Midsummer Night's Dream* is as proud of his hounds as the Dauphin in *Henry V* was of his horse. And he goes so far as to compare them with bulls (IV, i, 120):

> My hounds are bred out of the Spartan kind,
> So flew'd, so sanded; and their heads are hung
> With ears that sweep away the morning dew;
> Crook-knee'd, and dew-lapt like Thessalian **bulls**; ...

In *The Tempest* it is the sound of savage bulls, or maybe of lions, that wakes the shipwrecked noblemen from their first slumber on Prospero's island. The honest old counsellor, Gonzalo, gets the chance for a laugh from the last word in the passage (II, i, 302):

GONZALO: Now, good angels
  Preserve the king!

ALONSO: Why, how now? ho, awake!
... wherefore this ghastly looking?
GONZALO: What's the matter?
SEBASTIAN: Whiles we stood here securing your repose,
Even now, we heard a hollow burst of bellowing
Like **bulls**, or rather lions: did't not wake you?
It struck mine ear most terribly.
ALONSO: I heard nothing.
ANTONIO: O, 'twas a din to fright a monster's ear,
To make an earthquake! sure, it was the roar
Of a whole herd of lions.
ALONSO: Heard you this, Gonzalo?
GONZALO: Upon mine honour, sir, I heard a humming, ...

The isle is full of noises and hummings.

BUTTERFLIES

Five times only does a butterfly flutter into the great garden of Shakespeare's drama, and always with the prettiest and fleetest effect.

One of them is chased by the unseen little boy who is Coriolanus' son – unseen but vividly and naturally depicted by his mother and his wife, Volumnia and Virgilia, and the visiting lady, Valeria (*Coriolanus*, I, iii, 56):

VALERIA: How does your little son?
VIRGILIA: I thank your ladyship; well, good madam.
VOLUMNIA: He had rather see the swords, and hear a drum, than look upon his schoolmaster.
VALERIA: O' my word, the father's son: I'll swear, 'tis a very pretty boy. O' my troth, I lookt upon him o' Wednesday half an hour together: has such a confirm'd countenance. I saw him run after a gilded **butterfly**; and when he caught it, he let it go again; and after it again; and over and over he comes, and up again; catcht it

again: or whether his fall enraged him, or how 'twas, he did so
set his teeth, and tear it: O, I warrant, how he mammockt it!
VOLUMNIA: One on's father's moods.

Later in the same play, Cominius comments on Coriolanus
and his way with the Volscians to his friend Menenius (IV, vi,
91):

> He is their god: he leads them like a thing
> Made by some other deity than nature,
> That shapes man better; and they follow him,
> Against us brats, with no less confidence
> Than boys pursuing summer **butterflies**,
> Or butchers killing flies.

Titania has a charming behest to her attendant-fays that her
sleeping Bottom may not be disturbed (*M.N.D.*, III, i, 171):

> And pluck the wings from painted **butterflies**
> To fan the moonbeams from his sleeping eyes:
> Nod to him, elves, and do him courtesies.

Achilles philosophizes to Patroclus on the way of the world
(*Troilus and Cressida*, III, iii, 75):

> 'Tis certain, greatness, once faln out with fortune,
> Must fall out with men too: what the declined is,
> He shall as soon read in the eyes of others
> As feel in his own fall; for men, like **butterflies**,
> Show not their mealy wings but to the summer; ...

And the aged Lear, though in captivity, has the comfort of his
youngest daughter, and is too racked and buffeted to care even
for liberty (*King Lear*, V, iii, 7):

CORDELIA: Shall we not see these daughters and these sisters?
LEAR: No, no, no, no! Come, let's away to prison:
  We two alone will sing like birds i' the cage:
  When thou dost ask me blessing, I'll kneel down,

And ask of thee forgiveness: so we'll live,
And pray, and sing, and tell old tales, and laugh
At gilded **butterflies,** and hear poor rogues
Talk of court news; and we'll talk with them too,
Who loses and who wins; who's in, who's out;
And take upon's the mystery of things,
As if we were God's spies: ...

Of this century's four or five worthy Lears, Gielgud was here the most memorable and the most shattering.

BUZZARDS

If we permit ourselves to say that that ineffectual hawk, the Buzzard, buzzes through only two of the plays, we may also hasten to add that the word-play is not ours but that of the shrew-tamer, Petruchio (*The Taming of the Shrew*, II, i, 199):

KATHARINA: Asses are made to bear, and so are you.
PETRUCHIO: Women are made to bear, and so are you.
KATHARINA: No such jade as you, if me you mean.
PETRUCHIO: Alas, good Kate! I will not burthen thee!
 For, knowing thee to be but young and light –
KATHARINA: Too light for such a swain as you to catch;
 And yet as heavy as my weight should be.
PETRUCHIO: Should be! should – buzz!
KATHARINA: Well ta'en, and like a **buzzard.**
PETRUCHIO: O slow-wing'd turtle! shall a **buzzard** take thee?
KATHARINA: Ay, for a turtle, as he takes a **buzzard.**

The other mention comes from Hastings, just released from imprisonment in the Tower of London, to Gloster (*King Richard III*, I, i, 132):

More pity that the eagle should be mew'd,
While kites and **buzzards** prey at liberty.

138

Whereupon Gloster abruptly changes the awkward subject with the little question, 'What news abroad?'

CACODEMON

Again it is in *King Richard III* that old Queen Margaret, that past-mistress in the art of vituperation, comes away with this balefully splendid word for Gloster, when she rounds upon the bloody rogue who had killed her husband and not a few of her other close relatives (I, iii, 143):

> Hie thee to hell for shame, and leave this world,
> Thou **cacodemon!** there thy kingdom is.

Gloster himself had just come away with a line of his own which touches just about the high-water mark of his gloating hypocrisy and smiling villainy, 'I am too childish-foolish for this world.'

The word Cacodemon is Greek for an evil spirit; and it sounds like one.

CALIBAN

There are two remarkable facts about Caliban, the monster in *The Tempest*, which are never sufficiently dwelt upon. One is that it is an exceedingly small part – barely 180 lines in all – to have made so tremendous an impact. The other is that he is a character who speaks nothing but blank verse, even in his several scenes with two clowns, a jester and a butler, who speak nothing but prose. This second fact we owe to the observation of Schlegel, the German critic, who made the first German translation of Shakespeare's plays.

Another extraordinary circumstance about this character is that we get only the vaguest inklings about what happens to him when the play is ended. We suppose – but are given no good reasons for supposing – that he is left on the island, which anyhow he regards as his own property. Prospero's last word to him is little more than a command to go home and tidy up (v, i, 291):

> Go, sirrah, to my cell;
> Take with you your companions; as you look
> To have my pardon, trim it handsomely.

And Caliban's last word before he goes is hardly conclusive, though it suggests that he is transferring his loyalty from Trinculo and Stephano back to Prospero (v, i, 294):

> Ay, that I will; and I'll be wise hereafter,
> And seek for grace. What a thrice-double ass
> Was I, to take this drunkard for a god,
> And worship this dull fool!

But we are never to know whether he found his grace, his conscience, or his soul.

Prospero and Ariel between them have already given us Caliban's pedigree. His father was a half-god and half-devil called Setebos, whom Patagonian Indians are said to have worshipped. His mother was 'the foul witch Sycorax', whom Prospero describes as a 'blue-eyed hag', though one is inclined to prefer the emendation of the adjective to 'blear-eyed'. It is Prospero too who describes him as he was in the beginning (I, ii, 283):

> A freckled whelp hag-born – not honour'd with
> A human shape.

See also MONSTERS IN GENERAL.

CAMELS

In the great soliloquy that turns into his swan song, Richard II curiously misquotes Holy Scripture (*King Richard II*, v, v, 15):

> As thus, 'Come, little ones;' and then again,
> 'It is as hard to come as for a **camel**
> To thread the postern of a needle's eye.'

This is very odd, and no scholar has any comment. Nothing whatever about the rich man's difficulty in getting into Heaven!

Elsewhere the camel is just the symbol of a beast of burden, as when Pandarus (*Troilus and Cressida*, I, ii, 251) says, 'Achilles! a drayman, a porter, a very **camel**.' To which Cressida comments, 'Well, well.'

There is also that cloud said to be shaped like a camel in *Hamlet* where Polonius is humouring the mad Prince, saying, 'By th' mass, and 'tis like a **camel**, indeed' (III, ii, 395).

CATERPILLARS

> Where is the Earl of Wiltshire? where is Bagot?
> What is become of Bushy? where is Green?

asks King Richard II about his favourites when he is nearing his own piteous end (*King Richard II*, III, ii, 122).

Not long before this we have heard these same favourites scornfully described by Bolingbroke (II, iii, 166) as:

> The **caterpillars** of the commonwealth,
> Which I have sworn to weed and pluck away.

And not long after, a politically-minded gardener's boy tells his master (III, iv, 44) that the whole land

WSAM—C

> Is full of weeds; her fairest flowers choked up,
> Her fruit-trees all unpruned, her hedges ruin'd,
> Her knots disorder'd, and her wholesome herbs
> Swarming with **caterpillars**.

Whereon his even more politically-minded boss points the parallel (III, iv, 47):

> Hold thy peace:
> He that hath suffer'd this disorder'd spring
> Hath now himself met with the fall of leaf:
> The weeds that his broad-spreading leaves did shelter,
> That seem'd in eating him to hold him up,
> A **re** pluckt up root and all by Bolingbroke;
> Imean the Earl of Wiltshire, Bushy, Green.

The same figure of speech is used twice in *King Henry VI, Part Two*. First, where the Duke of York has an aside on hearing of territories lost in France (III, i, 89):

> Thus are my blossoms blasted in the bud,
> And **caterpillars** eat my leaves away:
> But I will remedy this gear ere long,
> Or sell my title for a glorious grave.

And again, when a Messenger tells the King himself of the approach of Jack Cade and his rebel army in Southwark (IV, iv, 32):

> His army is a ragged multitude
> Of hinds and peasants, rude and merciless: ...
> All scholars, lawyers, courtiers, gentlemen,
> They call false **caterpillars**, and intend their death.

CATS AND POLECATS

Cats provide their own concert. Let us be content, for the nonce, with three fantastic quartets and some very out-of-the-way solos.

First the solos. 'The **cat**, with eyne of burning coal, Now couches fore the mouse's hole,' are two lines in a nocturne by Gower the Chorus in *Pericles* (Act III, Prologue, line 5). In the poems Tarquin is said to play cat-and-mouse with Lucrece (lines 554–555):

> Yet, foul night-waking **cat**, he doth but dally,
> While in his hold-fast foot the weak mouse panteth.

And Launce in *The Two Gentlemen of Verona* tells Crab, his dog, what an upset there was when he left home to make his fortune (II, iii, 6):

> ... my mother weeping, my father wailing, my sister crying, our maid howling, our **cat** wringing her hands, and all our house in a great perplexity, ...

Second, the quartets. Mercutio in *Romeo and Juliet* (III, i, 100) calls Tybalt, who has just given him his death-wound, four animals in a row – 'A plague o' both your houses! Zounds, a dog, a rat, a mouse, a **cat**, to scratch a man to death!'

And among the 'deal of skimble-skamble stuff' with which Owen Glendower has been boring Hotspur are, as the latter tells us in *King Henry IV, Part One*, III, i, 150, 'a clip-wing'd griffin and a moulten raven, a couching lion and a ramping **cat**'.

Polecats? Mistress Quickly hears from Master William Page what she takes to be a mention of polecats in *The Merry Wives of Windsor* (IV, i, 29) and says, '**Polecats**! there are fairer things than **polecats**, sure.' Whereupon the intensely Welsh Sir Hugh Evans rebukes her, 'You are a very simplicity 'oman: I pray you, peace.'

CENTAURS

Centaurs, according to the English and the mythological dictionaries, as well as the Elgin Marbles, were men down to the waist and horses below the waist. King Lear in his madness envisaged their top halves as feminine (*King Lear*, IV, vi, 124):

> Down from the waist they are **centaurs**,
> Though women all above,
> But to the girdle do the gods inherit,
> Beneath is all the fiends';

Grimmer still is the second-last scene of *Titus Andronicus*, where Titus, with his one remaining hand, slits the throats of the two sons of Tamora, who had ravished and mutilated Lavinia. He proposes to bake their heads and serve them up to Tamora as a banquet, and he spares us no detail of the recipe (v, ii, 197):

> . . . Lavinia, come,
> Receive the blood: and when that they are dead,
> Let me go grind their bones to powder small,
> And with this hateful liquor temper it;
> And in that paste let their vile heads be baked.
> Come, come, be every one officious
> To make this banquet; which I wish may prove
> More stern and bloody than the **Centaurs'** feast.

It is a pleasure to turn away from this bloody kitchen scene and point out that The Centaur was the name of the inn at Ephesus where much of the action of *The Comedy of Errors* takes place. Also that 'The Battle of the Centaurs' was one of the *divertissements* offered to Theseus and Hippolyta for their wedding feast at the end of *A Midsummer Night's Dream* (v, i, 44). Theseus declined it, even though it was 'to be sung by an Athenian eunuch to the harp'.

CERBERUS

There are several allusions to Cerberus, the three-headed dog which guarded the gate of Hell in Greek mythology. It prevented the living from entering the infernal regions, and also the dead from escaping their confinement.

In *Love's Labour's Lost* the little page, Moth, is cast for Hercules in the elaborate masque within the play (v, ii, 581) and is so announced by the pedant, Holofernes:

> Great Hercules is presented by this imp,
> Whose club kill'd **Cerberus**, that three-headed canis; ...

In *Troilus and Cressida* the snarling Thersites rebukes Ajax (II, i, 31):

> Thou grumblest and railest every hour on Achilles;
> and thou art as full of envy at his greatness as
> **Cerberus** is at Proserpina's beauty, ay, that thou
> bark'st at him.

In *Titus Andronicus* the mutilated Lavinia is met in the forest by her uncle, Marcus Andronicus, who says of the unknown despoiler (II, iv, 48):

> ... had he heard the heavenly harmony
> Which that sweet tongue of thine hath often made,
> He would have dropt his knife, and fell asleep
> As **Cerberus** at the Thracian poet's feet.

But which of the Greek poets came from Thrace, which is approximately the modern Roumania?

CHAMELEON

Not much less horrible is the *Oxford English Dictionary*'s definition of the Chameleon: 'a saurian reptile, of the genus *Chamaeleo*, distinguished by a prehensile tail, long tongue, eyes moving independently, but especially by their power of changing the colour of the skin, varying through different shades of yellow, red, gray, brown, and dull inky blue'.

King Claudius, at the beginning of the Play Scene, says, 'How fares our cousin Hamlet?' to get the mad answer:

> Excellent, i' faith, of the **chameleon's** dish: I eat
> the air, promise-cramm'd: you cannot feed capons so.

The King replies, 'I have nothing with this answer, Hamlet' (*Hamlet*, III, ii, 94). But the King may be supposed, perhaps, to be unaware of the old legend that the chameleon lived on air.

Similarly in *The Two Gentlemen of Verona* the clownish servant, Speed, hints to his master, Valentine, that he wants his dinner (II, i, 165), 'Though the **chameleon** Love can feed on the air, I am one that am nourish'd by my victuals, and would fain have meat.' There is a reference to another of the creature's *outré* habits in a later scene in the same play (II, iv, 23):

SILVIA: What, angry, Sir Thurio? do you change colour?
VALENTINE: Give him leave, madam; he is a kind of **chameleon**.

And there is a final reference to the creature's changeability of colour in Gloster's long solo in *King Henry VI, Part Three* (III, ii, 191). It is that same speech which Olivier interpolated, in his film version of *King Richard III*, into the opening soliloquy. Copying it out, one can hear again the great actor's precise enunciation of every vowel and consonant, and reflect between the lines, that the performance as a whole recalls the Dictionary's definition of the chameleon itself:

> I can add colours to the **chameleon**;
> Change shapes with Proteus for advantages;
> And set the murderous Machiavel to school.
> Can I do this, and cannot get a crown?
> Tut, were it further off, I'll pluck it down.

The single word 'pluck' was like a sudden stab of steel.

COCK AND COCKEREL

For the most part the word 'cock' in Shakespeare simply means the male of the common domestic fowl, *Gallus domesticus*. This is the Cock that crows at break of day. In *King Henry V* it crows before the Battle of Agincourt: Chorus's Prologue to Act IV:

> The country **cocks** do crow, the clocks do toll,
> And the third hour of drowsy morning name.

In *King Richard III* it crows before the Battle of Bosworth Field when Ratcliff tells the ill-rested King (v, iii, 209):

> The early **village-cock**
> Hath twice done salutation to the morn;
> Your friends are up, and buckle on their armour.

In *King Lear* the fugitive Edgar hails his familiar, 'This is the foul fiend Flibbertigibbet; he begins at curfew, and walks till the first **cock**' (III, iv, 114).

In this same sense of the word, Horatio and the officers of the watch in the first act of *Hamlet* may be described as 'cock-ridden'. Within a dozen lines (I, i, 147) Bernardo says of the Ghost, 'It was about to speak when the **cock** crew.' Horatio tells us:

> I have heard,
> The **cock**, that is the trumpet to the morn,
> Doth with his lofty and shrill-sounding throat
> Awake the god of day; and at his warning . . .
> Th' extravagant and erring spirit hies
> To his confine: . . .

And Marcellus says:

> It faded on the crowing of the **cock**.
> Some say, that ever 'gainst that season comes
> Wherein our Saviour's birth is celebrated,
> The bird of dawning singeth all night long: . . .

And it is presumably from the private parts of the same fowl's lusty offspring that Juliet's Nurse draws her simile when describing how once upon a time the baby fell on her face, as a result of which (*Romeo and Juliet*, I, iii, 53)

> . . . I warrant, it had upon its brow
> A bump as big as a young **cockerel's** stone.

Jaques in *As You Like It* (II, vii, 30) tells of an occasion when Touchstone amused him greatly, so that 'my lungs began to crow like **chanticleer**'. And Ariel concludes the song, 'Come unto these yellow sands' in *The Tempest* (I, ii, 384) with the lines:

> Hark, hark! I hear
> The strain of strutting **chanticleer**
> Cry, Cock-a-diddle dow.

All these – and some others could be given – are so many references to *Gallus domesticus*, the male of the common domestic fowl.

But it is no such thing as the male fowl which bobs up in one of poor Ophelia's mad ditties. It is, rather, the male *member*, and one had better say so in this permissive day and age when frankness is so much the fashion (*Hamlet*, IV, v, 57):

> By Gis and by Saint Charity,
>   Alack, and fie for shame!
> Young men will do't, if they come to't;
>   By **cock**, they are to blame.
> Quoth she, before you tumbled me,
>   You promised me to wed.
> So would I ha' done, by yonder sun,
>   An thou hadst not come to my bed.

CORMORANT

Once upon a time one joined an amused crowd of Dubliners on a bridge over the River Liffey. They were watching a cormorant on the surface of the water. It was 'afther swallowin' an eel' at one gulp, and could not get it down for quite a time.

The Cormorant (*Phalacrocorax carbo*) is a huge sea-bird which was probably never seen by Shakespeare, though its reputation for voracity and greed certainly reached him. He uses the word only figuratively, sometimes as a noun and sometimes as an adjective.

Thus the King of Navarre in his opening speech in *Love's Labour's Lost* (I, i, 4) talks of '**cormorant** devouring Time'. And Nestor in a letter to Priam in *Troilus and Cressida* (II, ii, 6) has a reference to 'this **cormorant** war'. Vanity is called an 'insatiate **cormorant**' by John of Gaunt in *King Richard II* (II, i, 38). And in *Coriolanus* (I, i, 118) the First Citizen, in his curious colloquy with Menenius about the Human Belly and its strength and its weaknesses, describes that organ as 'the **cormorant** belly', and describes it furthermore as 'the sink o' the body'.

149

COW AND CALF

The Cow is the female of any bovine animal. It has never been satisfactorily explained why any woman must resent being called a cow, a bitch, a she-cat, a mare, a vixen, etc., whereas hardly any man would find it either abusive or offensive to be called a bull, a dog, a tom-cat, or a stallion. But this is by the way.

In *Antony and Cleopatra* it is Enobarbus' friend, Scarus, who dares to call Cleopatra a cow, but only behind her back and as a figure of speech. He is raging with anger at the flight of Cleopatra and Antony from the sea-fight at Actium when he uses the phrase (III, x, 14):

> Yon ribaudred nag of Egypt . . .
> The breese [gad-fly] upon her, like a **cow** in June,
> Hoists sails and flies.

Most other references in the plays are purely to the animal, as when Touchstone in *As You Like It* reminisces about one Jane Smile, presumably a former Audrey, and 'the **cow's** dugs that her pretty chopt hands had milkt' (II, iv, 46). And a very minor character called Second Goth in *Titus Andronicus* has an odd observation that is positively Mendelian concerning the blackness of the baby that the white Tamora, Queen of the Goths, bore to the blackamoor Aaron (v, i, 31):

> . . . where the bull and **cow** are both milk-white,
> They never do beget a coal-black calf.

As for the Calf so begotten, and of whatsoever colour, let us record only one of several mentions. This is the one in *Love's Labour's Lost* in a scene between Longaville and Katherine during the masquerade (v, ii, 247) – one of those interchanges which one would sooner transcribe than try to explain:

KATHERINE: Veal, quoth the Dutchman. Is not 'veal' a **calf**?
LONGAVILLE: A **calf**, fair lady?
KATHERINE:　　　　　　No, a fair lord **calf**.
LONGAVILLE: Let's part the word.
KATHERINE:　　　　　　　　No, I'll not be your half:
　Take all, and wean it, it may prove an ox.
LONGAVILLE: Look, how you butt yourself in these sharp mocks!
　Will you give horns, chaste lady? do not so.
KATHERINE: Then die a **calf**, before your horns do grow.
LONGAVILLE: One word in private with you, ere I die.
KATHERINE: Bleat softly then; the butcher hears you cry.

Fooling at its heaviest!

CRABS AND PRAWNS

By 'crab' Shakespeare almost always means not the crustacean crab but rather the 'crab apple'. Foolishly, being rather an anti-scholar than a scholar worthy of the name, one had hitherto imagined that the Winter Song at the end of *Love's Labour's Lost* had a cheerful reference to boiled crab as a supper dish (v, ii, 912):

> When roasted **crabs** hiss in the bowl,
> Then nightly sings the staring owl,
> 　Tu-who, tu-whit, tu-who.

But one now finds that Editor Hudson set us right about this as long ago as Edwardian times, when he provided the following delightful note, which really ought to have been quoted in the first volume of this series under APPLE:

This is the **crab apple**, which used to be roasted, and put hissing-hot into a bowl of ale, previously enriched with toast and spice and sugar. How much this was relished in old times may be guessed by those who appreciate the virtues of apple-toddy.

But at least Hamlet must have meant the crustacean (*Cancer pagurus*) and not the wild apple when he remarked to Polonius (*Hamlet*, II, ii, 200), 'For yourself, sir, shall grow old as I am, if, like a **crab**, you could go backward.' It is not really an intelligible remark: for Hamlet is here being mad rather than intelligible. But it is a fact that the crustacean in question can move in any direction – forwards, backwards, and (especially) sideways.

Prawns are much less equivocal and more straightforward. But here there is only a single reference to be discovered. It is buried in an immense prose-speech to Falstaff of Mistress Quickly – garrulous and breathless as Mrs Nickleby in Dickens – in *King Henry IV, Part Two* (II, i, 80):

Thou didst swear to me upon a parcel-gilt goblet, sitting in my Dolphin-chamber, at the round table, by a sea-coal fire, upon Wednesday in Wheeson-week, when the prince broke thy head for liking his father to a singing-man of Windsor, – thou didst swear to me then, as I was washing thy wound, to marry me, and make me my lady thy wife. Canst thou deny it? Did not goodwife Keech, the butcher's wife, come in then, and call me gossip Quickly? coming in to borrow a mess of vinegar; telling us she had a good dish of **prawns**; whereby thou didst desire to eat some; whereby I told thee they were ill for a green wound? And didst thou not, when she was gone down stairs, desire me to be no more so familiarity with such poor people; saying that ere long they should call me madam? And didst thou not kiss me, and bid me fetch thee thirty shillings? I put thee now to thy book-oath: deny it, if thou canst.

That these were prawns (*Palaemon senatus*) is as undeniable as Falstaff found Mistress Quickly's evidence.

CUCKOOS

The Cuckoo (*Cuculus manorus*) lays its eggs and has them hatched in the nests of other birds. For this reason – though it may not be a strictly logical reason – it is from the word 'cuckoo' that the once-common term 'cuckold' is directly derived. A cuckold, according to the *Oxford English Dictionary*, was – and is still – a husband whose wife is unfaithful to him with one or more other men. The word, it seems, applies only to the deceived husband, never to a deceived wife (surely quite as common a phenomenon?). The *O.E.D.* goes out of its way to add to its definition the comment, 'In English *cuckold* is not found applied to the adulterer.'

There seems much loose thinking and loose argument about this complicated etymology (though maybe there always is in sexual matters). One would only point out that the cuckoo bird – a hen, of course – is guilty not of infidelity but of sheer laziness when it lays its eggs in another bird's nest. The trouble is that we simply don't know enough about the domestic – or, rather, the non-domestic – life of a cuckoo couple. Are they more, or less, faithful than other bird couples? Is the cock cuckoo ever a cuckold?

Another oddity about the *O.E.D.*'s definition is that it declares the word to be 'derisory'. But is there anything less 'derisory' than Othello's use of the word about himself (*Othello*, IV, i, 198)? Othello is quite wrong about his cuckolding. But that is beside the point:

OTHELLO: I will chop her into messes! **cuckold** me!
IAGO: O, 'tis foul in her.
OTHELLO: With mine officer!
IAGO: That's fouler.
OTHELLO: Get me some poison, Iago; this night: – I'll not expostulate

with her, lest her body and beauty unprovide my mind again; – this night, Iago.

IAGO: Do it not with poison, strangle her in her bed, even the bed she hath contaminated.

There is no more terrifying, or less derisory, passage in the whole tragedy.

References in Shakespeare to the Cuckoo, without these adulterous overtones and double meanings, are few but all the more welcome. Thus, Portia is recognized by Lorenzo in the garden at Belmont by night (*The Merchant of Venice*, V, i, 110):

LORENZO: That is the voice,
Or I am much deceived, of Portia.
PORTIA: He knows me, as the blind man knows the **cuckoo**,
By the bad voice.

And the Fool's snatch of verse, amid the terrible scene between King Lear and his daughter Goneril (*King Lear*, I, iv, 212), indicates that Shakespeare was well aware of the Cuckoo's life-history and habits:

The hedge-sparrow fed the **cuckoo** so long,
That it had it head bit off by **it young.**

CYCLOPS

Mythology tells us that the Cyclopes were one-eyed giant blacksmiths who forged thunderbolts for the use of the gods. They were said to have worked for Vulcan in the vicinity of Mount Etna.

The First Player, giving Hamlet a taste of his quality in tragedy, has a striking allusion to them (*Hamlet*, II, ii, 488):

And never did the **Cyclops'** hammers fall
On Mars's armour, forg'd for proof eterne,

With less remorse than Pyrrhus' bleeding sword
Now falls on Priam.

And Titus Andronicus says to his own brother (*Titus Andronicus*, IV, iii, 45):

> Marcus, we are but shrubs, no cedars we,
> No big-boned men framed of the **Cyclops'** size;
> But metal, Marcus, steel to the very back,
> Yet wrung with wrongs more than our backs can bear.

This present commentator did once set eyes – both eyes – on a real-life Cyclops. He was a beggar-man in Istanbul. He was of no great height. But he was apparently dumb, and he had a single, round, and rather red eye, set in the middle of his forehead, close to the top of his nose. He opened the door of my taxi and mutely held out his hand for a coin, which was very quickly forthcoming. The British Council representative by my side was no less shocked, scared, and speedily generous.

DEER

Deer abound – and here we must be particularly selective. The aim now should be, as seemeth to me, to give one relishable, and not too familiar, example of the various forms and styles of Deer (of the order *Cervidae*), and to conclude with one or two particular *bonnes bouches* from the same source.

There is John Talbot, Earl of Shrewsbury, in *King Henry VI, Part One* (IV, ii, 45), though the allusion is only to his own troops:

> How are we parkt and bounded in a pale,
> A little herd of England's timorous **deer**.

There is Mrs Ford at the end of *The Merry Wives of Windsor* and in Windsor Park telling Falstaff that all is over between them (v, v, 114), 'Sir John we have had ill luck; we could never meet. I will never take you for my love again; but I will always count you my **deer** [so spelt].'

There is the Exiled Duke in *As You Like It* commenting on the philosopher Jaques (II, i, 64):

DUKE: And did you leave him in this contemplation?
SECOND LORD: We did, my lord, weeping and commenting
    Upon the sobbing **deer**.
DUKE: Show me the place:
    I love to cope him in these sullen fits,
    For then he's full of matter.
FIRST LORD: I'll bring you to him straight.

There is Mark Antony over Caesar's corpse (*Julius Caesar*, III, i, 208):

    O world! thou wast the forest to this **hart**;
    And this, indeed, O world, the heart of thee.
    How like a **deer**, strucken by many princes,
    Dost thou here lie!

There is Hamlet in his frenzy of excitement at the end of the Play Scene (*Hamlet*, III, ii, 290):

    Why, let the stricken **deer** go weep,
        The **hart** ungalled play;
    For some must watch, while some must sleep:
    So runs the world away.

There is Orlando, demanding food with drawn sword, and saying he must first succour his old servant Adam (*As You Like It*, II, vii, 127):

    Then but forbear your food a little while,
    Whiles, like a **doe**, I go to find my **fawn**,
    And give it food.

There is Octavius on Antony's service-fare in *Antony and Cleopatra* (I, iv, 63):

> ... Thy palate then did deign
> The roughest berry in the rudest hedge;
> Yea, like the **stag**, when snow the pasture sheets,
> The barks of trees thou browsed'st; ...

There is Page to Mistress Page in *The Merry Wives of Windsor* (I, i, 177):

> Wife, bid these gentlemen welcome. Come, we have a hot **venison**-pasty to dinner; come, gentlemen, I hope we shall drink down all unkindness.

DEVILS

One may make a rising crescendo out of only ten of the innumerable references –

Armado in *Love's Labour's Lost* (I, ii, 165): 'Love is a familiar; Love is a **devil**: there is no evil angel but love.'

Hotspur to Lady Hotspur in *King Henry IV, Part One* (III, i, 228): 'Now I perceive the **devil** understands Welsh.'

Theseus on the madman in *A Midsummer Night's Dream* (V, i, 9): 'One sees more **devils** than vast hell can hold.'

Lady Anne to Gloster in *King Richard III* (I, ii, 50): 'Foul **devil**, for God's sake, hence, and trouble us not.'

Lucrece on Tarquin (line 1555): 'Such **devils** steal effects from lightless hell.'

Ferdinand, leaping ashore from the shipwreck in *The Tempest* (I, ii, 215): 'Hell is empty, And all the **devils** are here.'

Macbeth to his Lady asking if he is still a man (*Macbeth* III, iv, 59): 'Ay, and a bold one, that dare look on that Which might appal the **devil**.'

WSAM–D

Prospero to Caliban in *The Tempest* (I, ii, 319): 'Thou poisonous slave, got by the **devil** himself, Upon thy wicked dam.'

Clown to Lafeu in *All's Well That Ends Well* (IV, v, 39): 'The black prince, sir; *alias*, the prince of darkness, *alias*, the **devil**.'

Lear fleeing from Goneril in *King Lear* (I, iv, 257): 'Darkness and **devils**!'

DOGS

One of the supreme things in Olivier's great Macbeth was the scene with the murderers he has hired to slay Banquo and Banquo's young son, Fleance. The First Murderer protests, 'We are men, my liege', and it is the cue for the tyrant's withering rejoinder which many a Macbeth in our time has thrown away. Not so Olivier, who loaded the lines with irony as well as scorn, his Macbeth being one who already felt his secret murders sticking on his hands (III, i, 91):

> Ay, in the catalogue ye go for men;
> As hounds, and greyhounds, mongrels, spaniels, curs,
> Shoughs, water-rugs, and demi-wolves, are clept
> All by the name of **dogs**: the valued file
> Distinguishes the swift, the slow, the subtle,
> The housekeeper, the hunter, every one
> According to the gift which bounteous nature
> Hath in him closed; whereby he does receive
> Particular addition, from the bill
> That writes them all alike: and so of men.
> Now, if ye have a station in the file,
> Not i' th' worst rank of manhood, say't;
> And I will put that business in your bosoms,
> Whose execution takes your enemy off,

Grapples you to the heart and love of us,
Who wear our health but sickly in his life,
Which in his death were perfect.

Edgar, the pretended madman in *King Lear* (III, vi, 63), has a less enthralling catalogue of dogs, but it is complementary to Macbeth's:

Avaunt, you **curs**!
Be thy mouth or black or white,
Tooth that poisons if it bite;
Mastiff, greyhound, mongrel grim,
Hound or spaniel, brach or lym,
Or bobtail tike or trundle-tail;
Tom will make them weep and wail:
For, with throwing thus my head,
Dogs leap the hatch, and all are fled.

Of actual dogs, appearing or mentioned in the plays, there is in *The Two Gentlemen of Verona* (II, iii, 5) 'the sourest-natured **dog** that lives' – Launce's dog, Crab. There are King Lear's little dogs, Tray, Blanch and Sweetheart, which bark at him; there is also in the same play the Fool's 'brach' or **scent-hound** called Lady, which does nothing but 'stand by the fire and stink' (I, iv, 115). Hotspur, in *King Henry IV, Part One*, has another **scent-hound** called Lady which he would like to hear 'howl in Irish'.

The Hunting Lord in the Induction to *The Taming of the Shrew* mentions some of his hounds by name – Merriman, Clowder, Silver, Belman and Echo. Of all these it is only Launce's dog, Crab, which actually appears – when it invariably runs away with the play, what there is of it.

DOLPHIN and PORPOISE

Cleopatra does nobly by the Dolphin when she makes mention of it in connection with the dead Antony and his pleasures when alive (*Antony and Cleopatra*, v, ii, 86):

> ... For his bounty,
> There was no winter in't; an autumn 'twas
> That grew the more by reaping: his delights
> Were **dolphin**-like; they show'd his back above
> The element they lived in: ...

In its other two significant mentions the Dolphin is cavorting at sea with a passenger bestriding it. Thus Oberon in *A Midsummer Night's Dream* (II, i, 149) tells his gentle Puck:

> ... once I sat upon a promontory,
> And heard a mermaid, on a **dolphin's** back,
> Uttering such dulcet and harmonious breath,
> That the rude sea grew civil at her song, ...

And then the Captain in *Twelfth Night* (I, ii, 14) tells Viola of her lost brother, Sebastian, that he was seen binding himself

> To a strong mast that lived upon the sea;
> Where, like Arion on the **dolphin's** back,
> I saw him hold acquaintance with the waves
> So long as I could see.

The Dolphin is described by biologists as a cetacean mammal. So, too, is the no less playful porpoise which appears with the old name of 'porpus' and has only a single mention. This is at the opening of the second act of *Pericles, Prince of Tyre*, when that wandering hero is thrown up by the sea on the shore at Pentapolis and found by three fishermen (II, i, 20):

160

FIRST FISHERMAN: Alas, poor souls, it grieved my heart to hear what pitiful cries they made to us to help them, when, well-a-day, we could scarce help ourselves.

THIRD FISHERMAN: Nay, master, said not I as much when I saw the **porpus,** how he bounced and tumbled? they say they're half-fish, half-flesh: . . .

DOVES AND PIGEONS

Hermia in *A Midsummer Night's Dream* (I, i, 171) swears very prettily 'by the simplicity of Venus' **doves**'.

Juliet's Nurse in *Romeo and Juliet* (I, iii, 27) tells how she was once 'sitting in the sun under the **dove-house** wall'.

Perdita in *The Winter's Tale* (IV, iii, 367) is told that her hand is 'as soft as **dove's** down, and as white as it'.

Gertrude after Ophelia's funeral and at the end of Hamlet's rant by the grave (*Hamlet*, V, i, 278) has her strange and lovely speech:

> This is mere madness:
> And thus awhile the fit will work on him;
> Anon, as patient as the female **dove**
> When that her golden couplets are disclosed,
> His silence will sit drooping.

Paris in *Troilus and Cressida* (III, i, 122) exclaims to Helen (and sounds much more like Pandarus as he does so): 'He eats nothing but **doves**, love; and that breeds hot blood, and hot blood begets hot thoughts, and hot thoughts beget hot deeds, and hot deeds is love.'

These are but a few of the references to the Dove, incessant as his cooing. Two references to the Pigeon, as distinct from the Dove, are much less passionate and much more prosaic. They occur respectively in *Love's Labour's Lost* (V, ii, 315) and *King Henry IV, Part Two* (V, i, 23). They are Berowne's 'This fellow pecks up wit as **pigeons** pease,' and Justice Shallow's order to his servant while entertaining Falstaff in Gloucester-shire, 'Some **pigeons**, Davy, a couple of short-legg'd hens, a joint of mutton, and any pretty little tiny kickshaws, tell William cook.'

DRAGONS

A Dragon contributes one of its scales to the Witches' Brew in *Macbeth* (IV, i, 22), and 'a **dragon** and a finless fish' are among the properties of Glendower which Hotspur finds so tedious in *King Henry IV, Part One* (III, i, 150).

But the most interesting usages of the word are less direct and more symbolic, and spring from what is apparently self-knowledge. 'Come not between the **dragon** and his wrath,' says King Lear to Kent, when the latter tries to interfere with the old man's unjust spurning of Cordelia (I, i, 122). But another character in the same play who has far more of genuine self-knowedge is Gloster's natural son, Edmund, who has no illusions whatever about heredity, and gives his conviction brilliant expression (*King Lear*, I, ii, 130) with a dragon dramatically participating:

An admirable evasion of whoremaster man, to lay his goatish disposition to the charge of a star! My father compounded with my mother under the **dragon's tail**; and my nativity was under *ursa major*; so that it follows, I am rough and lecherous. Fut, I should have been that I am, had the maidenliest star in the firmament twinkled on my bastardizing.

Coriolanus is twice likened to a dragon, once by himself, once by his friend Menenius. The great man addresses his friends and relatives in turn, concluding with Volumnia (*Coriolanus*, IV, i, 27):

My mother, you wot well
My hazards still have been your solace: and

Believe't not lightly, though I go alone,
Like to a lonely **dragon**, that his fen
Makes fear'd and talkt of more than seen, . . .

Menenius in a later passage vividly describes Coriolanus near the end of the heyday of his pride (v, iv, 10):

MENENIUS: This Marcius is grown from man to **dragon**: he has wings; he's more than a creeping thing.

SICINIUS: He loved his mother dearly.

MENENIUS: But so did he me: and he no more remembers his mother now than an eight-year-old horse. The tartness of his face sours ripe grapes: when he walks, he moves like an engine, and the ground shrinks before his treading: . . . He sits in his state, as a thing made for Alexander. What he bids be done, is finisht with his bidding. He wants nothing of a god but eternity, and a heaven to throne in. . . . I paint him in the character. Mark what mercy his mother shall bring from him: there is no more mercy in him than there is milk in a male tiger.

DUCK AND MALLARD

Almost the only mention of the Duck (*Anas*), excepting in its secondary sense as a term of endearment, is in *The Tempest*. It is in a marvellously characterized little scene between Caliban and the butler Stephano and the jester Trinculo, the latter two having just been reunited after the shipwreck (II, ii, 112):

CALIBAN (*aside*): These be fine things, an if they be not sprites. That's a brave god, and bears celestial liquor: I will kneel to him.

STEPHANO: How didst thou 'scape? How camest thou hither? swear, by this bottle, how thou camest hither. I escaped upon a butt of sack, which the sailors heaved o'erboard, by this bottle! which I made of the bark of a tree with mine own hands, since I was cast ashore.

CALIBAN: I'll swear, upon that bottle, to be thy true subject, for the liquor is not earthly.

STEPHANO: Here; swear, then, how thou escapedst.

TRINCULO: Swam ashore, man, like a **duck**: I can swim like a **duck**, I'll be sworn.

STEPHANO: Here, kiss the book. Though thou canst swim like a **duck**, thou art made like a goose.

TRINCULO: O Stephano, hast any more of this?

STEPHANO: The whole butt, man: my cellar is in a rock by the sea-side, where my wine is hid. – How now, moon-calf! how does thine ague?

CALIBAN: Hast thou not dropt from heaven?

STEPHANO: Out o' the moon, I do assure thee: I was the man-i'-the-moon when time was.

CALIBAN: I've seen thee in her, and I do adore thee.

Such scenes ought to 'come off' in the theatre better than they usually do. They are simple in language (unlike similar scenes of fooling in, for example, *Twelfth Night* and *As You Like It*). They even have a positively 'pop' flavour with the foolishly repetitive 'man', but still they *read* much better than they usually *act*.

The Mallard or wild duck (*Anas boscas*) gets only a solitary quack, though it is in surely the greatest and largest of all the plays, *Antony and Cleopatra*. The queen is seized with panic and flies from the sea-fight at Actium, closely followed by Antony, to the disgust of Scarus (III, x, 20) who says that Antony has behaved 'like a doting **mallard**'.

EAGLE

The Eagle (*Aquila*), the royal bird, can easily provide us with a dozen lofty images. Some of the best are some of the least familiar. Thus Warwick, dying at the Battle of Barnet (*King Henry VI, Part Three*, v, ii, 11):

Thus yields the cedar to the axe's edge,
Whose arms gave shelter to the princely **eagle**, . . .
Why, what is pomp, rule, reign, but earth and dust?
And, live we how we can, yet die we must.

And thus Philip Falconbridge speaks to the French on behalf of the English king in *King John* (v, ii, 148):

  . . . Know the gallant monarch is in arms,
  And, like an **eagle** o'er his aery, towers,
  To souse annoyance that comes near his nest.

And thus the Earl of Westmoreland reminds his king how the Scots customarily behave when the English back is turned on them as they face France (*King Henry V*, i, ii, 169):

  For once the **eagle** England being in prey,
  To her unguarded nest the weasel Scot
  Comes sneaking, and so sucks her princely eggs;
  Playing the mouse in absence of the cat,
  To spoil and havoc more than she can eat.

And Gloster, more familiarly but with irresistible *diablerie*, assumes a virtue when he has it not (*King Richard III*, i, iii, 70):

  I cannot tell: the world is grown so bad,
  That wrens may prey where **eagles** dare not perch:
  Since every Jack became a gentleman,
  There's many a gentle person made a Jack.

The rest of the military parade are as nothing to Pandarus when Troilus has passed in the procession (*Troilus and Cressida*, i, ii, 239) and his speech to Cressida, even with its repeated phrases, is intensely characteristic:

Asses, fools, dolts! chaff and bran, chaff and bran! porridge after meat! I could live and die i' th' eyes of Troilus. Ne'er look, ne'er look; the **eagles** are gone; crows and daws, crows and daws! I had rather be such a man as Troilus than Agamemnon and all Greece.

And near the end of *Cymbeline* (v, iv, 113) no less a god than Jupiter descends upon an eagle from Olympus, utters a fine oration in honour of Imogen, and ascends to Olympus again with the absolutely transcendent final line:

> Mount, **eagle**, to my palace crystalline.

EEL AND CONGER

Marina, the daughter of Pericles, is a lost soul, but wanders unsullied and 'in strong proof of chastity well armed' (like Romeo's Rosaline). It is admittedly – as the workaday world would say – a very near thing when she finds herself in captivity in a brothel, and when she has to take part in this snatch of conversation with a Bawd (unnamed) and one Boult (who is a Pander's servant – as low a calling as one could come by). The play is *Pericles, Prince of Tyre* (IV, ii, 133):

BAWD: Come, young one, I like the manner of your garments well.

BOULT: Ay, by my faith, they shall not be changed yet.

BAWD: Boult, spend thou that in the town: report what a sojourner we have; you'll lose nothing by custom. When nature framed this piece, she meant thee a good turn; therefore say what a paragon she is, and thou hast the harvest out of thine own report.

BOULT: I warrant you, mistress, thunder shall not so awake the beds of **eels** as my giving out her beauty stir up the lewdly-inclined. I'll bring home some to-night.

BAWD: Come your ways, follow me.

MARINA: If fires be hot, knives sharp, or waters deep,
Untied I still my virgin knot will keep.
Diana, aid my purpose!

BAWD: What have we to do with Diana? Pray you, will you go with us?   [*Exeunt*

But the goddess – and Marina – had the last word all the same.

Conger, the outsize in eels or sea-eels, has two mentions,

both in *King Henry IV, Part Two*. Doll Tearsheet calls Falstaff 'a muddy **conger**', while telling him to go and hang himself (II, iv, 54); and Falstaff tells Doll Tearsheet that the somewhat nondescript character called Pointz (II, iv, 243) plays quoits well and 'eats **conger** and fennel,' which is said to have been a high old mixture. Conger, incidentally, is a high old dish.

ELEPHANT

One of the conspirators against Caesar, Decius Brutus, has a remark to Cassius which indicates some grounding in elementary psychology (*Julius Cáesar*, II, i, 202). Cassius has just been opining that several bad omens may prevent Caesar going to the Capitol on that fatal day. But Decius Brutus is firmly and shrewdly of the opposite opinion:

> Never fear that: if he be so resolved,
> I can o'ersway him; for he loves to hear
> That unicorns may be betray'd with trees,
> And bears with glasses, **elephants** with holes,
> Lions with toils, and men with flatterers:
> But when I tell him he hates flatterers,
> He says he does, being then most flattered.
> Let me work;
> And I will bring him to the Capitol.

The Elephant is the often-mentioned name of the inn 'in the south suburbs' in Illyria (*Twelfth Night*, III, iii, 39). But the animal itself is only referred to, figuratively, in one other play, *Troilus and Cressida*. Cressida hears Ajax described by her eloquent servant, Alexander, as being 'valiant as the lion, churlish as the bear, slow as the **elephant**' (I, ii, 20). The blunt-tongued Thersites bluntly calls the same character 'the **elephant** Ajax,' though behind his back (II, iii, 2). And later, within the same scene, Ulysses comes away – for no reason at all – with his own expression of the old legend that elephants never kneel or lie down: 'The **elephant** hath joints, but none for courtesy: his legs are legs for necessity, not for flexure' (II, iii, 99).

It is one's own observation that that much more familiar animal, the horse (which see), seldom lies down when well, and usually sleeps standing. Moreover, when a horse falls down by accident it cannot wait to get on all fours again, unless it be grievously hurt.

FALCON AND KITE

Both are of the falcon family (*Falconidae*). The Falcon, more fully the peregrine falcon, plays its part in the unnatural happenings in nature on the night of King Duncan's murder. An unnamed Old Man tells Ross (*Macbeth* II, iv, 12) how on the previous Tuesday –

> A **falcon**, towering in her pride of place,
> Was by a mousing owl hawk'd at and kill'd.

The same bird's assurance is cited by Bolingbroke in *King Richard II* (I, iii, 59):

> O, let no noble eye profane a tear
> For me, if I be gored with Mowbray's spear:
> As confident as is the **falcon's** flight
> Against a bird, do I with Mowbray fight.

Lord Clifford in *King Henry VI, Part Three* has an observation to the effect that even the most overpowered creature may still have a little game struggle left in it (I, iv, 40):

> So cowards fight when they can fly no further;
> So doves do peck the **falcon's** piercing talons;
> So desperate thieves, all hopeless of their lives,
> Breathe out invectives 'gainst the officers.

And Touchstone, in one of his too few colloquies with the philosopher Jaques, tells us how he is threatened with wedlock, and in passing mentions that falcons were supplied with bells, as they still are when one sees any (*As You Like It*, III, iii, 73):

JAQUES: Will you be married, motley?
TOUCHSTONE: As the ox hath his bow, sir, the horse his curb, and the **falcon** her bells, so man hath his desires; and as pigeons bill, so wedlock would be nibbling.

All the references to the Kite are much unpleasanter. Antony is clearly in a dangerous rage when he discovers Caesar's messenger bending over Cleopatra's hand (III, xiii, 89):

Approach, there! – Ah, you **kite**! – Now, gods and devils!
Authority melts from me: ...

And Macbeth, facing the stare of the blood-boltered Banquo's ghost, is almost incoherent with terror (*Macbeth*, III, iv, 69):

Prithee, see there! behold! look! lo! how say you?
Why, what care I? If thou canst nod, speak too.
If charnel-houses and our graves must send
Those that we bury back, our monuments
Shall be the maws of **kites**.

A far from ideal Macbeth, Charles Laughton was unforgettable in this scene, and in this particular speech.

FIEND AND FLIBBERTIGIBBET

Gloster's son, Edgar, in his naked guise as Poor Tom (*King Lear*), more than once conjures up various fiends and familiars, the friendliest of which he calls Flibbertigibbet (III, iv, 118):

This is the foul **fiend Flibbertigibbet**: he begins at curfew, and walks till the first cock; he gives the web and the pin [= eye distempers], squints the eye, and makes the hare-lip; mildews the white wheat, and hurts the poor creature of earth.

Edgar has still worse company (III, iv, 145):

> Beware my follower. Peace, Smulkin; peace, thou **fiend**! ... The prince of darkness is a gentleman: Modo he's called, and Mahu.

And, later, Edgar raves on and on to his father, who has been cruelly blinded and does not recognize him (IV, i, 59):

> Poor Tom hath been scared out of his good wits: bless thee, good man's son, from the foul **fiend**! five **fiends** have been in poor Tom at once: of lust, as Obidicut; Hobbididence, prince of dumbness; Mahu, of stealing; Modo, of murder; and **Flibbertigibbet**, of mopping and mowing, who since possesses chambermaids and waiting-women. So, bless thee, master!

Fiends, more or less foul, swarm in Shakespeare, as in one of those proverb-canvases of Bosch or the elder Bruegel or Breugel (he spells it both ways). 'They are devils' additions, the names of **fiends**,' says Ford in *The Merry Wives of Windsor* (II, ii, 298). 'The **fiend** is at mine elbow, and tempts me,' says Launcelot Gobbo in *The Merchant of Venice* (II, ii, 2). 'Out, hyperbolical **fiend**! how vexest thou this man!' says Feste, when confronted with Malvolio, who is said to be mad and therefore possessed by a fiend (*Twelfth Night*, IV, ii, 27). '**Fiend**, thou torment'st me ere I come to hell!' says Richard II to Bolingbroke (*King Richard II*, IV, i, 270).

And so on, by the score. The marvel is that the most evil and pernicious character in all the plays, Iago, is nowhere called a fiend, either to his face or behind his back. Till the end he conceals his innate fiendishness only too well, not only from his master and mistress, but even from his wife Emilia; and it is perhaps Shakespeare's fault that he has made Emilia too shrewd a woman to have been deceived by that specious fiend for quite so long.

FISHES IN GENERAL

Respecting fish, there is no lovelier image in all the plays than the one in the long poem *Venus and Adonis* (line 1099) where Venus envisages her shepherd bathing:

> When he beheld his shadow in the brook,
> The **fishes** spread on it their golden gills; ...

But there are marvellous other effects in the plays. The effect sinister, as in Clarence's account of his under-water dream in *King Richard III* (I, iv, 24):

> Methought I saw a thousand fearful wrecks;
> Ten thousand men that **fishes** gnaw'd upon;
> Wedges of gold, great anchors, heaps of pearl,
> Inestimable stones, unvalued jewels,
> All scatt'red in the bottom of the sea: ...

The effect philosophic, as in *Hamlet* in the Prince's rapid interchange with Claudius (IV, iii, 28):

HAMLET: A man may **fish** with the worm that hath eat of a king, and eat of the **fish** that hath fed of that worm.
KING: What dost thou mean by this?
HAMLET: Nothing but to show you how a king may go a progress through the guts of a beggar.

And the effect plainly comical, as when Trinculo comes upon the sleeping Caliban in *The Tempest* when another tempest seems imminent (II, ii, 20):

> Yond same black cloud, yond huge one, looks like a foul bombard that would shed his liquor. If it should thunder as it did before, I

know not where to hide my head: yond same cloud cannot choose but fall by pailfuls. What have we here? a man or a **fish**? dead or alive? A **fish**: he smells like a **fish**; a very ancient and **fish-like** smell; ...

And so Trinculo goes on and on till he arrives at a sentence which compensates us richly for his verbosity: 'Misery acquaints a man with strange bedfellows.'

FLEAS, FLIES AND GNATS

These again abound, and again one has to pick and choose – and scratch.

Petruchio with his wife's Tailor lets out a nice stream of dog's abuse in *The Taming of the Shrew* (IV, iii, 109): 'Thou **flea**, thou nit, thou winter-cricket thou!' Sir Toby tells Fabian what he thinks of Sir Andrew's valour, or lack of it, in *Twelfth Night* (III, ii, 50): 'For Andrew, if he were open'd, and you find so much blood in his liver as will clog the foot of a **flea**, I'll eat the rest of th' anatomy.' And in *King Henry V* the followers of Falstaff, after his death, indulge in affectionate reminiscence (II, iii, 42). The Boy says: 'Do you not remember, a' saw a **flea** stand upon Bardolph's nose, and a' said it was a black soul burning in hell-fire?' This usually wins a laugh in the theatre which drowns Bardolph's very characteristic answer: 'Well, the fuel is gone that maintain'd that fire: that's all the riches I got in his service.'

Around the subject of Flies, Lear's Gloster is absolute, Othello terrifying, and Cleopatra tremendous. Gloster (*King Lear*, IV, i, 37) declares:

> As **flies** to wanton boys, are we to the gods,
> They kill us for their sport.

Othello answers the doomed Desdemona's utterance, 'I hope

my noble lord esteems me honest,' in this sort (*Othello*, IV, ii, 66):

> O, ay; as summer **flies** are in the shambles,
> That quicken even with blowing.

And Cleopatra to Antony, just before they choose to have 'one other gaudy night', very nearly transcends language in the lines (*Antony and Cleopatra*, III, xiii, 161):

> . . . as it determines, so
> Dissolve my life! The next Caesarion smite!
> Till, by degrees, the memory of my womb,
> Together with my brave Egyptians all,
> By the discandying of this pelleted storm,
> Lie graveless, till the **flies** and **gnats** of Nile
> Have buried them for prey!

After this any Gnats of any sort must flutter in anti-climax – for example, those in *The Comedy of Errors*. In this observation of Antipholus of Syracuse (II, ii, 30) their behaviour is seen to be not very different from that of humankind:

> When the sun shines let foolish **gnats** make sport,
> But creep in crannies when he hides his beams.

FOWL AND WILDFOWL

In his superb answer to the psycho-analyst Feste, the locked-up Malvolio proves himself as right-minded as anybody else in *Twelfth Night* (IV, ii, 47):

MALVOLIO: I say, this house is as dark as ignorance, though ignorance were as dark as hell; and I say, there was never man thus abused. I am no more mad than you are: make the trial of it in any constant question.

WSAM–E

FESTE: What is the opinion of Pythagoras concerning **wildfowl**?
MALVOLIO: That the soul of our grandam might haply inhabit a bird.
FESTE: What think'st thou of his opinion?
MALVOLIO: I think nobly of the soul, and no way approve his opinion.

In out-of-the-way places two haunting phrases about fowl should here be noted. The one is in the last scene of *Titus Andronicus* (v, iii, 67) where, with the stage strewn with bleeding corpses, Lucius Andronicus addresses the Romans:

> You sad-faced men, people and sons of Rome,
> By uproar sever'd, like a flight of **fowl**
> Scatter'd by winds and high tempestuous gusts,
> O, let me teach you . . .

The other is early on in the action of *Cymbeline*, when Iachimo is telling Posthumus that he need not be too complacent or cocksure about his wife Imogen's integrity and fidelity (I, iv, 87): 'You know, strange **fowl** light upon neighbouring ponds.' Here Shakespeare is being positively Strindbergian.

But these are unfamiliar things. Among the familiar ones, we simply cannot ignore that sublimely stupid leading man, Bottom, and his sensibility about scaring his audience with the sight and sound of a real lion (*A Midsummer Night's Dream*, III, i, 29): 'Masters, you ought to consider with yourselves: to bring in, – God shield us! – a lion among ladies is a most dreadful thing; for there is not a more fearful **wild-fowl** than your lion living; and we ought to look to't.'

FOX AND VIXEN

The Fox is famed for its craftiness and cunning, the Vixen solely for its short temper. The vixen is mentioned only in *A Midsummer Night's Dream* (III, ii, 323) where Helena comments on Hermia who is sharper as well as shorter than herself:

> O, when she's angry, she is keen and shrewd!
> She was a **vixen** when she went to school;
> And though she be but little, she is fierce.

When Hermia protests warmly at this, Lysander adds insult to the injury: 'Get you gone, you dwarf; You minimus, of hind'ring knot-grass made; You bead, you acorn.'

But Shakespeare, oddly enough, has no mention of craft or cunning in his many mentions of the fox. 'Subtle', in the old sense of the word, is the nearest he comes to the traditional attribute, and this is best instanced not in any of the plays but in that lovely long poem, *Venus and Adonis*, which will never belong to the popular taste because it is about frustration, not gratification.

In an uninterrupted speech of more than a hundred lines Venus has a flying reference to 'the **fox** which lives by subtlety' (line 675). But Adonis, who would infinitely rather hunt the boar than be bored by Venus, practically tells her so to her importunate face (lines 773–774):

> For, by this black-faced night, desire's foul nurse,
> Your treatise makes me like you worse and worse.

FROGS AND TOADS

We are again in the world of reptilian familiars. They have their liveliest orgy, both the living and the dead familiars, in the opening scene of the fourth act of *Macbeth*. Some relegate this scene to the cruder pen of Thomas Middleton. But those who do so unthinkingly might like to reassess Middleton. He may have been a much inferior playwright. He was. But he was a far better dog at a title. Only an insane bias in favour of Shakespeare over all other Elizabethans and Jacobeans put together could make out that *Twelfth Night, As You Like It,* and *Much Ado About Nothing* are anything like such promising play-titles as *The Roaring Girl, A Chaste Maid in Cheapside,* and *A Mad World, My Masters,* which are plays by Middleton. (Pursuing this matter a step further, we may opine that *The Tempest* is a poor reach-me-down sort of title for what is perhaps the most magical and metaphysical fantasy ever written to be acted or merely read.)

The Frog (*Rana*) has an edible species, and the Toad (*Bufo*) has none such. But both come into the regular menu, with some other non-delicacies, of Edgar masquerading as Poor Tom in *King Lear* (III, iv, 132):

Poor Tom; that eats the swimming **frog**, the **toad**, the tadpole, the wall-newt and the water [newt]; that in the fury of his heart, when the foul fiend rages, eats cow-dung for sallets; swallows the old rat and the ditch-dog; drinks the green mantle of the standing pool; ...

There are, again, dire and dreadful things about toads in the rarer plays. Thus Ajax in *Troilus and Cressida* (II, iii, 158) declares: 'I do hate a proud man, as I hate the engendering of **toads**.' And the fiend-like Tamora in *Titus Andronicus* (II, iii, 101) tells how she was left in an evil spot in the forest, where

Ten thousand swelling **toads**, as many urchins [= hedgehogs],
Would make such fearful and confused cries,
As any mortal body hearing it
Should straight fall mad, or else die suddenly.

But yet we need go no further than *Othello* – Olivier's superb in recent memory – to note the Moor's most sinister emphases in two scenes, both with Desdemona, where he mentions 'a cistern for foul **toads** to knot and gender in'

(*Othello*, IV, ii, 61), and where with infinite yearning he breathes the words (III, iii, 270):

> ... I had rather be a **toad**,
> And live upon the vapour of a dungeon,
> Than keep a corner in the thing I love
> For others' uses.

See also under HEDGEHOG AND PADDOCK.

GARGANTUA AND GORGON

The sole reference to Rabelais in Shakespeare – the possessive form of the name 'Gargantua' – is no proof that the poet had read the great French scholar-buffoon who died eleven years before his own birth.

The reference is in *As You Like It* (III, ii, 221) when Celia tells Rosalind that she has encountered no less a man than Orlando in the forest:

ROSALIND: Orlando?
CELIA: Orlando.
ROSALIND: Alas the day! what shall I do with my doublet and hose? What did he when thou saw'st him? What said he? How lookt he? Wherein went he? What makes he here? Did he ask for me? Where remains he? How parted he with thee? and when shalt thou see him again? Answer me in one word.

This is the excitement of one 'many fathom deep in love', as she describes herself elsewhere. And Celia has her good Rabelaisian answer: 'You must borrow me **Gargantua's** mouth first: 'tis a word too great for any mouth of this age's size. ...'

Those monster-sisters of Greek mythology, the Gorgons, have two fleeting mentions. Cleopatra says of Antony, when she hears of his marriage to Octavia (*Antony and Cleopatra*, II, v, 116):

> Though he be painted one way like a **Gorgon**,
> The other way's a Mars.

And Macduff, having found King Duncan murdered, urges the others to go and see for themselves (*Macbeth*, II, iii, 73):

> Approach the chamber, and destroy your sight
> With a new **Gorgon**: do not bid me speak;
> See, and then speak yourselves.

Medusa, the best-known of these sight-destroying Gorgons, gets no mention at all in Shakespeare.

GEESE AND WILD GEESE

What is, or was, a Winchester Goose? It is mentioned in *King Henry VI, Part One*, where Gloster, the King's uncle, and Henry Beaufort, both a Bishop and a Cardinal, are having a public brawl before the Tower of London. Gloster calls Beaufort such things as 'peel'd [=bald] priest', 'manifest conspirator' and 'scarlet hypocrite', but the crowning insult is when he calls him 'Winchester goose' (I, iii, 53). In their efforts to explain this all the editors, like sheep, go back to a Victorian scholar, the Rev. Alexander Dyce, who died 100 years ago and who opined that the term was venereal and referred to a 'certain stage' in syphilis. It would seem that the Bishop of Winchester was in control also of Southwark, where were the worst stews in London.

So far, so bad. But Winchester Goose is mentioned also in, of all unlikely places, the last few lines of *Troilus and Cressida*. Usually, in the theatre, this play ends with Troilus rounding on and dismissing Pandarus. But in the text – and indeed in the First Folio – Pandarus has a concluding soliloquy about which nothing is very clear except its gracelessness (v, x, 45):

> Good traders in the flesh, set this in your painted cloths:
> As many as be here of Pander's hall,
> Your eyes, half out, weep out at Pandar's fall;
> Or if you cannot weep, yet give some groans,
> Though not for me, yet for your aching bones.
> Brethren and sisters of the hold-door trade,
> Some two months hence my will shall here be made:
> It should be now, but that my fear is this,
> Some gallèd **goose** of Winchester would hiss:
> Till then I'll sweat, and seek about for eases;
> And at that time bequeath you my diseases.

This probably is not Shakespeare. But whoever the writer may be, what is this debased mention of Winchester doing in ancient Troy?

There are some picturesque images of the wild goose. In *King Henry IV, Part One* (II, iv, 138) Falstaff declares to Prince Hal: 'A king's son! If I do not beat thee out of thy kingdom with a dagger of lath, and drive all thy subjects afore thee like a flock of **wild-geese**, I'll never wear hair on my face more. You Prince of Wales!' And the Fool says to King Lear when on the very verge of his madness (*King Lear*, II, iv, 46): 'Winter's not gone yet, if the **wild-geese** fly that way.'

GOATS

Goats are goatish, as men can be. And Audrey, whom Touchstone was eventually to take in marriage, was – as is not usually remembered – a goatherdess as distinct from a shepherdess.

The first of these facts is expressed by Edmund, Gloster's bastard son, in *King Lear* (I, ii, 130): 'An admirable evasion of whoremaster man, to lay his **goatish** disposition to the charge of a star!'

The second is told us, twice over, by Touchstone himself in the heart of *As You Like It* (III, iii, 1):

TOUCHSTONE: Come apace, good Audrey: I will fetch up your **goats**, Audrey. And how, Audrey? am I the man yet? doth my simple feature content you?

AUDREY: Your features! Lord warrant us! what features?

TOUCHSTONE: I am here with thee and thy **goats,** as the most capricious poet, honest Ovid, was among the Goths.

JAQUES (*aside*): O knowledge ill-inhabited, worse than Jove in a thatch'd house!

GRIFFIN AND GOBLIN

The Griffin is a fabulous animal with the head and wings of an eagle and the body and hindquarters of a lion. It seems somehow very right and proper that this rather endearing monster should be the symbol of Wales, just as the rampant red lion – shaped not at all unlike Caledonia itself – should be the standard of Scotland.

Its one, somewhat involved, appearance in Shakespeare is in *A Midsummer Night's Dream*, in Helena's speech as she pursues Demetrius, who no longer wants her (II, i, 231):

> Apollo flies, and Daphne holds the chase;
> The dove pursues the **griffin**; the mild hind
> Makes speed to catch the tiger, bootless speed,
> When cowardice pursues, and valour flies!

The *Dictionary* sense of the word 'goblin' is 'a mischievous and ugly sprite or demon'. But the word has largely lost its original force through two centuries or so of fairy tales. In Elizabethan times it could still have a more sinister power, far

more of the genuine ghostly quality. Note well Hamlet's first
address to his father's spirit at Elsinore (I, iv, 39):

> Angels and ministers of grace defend us!
> Be thou a spirit of health or **goblin** damn'd,
> Bring with thee airs from heaven or blasts from hell,
> Be thy intents wicked or charitable,
> Thou com'st in such a questionable shape,
> That I will speak to thee: I'll call thee Hamlet,
> King, father, royal Dane: O, answer me! . . .

There is more of the childish or harmless sense of 'goblin'
in little Mamillius' bedtime story in *The Winter's Tale* (II, i,
23). His mother Hermione requests it:

MAMILLIUS: Merry or sad shall't be?
HERMIONE: As merry as you will.
MAMILLIUS: A sad tale's best for winter: I have one
  Of sprites and **goblins**.
HERMIONE: Let's have that, good sir.
  Come on, sit down: come on, and do your best
  To fright me with your sprites; you're powerful at it.
MAMILLIUS: There was a man –
HERMIONE: Nay, come, sit down; then on.
MAMILLIUS: Dwelt by a churchyard: . . .

Alas that the story, so marvellously begun, got no farther since
into the scene burst Leontes in a jealous rage.

HARES

On the subject of the Hare (or *Lepus*) Shakespeare is thoroughly
outclassed by many subsequent poets. Robert Burns can coin
the perfect phrase for this animal's sportiveness in 'amorous
whids', and can turn out the perfect Scottish word for its

swift, wide-paced gait in 'hirpling'. Keats can freeze it in winter:

> St Agnes' Eve – Ah, bitter chill it was!
> The owl, for all his feathers, was a-cold;
> The **hare** limp'd trembling through the frozen grass,
> And silent was the flock in woolly fold. . . .

Wordsworth can follow it around on a spring morning (in the lovely poem about the old leech-gatherer on the moor):

> All things that love the sun are out of doors;
> The sky rejoices in the morning's birth;
> The grass is bright with rain-drops; – on the moors
> The **hare** is running races in her mirth;
> And with her feet she from the plashy earth
> Raises a mist; that, glittering in the sun,
> Runs with her all the way, wherever she doth run.

Against such delights Shakespeare can offer only some commonplace similes about the beast's cowardice and timidity, and Mercutio's abominable humour at its punning worst (*Romeo and Juliet*, II, iii, 141):

> An old **hare** hoar,
> And an old **hare** hoar,
> Is very good meat in Lent:
> But a **hare** that is hoar
> Is too much for a score,
> When it hoars ere it be spent.

Well may Juliet's Nurse say 'Scurvy knave!' twice over, when Mercutio has marched out singing this stuff. In the mind's ear, I can still hear Edith Evans's matchless old Nurse uttering the words in crackling fury. Scurvy knave!

HARPY AND HARPIER

There is something about the Harpy repellent above all other mythological or supernatural monsters. It may be the element of filth, which the *Oxford Dictionary* emphasizes: 'a fabled monster, rapacious and filthy, having a woman's face and body and a bird's wings and claws'.

There is also a Harpy-Bat in the East Indies, and a Harpy-Eagle, which is a South American bird of prey. Doubtless they are well-named, but they come not into Shakespeare. Benedick, of course, is merely fooling when he tells Don Pedro that he will go errands to the ends of the earth 'rather than hold three words' conference with this **harpy**', meaning Beatrice (*Much Ado About Nothing*, II, i, 260). And Prospero commends Ariel for assuming the disguise of a Harpy to make a banquet vanish before it is tasted (*The Tempest*, III, iii, 83): 'Bravely the figure of this **harpy** hast thou Perform'd, my Ariel.'

But the most alarming form of the word is Harpier, which is heard and not seen. It is a familiar of the Witches in *Macbeth* (IV, i, 3). The Brinded Cat at least mewed, the Hedge-Pig at least whined, but Harpier, simply and appallingly, cried, ''Tis time, 'tis time.' Forty lines later Macbeth says to the Witches:

> How now, you secret, black, and midnight hags!
> What is't you do?

and gets the paralysing answer, 'A deed without a name.'

Harpier, their most intense familiar, may be called a shape without a name.

HAWK AND HERNSHAW

In the Induction to *The Taming of the Shrew* a drunken tinker, Christopher Sly, is treated as though he were a noble lord who had lost his reason. Shakespeare was not yet a Pirandello; he could not sustain the joke for more than a scene or two. But the fantasy certainly has its moments till it vanishes to make way for the farce itself. Sly is offered luxuries, music, horses:

> Dost thou love hawking? thou hast **hawks** will soar
> Above the morning lark: . . .

And so on, from the Induction, Scene 2 (line 43).

The Hawk is used also in a comparison made by the horse-proud Dauphin of France in *King Henry V* (III, vii, 11). This Dauphin is more lyrical about his horse than Romeo about his Juliet:

> I will not change my horse with any that treads but on four pasterns. . . . When I bestride him, I soar, I am a **hawk**: he trots the air; the earth sings when he touches it; . . . It is a beast for Perseus: he is pure air and fire; and the dull elements of earth and water never appear in him, but only in patient stillness while his rider mounts him: he is, indeed, a horse; and all other jades you may call beasts. . . .

Hamlet in his pretended madness says to Guildenstern (*Hamlet*, II, ii, 383): 'I am but mad north-north-west: when the wind is southerly I know a **hawk** from a handsaw.' The last word is corrupt, and has raised a hubbub of conjecture, and has variously appeared as 'heron', 'hernshaw' and 'heronshaw'. It is not generally known, even to the dramatic critics, that Barry Sullivan – a sonorous Irish tragedian whom Bernard Shaw injudiciously preferred to Henry Irving – accepted 'heronshaw' when he played Hamlet. He went so far as to pronounce the word 'heron . . . pshaw!' When on one occa-

sion he brought his Hamlet to Manchester, that city's great
newspaper coldly advised him to desist from this malpractice.

HEDGEHOG AND PADDOCK

They are all things of evil, witches' familiars. The fairies sing
to keep them away while their Queen lies sleeping (*A Midsummer Night's Dream*, ii, ii, 9):

> You spotted snakes with double tongue,
> Thorny **hedgehogs**, be not seen;
> Newts and blind-worms, do no wrong,
> Come not near our fairy queen.

Caliban in *The Tempest* (ii, ii, 8) sees them among the
spirits with which Prospero torments and prods him:

> For every trifle are they set upon me;
> Sometimes like apes, that mow and chatter at me,
> And after bite me; then like **hedgehogs**, which
> Lie tumbling in my barefoot way, and mount
> Their pricks at my footfall; . . .

Frogs or toads in the form of 'puttock' are met with elsewhere. Warwick, amid the lords with their never-ending
quarrel in *King Henry VI, Part Two*, has a picturesque phrase
(iii, ii, 191):

> Who finds the partridge in the **puttock's** nest,
> But may imagine how the bird was dead,
> Although the kite soar with unbloodied beak?
> Even so suspicious is this tragedy.

But it is the same reptile in yet another form, that of Paddock, that is most sinister of all. It is mentioned – hardly more
than mentioned – in *Macbeth* (i, i, 9) when one of the Witches

185

(the various editions of the play have not settled which one) says, '**Paddock** calls – anon!'

Yet another form of the word, 'Puddock', is how the frog is generally known to this day to children all over Scotland.

See under FROGS AND TOADS.

HEN AND CHICKS

The Hen is a much less nefarious creature (much less assertive and flamboyant) than the Cock. It has not even very much emotion to display as a general rule, aside from a curious trick of indignant iteration and reiteration in the announcement of the fact that it has just laid an egg. Egg-laying, indeed, may be said to go to a hen's head. But nothing else does. The Cock can be both loud and demanding, chicks querulous and in-clined to twitter unendingly, but the Hen is apt to be dumb in all of that word's meanings.

Volumnia, conversing with her son, Coriolanus, compares herself to a hen without doing herself any disservice (v, iii, 160):

> ... There's no man in the world
> More bound to's mother; yet here he lets me prate
> Like one i' the stocks. Thou hast never in thy life
> Show'd thy dear mother any courtesy;
> When she, poor **hen**, fond of no second brood,
> Has cluckt thee to the wars, and safely home,
> Loaden with honour. ...

(One admiringly recalls Sybil Thorndike in the part gazing upon her Coriolanus – it was Olivier – and priding herself upon his very pride.)

The hen clucks again in a very different sort of interchange between Katharine and Petruchio (*The Taming of the Shrew*, II, i, 222):

PETRUCHIO: O, put me in thy books!
KATHARINA: What is your crest? a coxcomb?
PETRUCHIO: A combless cock, so Kate will be my **hen.**
KATHARINA: No cock of mine; you crow too like a craven.

There is Falstaff, too – in *King Henry IV, Part One*, III, iii, 54 – saying to Mistress Quickly: 'How now, Dame Partlet the **hen**! have you inquired yet who pickt my pocket?' Can there be an indication here at last that Shakespeare knew his Chaucer – Partlet being the same as Pertelote, which is the name of the hen in the Nonnes Preestes Tale? But, alas, there can be no such indication. Pertelote is ancient pre-Chaucer French for a hen, just as Chauntecleer is ancient pre-Chaucer French for a cock.

Shakespeare's few references to chicks and chickens are mainly figurative. Prospero calls Ariel 'chick' just once, at the end of the play when about to return his servant to his natural element, the air (*The Tempest*, V, i, 317):

> ... My Ariel, **chick,**
> That is thy charge: then to the elements
> Be free, and fare thou well! ...

This is touching. But more than touching, indeed very moving, is what Macduff says when told that his wife and children have been slaughtered by Macbeth (*Macbeth*, IV, iii, 218):

> What, all my pretty **chickens** and their dam
> At one fell swoop?

HORSE AND FOAL

Horses provide almost too broad and wide a subject for choice.

One might be dark and terrible like King Lear: 'Darkness and devils! saddle my **horses**' (*King Lear*, I, iv, 257).

Or passionate like Cleopatra: 'O happy **horse**, to bear the weight of Antony! Do bravely, horse!' (*Antony and Cleopatra*, I, v, 21).

Or impetuous like Hotspur: 'Come, let me taste my **horse**, Who is to bear me, like a thunderbolt, . . .' (*King Henry IV, Part One*, IV, i, 119).

Or desperate like Richard III: 'Give me another **horse**, bind up my wounds' (*King Richard III*, v, iii, 178).

Or mystical and Blake-like as Macbeth with his 'Heaven's cherubin, **horsed** Upon the sightless couriers of the air' (*Macbeth*, I, vii, 22).

Or imaginative like the Prologue to *Henry V* (line 26):

> Think, when we talk of **horses**, that you see them
> Printing their proud hoofs i' th' receiving earth; . . .

Or detailed and particular like the description of the perfect steed in *Venus and Adonis* (lines 295–300):

> Round-hooft, short-jointed, fetlocks shag and long,
> Broad breast, full eye, small head, and nostril wide,
> High crest, short ears, straight legs, and passing strong,
> Thin mane, thick tail, broad buttock, tender hide:
> Look, what a **horse** should have he did not lack,
> Save a proud rider on so proud a back.

(Hazlitt, who thought poorly of the poems as compared with the plays, said of this stanza: 'This inventory of perfections shows great knowledge of the horse; and it is good matter-of-fact poetry.')

Alternatively one might give so many single instances of other grades of horseflesh.

For example, cite Falstaff's curious and quaint question in *King Henry IV, Part Two* (II, i, 43): 'How now! whose **mare**'s dead? what's the matter?'

Or repeat Lysander's criticism of Quince's delivery of the

Prologue to the play (in *A Midsummer Night's Dream*, v, i, 119): 'He hath rid his prologue like a rough **colt**.'

Or simply, like Puck, in the same play (ii, i, 46), neigh 'in likeness of a **filly foal**'.

INSECTS IN GENERAL

Such insects (of the phylum *Arthropoda*) as are not dealt with elsewhere may here be dealt with severally and in alphabetical order. Here again the examples may be said to *teem*, so that choice of each single example has been the selector's.

A NTS. The *Dictionary*, not unamusingly, defines the ant as 'a small social insect of the Hymenopterous order, celebrated for its industry; an emmet, a pismire'. It is more than once mentioned by Hotspur in *King Henry IV, Part One*. Talking of Owen Glendower (iii, i, 146):

> I cannot choose: sometime he angers me
> With telling me of the moldwarp [or mole] and the **ant**,
> Of the dreamer Merlin and his prophecies, ...

And, still more characteristically (i, iii, 238):

> Why, look you, I am whipt and scourged with rods,
> Nettled, and stung with **pismires**, when I hear
> Of this vile politician, Bolingbroke. ...

CRICKETS. The cricket on the hearth is *Acheta domestica*, and it is defined as a 'saltatorial orthopterous insect', which merely means that it goes by leaps and bounds, and that its wings fold lengthwise down its body. The little Prince Mamillius in *The Winter's Tale* (ii, i, 30), beginning and ending his ghost story with the single sentence, 'There was a man dwelt by a churchyard', breaks off to add the words, 'I will tell it softly – Yond **crickets** shall not hear it.' A touch of genius, if one likes.

GRASSHOPPERS. The common grasshopper (*Chorthippus brunneus*) is equally saltatorial, no less orthopterous, and just as merry. Incidentally, the *Oxford Dictionary* traces this proverbial cheerfulness of the cricket only as far back as one century – 'as cheerful and lively as a cricket, 1873'. But it can be traced at least as far back as Shakespeare himself, that is to *King Henry IV, Part One* (II, iv, 88):

PRINCE HENRY: Sirrah, Falstaff and the rest of the thieves are at the door: shall we be merry?
POINTZ: As merry as **crickets**, my lad.

Elements of both these insects come into the description of Queen Mab's coach in Mercutio's celebrated scherzo for the voice (*Romeo and Juliet*, I, iv, 59). This is a synthesis of some of the finest and smallest things observable before the discovery of the microscope:

> Her wagon-spokes made of long spinners' legs;
> The cover, of the wings of **grasshoppers**;
> The traces, of the moonshine's watery beams;
> The collars **crickets'** bones; the lash, of film . . .

That this 'scurvy knave' Mercutio should have so delicate an imagination!

HONEY BEES. The distinction and the difference between, for example, a humble bee and a bumble bee is not readily made by the merely amateur hymenopterist. But it is made possible and pleasurable by John Barton's recently published *Oxford Book of Insects* (1968), especially as the illustrations are by a brilliant team led by the felicitously named Joyce Bee.

It is, oddly enough, King Henry V's Archbishop of Canter-

bury who gives us the poet's most elaborate metaphor on the
subject of honey bees in general (*King Henry V*, I, ii, 187):

> ... so work the **honey-bees**,
> Creatures that, by a rule in nature, teach
> The act of order to a peopled kingdom.
> They have a king, and officers of sorts:
> Where some, like magistrates, correct at home;
> Others, like merchants, venture trade abroad;
> Others, like soldiers, armed in their stings,
> Make boot upon the summer's velvet buds;
> Which pillage they with merry march bring home
> To the tent-royal of their emperor:
> Who, busied in his majesty, surveys
> The singing masons building roofs of gold;
> The civil citizens kneading-up the honey;
> The poor mechanic porters crowding in
> Their heavy burdens at his narrow gate;
> The sad-eyed justice, with his surly hum,
> Delivering o'er to executors pale
> The lazy yawning **drone**. . . .

And so on for almost as long again. Henry V, who was apparently no hymenopterist, almost before His Eminence has
come to a full stop, interposes, 'Call in the messengers sent
from the Dauphin.'

But equally interesting, and very much less verbose, is a
parallel drawn by Lucrece between herself, Collatine her
husband, and Tarquin her ravisher, the parallel being with the
bees (*The Rape of Lucrece*, lines 834–840). This stanza is part of
the desolated Lucrece's long monody addressed to her absent
husband:

> If, Collatine, thine honour lay in me,
> From me by strong assault it is bereft.
> My honey lost, and I, a **drone-like bee**,
> Have no perfection of my summer left,

> But robb'd and ransack'd by injurious theft:
> In thy weak hive a wandering **wasp** hath crept,
> And suck'd the honey which thy chaste **bee** kept.

The bee is, of course, herself, and the wasp Tarquin the
ravisher.

WASPS. The wasp, which is *Vespa vulgaris*, has little in its
favour except that it infinitely prefers sweetness to putrefac-
tion. The prettiest reference to it in Shakespeare is in *The
Two Gentlemen of Verona*, the nastiest in *The Winter's Tale*. In
the former comedy Julia abuses herself for having torn up
Proteus's love-letter to her (i, ii, 105):

> O hateful hands, to tear such loving words!
> Injurious **wasps**, to feed on such sweet honey,
> And kill the **bees,** that yield it, with your stings!
> I'll kiss each several paper for amends.

In the much later drama of jealousy Leontes, that brain-
sickly and positively Strindbergian husband, tries to assure his
courtier Camillo that there is method in his madness (i, ii,
326):

> Dost think I am so muddy, so unsettled,
> To appoint myself in this vexation; sully
> The purity and whiteness of my sheets,
> Which to preserve is sleep, which being spotted
> Is goads, thorns, nettles, tails of **wasps**;
> Give scandal to the blood o' the prince my son,
> Who I do think is mine, and love as mine,
> Without ripe moving to't? Would I do this?
> Could man so blench?

None who saw John Gielgud in the play's record-making
revival (in 1951) will ever forget the quality of exquisite self-
torture he put into such scenes.

Talking of torture, we must quote a killing devised by

192

Autolycus in this same play, the more so since it introduces wasps yet again. This speech is almost invariably cut in stage performance, and quite rightly too. It is in *The Winter's Tale*, IV, iii, 793:

CLOWN: Has the old man e'er a son, sir, do you hear, an't like you, sir?

AUTOLYCUS: He has a son, who shall be flay'd alive; then, 'nointed over with honey, set on the head of a **wasps'** nest; then stand till he be three quarters and a dram dead; then recover'd again with aqua-vitae or some other hot infusion; then, raw as he is, and in the hottest day prognostication proclaims, shall he be set against a brick-wall, the sun looking with a southward eye upon him, where he is to behold him with flies blown to death. . . .

But it may be that to take this over-seriously is like taking Gilbert's Mikado over-seriously.

LAPWING

The Lapwing is a crested bird (*Vanellus cristatus*) of the plover family, and its eggs are the 'plovers' eggs' of the London markets. It is also called the Pewit from its characteristic cry (Peesie in Scotland). Shakespeare uses it in one of his most endearing similes in *Much Ado About Nothing* (III, i, 24):

> For look where Beatrice, like a **lapwing**, runs
> Close by the ground, to hear our conference.

But hardly less endearing are other references. Adriana in *The Comedy of Errors* (IV, ii, 27) says, 'Far from her nest the **lapwing** cries away.' The rake Lucio, confronting the chaste Isabella in *Measure for Measure*, is moved out of his usual levity (I, iv, 31):

> I would not – though 'tis my familiar sin
> With maids to seem the **lapwing**, and to jest,

Tongue far from heart – play with all virgins so:
I hold you as a thing ensky'd and sainted;
By your renouncement, an immortal spirit;
And to be talk'd with in sincerity,
As with a saint.

And Horatio on Osric's exit says, 'This **lapwing** runs away with the shell on his head' (*Hamlet*, v, ii, 185).

But then, it is a gentle bird with a gentle name, and Shakespeare obviously knew it well by sight.

LARKS

He knew the Lark well likewise. But before we begin to choose from his murmuration of lovely lines and phrases on the subject, let us turn to an earlier poet's couplet on this earliest of the morning's birds. One cannot swear to it that it is Chaucer (1340–1400) or Skelton (1460–1530). But it was one or the other, and both are much earlier than Shakespeare; and without being able to find or verify, one will swear to the words if not to their spelling:

The bisy **larke,** messager of daye,
Salueth in hir song the morwe graye

Let the poems come before the plays. From the Sonnets (No. 29) comes:

Haply I think on thee, – and then my state,
Like to the **lark** at break of day arising
From sullen earth, sings hymns at heaven's gate; ...

And from *Venus and Adonis* (lines 853–855):

Lo, here the gentle **lark,** weary of rest,
From his moist cabinet mounts up on high,
And wakes the morning, ...

The plays are not a whit less poetical on the subject. For Juliet it was the nightingale and not the lark; and for Romeo it was the lark and not the nightingale (*Romeo and Juliet*, III, v, 2, 6–7).

In the song of spring at the end of *Love's Labour's Lost* we hear that 'merry **larks** are ploughmen's clocks'. In the song of early morning in the middle of *Cymbeline* 'the **lark** at heaven's gate sings'. In the best of Autolycus's songs in *The Winter's Tale* it is the lark 'that tirra-lirra chants'.

Troilus at dawn says to his heart-breaker (*Troilus and Cressida*, IV, ii, 8):

> O Cressida! but that the busy day,
> Waked by the **lark**, hath roused the ribald crows,
> And dreaming night will hide our joys no longer,
> I would not from thee.

And the Dauphin, in the French camp near Agincourt (*King Henry V*, III, vii, 32), wants to hear praise of his horse from morn to night, which he calls 'from the rising of the **lark** to the lodging of the lamb'.

The skylark is in Scotland the laverock, and in Latin *Alauda arvensis*.

LEOPARD AND PANTHER

Talbot in *King Henry VI, Part One*, finds himself in battle near Orleans with Joan La Pucelle, and almost literally does not know where he is (I, v, 20):

> I know not where I am, nor what I do:
> A witch by fear, not force, like Hannibal,
> Drives back our troops, and conquers as she lists:
> So bees with smoke, and doves with noisome stench,
> Are from their hives and houses driven away.
> They call'd us, for our fierceness, English dogs;
> Now, like to whelps, we crying run away.

> Hark, countrymen! either renew the fight,
> Or tear the lions out of England's coat;
> Renounce your soil, give sheep in lions' stead:
> Sheep run not half so timorous from the wolf,
> Or horse or oxen from the **leopard**,
> As you fly from your oft-subduèd slaves. . . .

It is a fine zoological mêlée, and we behold in it the Leopard.

It is seen again in *Timon of Athens* (IV, iii, 327) where, as is justly said by Apemantus, 'the commonwealth of Athens is become a forest of beasts', and Timon himself surveys it: 'If thou wert the lion, the fox would beguile thee; if thou wert the lamb, the fox would eat thee: if thou wert the fox, the lion would suspect thee, when, peradventure, thou wert accused by the ass: if thou wert the ass, thy dulness would torment thee; and still thou livedst but as a breakfast to the wolf: if thou wert the wolf, thy greediness would afflict thee, and oft thou shouldst hazard thy life for thy dinner: wert thou the unicorn, pride and wrath would confound thee, and make thine own self the conquest of thy fury: wert thou a bear, thou wouldst be kill'd by the horse: wert thou a horse, thou wouldst be seized by the **leopard**; wert thou a **leopard**, thou wert german to the lion, and the spots of thy kindred were jurors on thy life: . . .'

All the Shakespearean Panthers there are occur within the same play, *Titus Andronicus*. First Titus proposes a day's hunting to the Emperor Bassianus (I, i, 491):

> To-morrow, an it please your majesty
> To hunt the **panther** and the hart with me,
> With horn and hound we'll give your Grace *bonjour*.

The hunt duly proceeds with Marcus Andronicus saying to his same lord (II, ii, 20):

> I have dogs, my lord,
> Will rouse the proudest **panther** in the chase.

It is in the same forest that Aaron the Moor leads Titus's two sons to their doom (II, iii, 191) in that baleful play:

> Straight will I bring you to the loathsome pit
> Where I espied the **panther** fast asleep.

Both the leopard and the panther are *Felis pardus*.

LION AND LIONESS

The only two examples of *Felis leo* that one meets in all the plays – apart from countless metaphorical and figure-of-speech and heraldic lions – are the unimpressive lioness in *As You Like It* and the not unimpressive lion in *Julius Caesar*. The first beast we giggled at even in schooldays – 'a **lioness**, with udders all drawn dry' (IV, iii, 115) – and still cannot take wholly seriously in Arden, although it nearly ate Oliver de Boys, and would have done had it not been dispatched by his ill-dealt-with younger brother, Orlando.

There is, on the other hand, a kind of potency and earnestness in the Roman lion which was one of several strange portentous things seen by Cicero in the streets of Rome, a day or so before Caesar's assassination. Cicero himself describes it (*Julius Caesar*, I, iii, 19):

> Besides – I ha' not since put up my sword, –
> Against the Capitol I met a **lion**,
> Who glared upon me, and went surly by,
> Without annoying me: . . .

For the rest we can but instance six out of many leonine images:

From *King Henry V* (IV, iii, 93) the king's own cryptic but arresting:

The man that once did sell the **lion's** skin
While the beast lived, was kill'd with hunting him.

From *Measure for Measure* (I, iii, 21) the Duke's mention to
Friar Thomas of one of Vienna's unenforced laws:

Which for this fourteen years we have let slip;
Even like an o'ergrown **lion** in a cave,
That goes not out to prey.

From Patroclus to Achilles in *Troilus and Cressida* with one
marvellous image (III, iii, 222):

Sweet, rouse yourself; and the weak wanton Cupid
Shall from your neck unloose his amorous fold,
And, like a dew-drop from the **lion's** mane,
Be shook to air.

From Aaron the Moor in *Titus Andronicus* (IV, ii, 136), proclaiming his own valour:

Why, so, brave lords! when we join in league,
I am a lamb: but if you brave the Moor,
The chafed boar, the mountain **lioness**,
The ocean swells not so as Aaron storms.

From Bottom the Weaver in *A Midsummer Night's Dream*
(III, i, 31):

For there is not a more fearful wild-fowl than your **lion** living.

From *Antony and Cleopatra* where another Messenger is
whipped and Enobarbus has an aside or two (III, xiii, 89):

ANTONY: Approach, there! Ah, you kite! Now, gods and devils!
Authority melts from me: of late, when I cried 'Ho!'
Like boys unto a muss [= scramble *or* scrum], kings would start
forth,
And cry 'Your will?' Have you no ears? I am
Antony yet. Take hence this Jack and whip him.

ENOBARBUS (*aside*): 'Tis better playing with a **lion's** whelp
Than with an old one dying.
ANTONY: Moon and stars!
Whip him.

MACKEREL AND DOGFISH

The sole reference to Mackerel requires much annotation. It is
in *King Henry IV, Part One* (II, iv, 366) in one of Falstaff's
meaty colloquies with Prince Hal:

Well, he [Douglas] is there too, and one Mordake, and a thousand
blue-caps more [blue bonnets ower the Border!]: Worcester is stolen
away to-night: thy father's beard is turn'd white with the news:
you may buy land now as cheap as stinking **mackerel**.

This could be, quite conceivably, the origin of our unidenti-
fiable proverb to the effect that 'no man cries stinking fish'.
    The sole reference to Dogfish turns out, after severe annota-
tion, to be not fishy at all but a mere term of contempt. It is
used by Talbot against the French troops led by Joan La
Pucelle in *King Henry VI, Part One* (I, iv, 107):

Pucelle or puzzel, dolphin or **dogfish**,
Your hearts I'll stamp out with my horse's heels,
And make a quagmire of your mingled brains.

M.R.Ridley's note (New Temple) is perfectly adequate:
'*Puzzel* means a drab, *dolphin* is the normal Elizabethan
spelling of Dauphin, and *dog-fish* was used as a common term
of abuse.' Henry Hudson (Windsor) goes much further back
and quotes ancient books to the effect that *puzzels*, 'especially
our puzzels of Paris,' were 'filthy queans' who 'carried nosegays' and needed them.

MANDRAKE AND SALAMANDER

We arrive at two of the most mysterious of the Devil's creatures or creations (for assuredly they cannot be God's). They are the Mandrake and the Salamander.

Mandrakes were said to be aphrodisiacal and were thence called love-apples. The Emperor Julian tells Callixenes in his epistles that he drank the mandrake's juice as a nightly love-potion. Mandragora one supposes to be, or to have been, the essence of mandrake. The *Oxford Dictionary* begins its definition with the slightly alarming word '*Hist.*' This turns out to be merely an abbreviation for 'in historical use'. But does this mean that the mandrake is extinct nowadays?

Another valuable reference – the Centenary Edition of Brewer's *Dictionary of Phrase and Fable* – assures us that a small dose of mandragora was held to produce vanity in one's appearance, and a large dose idiocy. One would like to know what happens after a medium dose, and how *any* kind of dose is measured. Is it true that human figures used to be cut out of a mandrake root? Or that the mandrake used to scream when it was uprooted?

Shakespeare, who is often – and often deservedly – declared to tell us about everything, does at least repeat some of these legends in most pungent form. In *King Henry IV, Part Two* (III, ii, 324) we are told by Falstaff that Justice Shallow when at Clement's Inn was 'the very genius of famine; yet lecherous as a monkey, and the whores call'd him **mandrake**'. In the same play Falstaff addresses his own Page as 'thou whoreson **mandrake**' (I, ii, 15). In *King Henry VI, Part Two* (III, ii, 310) the Duke of Suffolk, a character who can be a cataract of execration, remarks:

> Would curses kill, as doth the **mandrake's** groan,
> I would invent as bitter-searching terms,

As curst, as harsh, and horrible to hear,
Deliver'd strongly through my fixèd teeth,
With full as many signs of deadly hate,
As lean-fac'd Envy in her loathsome cave: ...

And Juliet (*Romeo and Juliet*, IV, iii, 47) is fearful of the effects her drug may have:

So early waking, what with loathsome smells;
And shrieks like **mandrakes'** torn out of the earth,
That living mortals, hearing them, run mad; ...

The drug mandragora has two distinct references in lines still more striking. Cleopatra asks her tactful maid Charmian for the drug, so that she may sleep through Antony's absence (*Antony and Cleopatra*, I, v, 4):

CLEOPATRA: Give me to drink **mandragora**.
CHARMIAN: Why, madam?
CLEOPATRA: That I might sleep out this great gap of time
  My Antony is away.
CHARMIAN: You think of him too much.
CLEOPATRA: O, 'tis treason!
CHARMIAN: Madam, I trust, not so.

Cleopatra does not question the drug's potency as an opiate.

But Iago does. He has been telling us how he has been busily inflaming Othello's jealousy, when the latter enters, burning like 'the mines of sulphur' and looking red-black with rage (*Othello*, III, iii, 330):

Look, where he comes! Not poppy, nor **mandragora**,
Nor all the drowsy syrups of the world,
Shall ever medicine thee to that sweet sleep
Which thou owedst yesterday.

The Salamander is a sinister creature also. It *was* a lizard-like animal and mythological, supposed to be able to live in fire.

It *is* a lizard-like animal of the *Urodela* (newts, etc.). It has the tertiary sense of being a spirit supposed to live in fire, and only in fire. Dr Brewer tells us that Francis I of France adopted as his badge the salamander, a lizard in the midst of flames, with the legend, *Nutrisco et extinguo*. This he translates for us very roughly as 'Fire purifies good metal, but consumes rubbish.' It logically follows that the salamander is, or was, good metal, and cannot, or could not, have been rubbish.

Shakespeare takes it very much less seriously than he does the Mandrake. He has but one allusion to the Salamander: he is reminded of it by the flaming red of Bardolph's nose, whose owner is called the Knight of the Lamp, for his 'face is all bubukles, and whelks, and knobs, and flames o' fire' (*King Henry V*, III, vi, 106). But in *King Henry IV, Part One* (III, iii, 31) Falstaff declares to the owner of this same flaming organ, 'I never see thy face but I think upon hell fire . . . thou wert indeed, but for the light in thy face, the son of utter darkness. . . . I have maintain'd that **salamander** of yours with fire any time this two-and-thirty years.'

MERMAIDS AND NEPTUNE

King Henry IV is no actor's favourite part. Falstaff and Hotspur, Prince Hal and his adorably human hangers-on steal from him both the great plays to which he gives his name. But the King has his depth as well as his dignity (and one well remembers a Stratford-on-Avon season when that valuable actor, Harry Andrews, fulfilled him to perfection, and made him nowhere dull in spite of the character's humourlessness). He has difficult but rewarding things to say like this (*Part Two*, III, i, 45):

> O God! that one might read the book of fate,
> And see the revolution of the times

Make mountains level, and the continent,
Weary of solid firmness, melt itself
Into the sea! and, other times, to see
The beachy girdle of the ocean
Too wide for **Neptune's** hips; how chances mock,
And changes fill the cup of alteration
With divers liquors! O, if this were seen,
The happiest youth, viewing his progress through,
What perils past, what crosses to ensue,
Would shut the book, and sit him down and die.

In his famous description of the royal barge, Enobarbus (Ralph Richardson was ever the actor for this superb part) has his reference to the Nereides, who were Neptune's sea-goddesses, and at least fifty in number (*Antony and Cleopatra*, II, ii, 210). We have just been hearing how Antony was being fanned by 'pretty dimpled boys, like smiling Cupids', and Agrippa interrupts with his usual witty and brief comment:

AGRIPPA: O, rare for Antony!
ENOBARBUS: Her gentlewomen, like the Nereides,
  So many **mermaids**, tended her i' the eyes,
  And made their bends adornings: at the helm
  A seeming **mermaid** steers: the silken tackle
  Swell with the touches of those flower-soft hands,
  That yarely frame the office. From the barge
  A strange invisible perfume hits the sense
  Of the adjacent wharfs. . . .

The effect is some great canvas that Tiepolo was never to paint.

Editor Ridley (of the New Temple edition) rightly makes light of the many difficulties raised here, and in his explanation does homage to two great scholars of past time: 'There seems no sort of reason for going beyond the straightforward meaning, accepted by the straightforward Steevens and Warburton, namely, that the gentlewomen as they moved gracefully (one might say even sinuously, as befitting mermaids) made a lovely frame for the lovelier picture.'

Elsewhere Neptune is simply synonymous with the sea, though often very strikingly as in *King Richard II* where John of Gaunt has these among his splendid last words (II, i, 61):

> England, bound in with the triumphant sea,
> Whose rocky shore beats back the envious siege
> Of watery **Neptune**, is now bound in with shame, . . .

Mermaids disport themselves in many other plays and places, and lure sailors to their doom. With gloating relish does Gloster promise to do this latter in *King Henry VI, Part Three* (III, ii, 186), 'I'll drown more sailors than the **mermaid** shall; . . .' The whole soliloquy was transferred into the opening of the film of *Richard III*, and Olivier made it one of the best things in one of the best of all his performances.

MINOTAUR AND TITAN

The Minotaur was a monstrous creature with the head of a bull and the body of a man, who expected and received human sacrifices, apparently quite indifferent whether male or female, so long as they were plentiful. Titan was the god of the Sun – alternatively supposed to be twelve giants in all, six male and six female.

Shakespeare tells us very little more about either the Minotaur or Titan (or the Titans). To the former he has only a fleeting allusion in *King Henry VI, Part One* (v, iii, 187) where Suffolk says to himself about Queen Margaret who has just left his company:

> . . . Suffolk, stay;
> Thou mayst not wander in that labyrinth;

There **Minotaurs** and ugly treasons lurk.
Solicit Henry with her wondrous praise: ...

Titan he tends to use merely as synonymous with Sun.
Thus Friar Laurence in *Romeo and Juliet* (ii, ii, 1) begins his
lovely speech in his cell:

The gray-eyed morn smiles on the frowning night,
Chequering the eastern clouds with streaks of light;
And flecked darkness like a drunkard reels
From forth day's path and **Titan's** fiery wheels: ...

It would be interesting to find out whether the Elizabethan
poet, William Drummond of Hawthornden, borrowed an
idea from this when he wrote his *Summons to Love*, which has
the lines:

The winds all silent are,
And Phoebus in his chair
Ensaffroning sea and air
Makes vanish every star:
Night like a drunkard reels
Beyond the hills, to shun his flaming wheels.

MONSTERS IN GENERAL

Caliban is called 'monster' by the other characters repeatedly.
Trinculo, first discovering him on the shore, has this (*The
Tempest*, ii, ii, 25):

What have we here? a man or a fish? dead or alive? A fish: he
smells like a fish; a very ancient and fish-like smell; ... A strange
fish! Were I in England now, as once I was, and had but this fish
painted, not a holiday fool there but would give a piece of silver:
there would this **monster** make a man; any strange beast there makes
a man: when they will not give a doit to relieve a lame beggar, they
will lay out ten to see a dead Indian. Legg'd like a man! and his fins

like arms! Warm, o' my troth!... this is no fish, but an islander, that hath lately suffer'd by a thunderbolt....

Stephano, discovering Trinculo and Caliban sheltering under the same gaberdine (II, ii, 67), says, 'This is some **monster** of the isle with four legs, who hath got, as I take it, an ague.' And a few lines later, 'Four legs and two voices, a most delicate **monster**.' And he is called many other kinds of monster – shallow, weak, credulous, perfidious, drunken, puppy-headed, most scurvy, abominable, ridiculous, howling, brave, ignorant, lost, and even Monsieur Monster.

But in the end Caliban is more man than monster, however base, degraded and witch-born. And all the best Calibans on the stage – memorably that of the veteran Robert Atkins – have this quality of a creature aching to be human.

Elsewhere the word is mostly used in the absolute sense. To the pedants in *Love's Labour's Lost* it is Ignorance, to Coriolanus it is Rabble or Multitude, to Hamlet it is Custom, to Lear it is Ingratitude, to Iago it is Jealousy, 'the green-eyed **monster**'. Othello himself, nevertheless, has reference to actual physical monsters (*Othello*, I, iii, 143), and he names certain incredible creatures which came into Elizabethan cognition with the publication in 1595 of Sir Walter Raleigh's account of his travels:

> And of the Cannibals that each other eat,
> The Anthropophagi, and men whose heads
> Do grow beneath their shoulders.

MOUSE AND MOLE

Somewhere in the works of the past masters of English prose – either in Sir Thomas Browne or Robert Burton, as one remembers – there is this marvellous sentence, 'It is as a thing of naught in a great immensity, like unto a mouse in Africa.'

Shakespeare has nothing so tremendous about the mere Mouse. His similes emphasize its minuteness and its quietness. 'Have you had quiet guard?' asks Bernardo on the battlements at Elsinore; and Francisco answers, 'Not a **mouse** stirring' (*Hamlet*, I, i, 10). Falstaff says to the 'most forcible Feeble', one of his recruits, 'Thou wilt be as valiant as the wrathful dove or most magnanimous **mouse**' (*King Henry IV, Part Two*, III, ii, 164). And Lion, explaining that he is really no Lion but only Snug the Joiner, does so to the ladies in his audience (*M.N.D.*, v, i, 212), 'You, ladies, you whose gentle hearts do fear/The smallest monstrous **mouse** that creeps on floor.'

The Mole (*Talpa europaea*) is a burrowing mammal and just as 'sleekit, cowrin', timorous' as Burns called the mouse. Caliban, approaching Prospero's cell with his two new man-gods, Trinculo and Stephano, says to them (*The Tempest*, IV, i, 194):

> Pray you, tread softly, that the blind **mole** may not
> Hear a foot fall: we now are near his cell.

Hamlet says to his father's Ghost (*Hamlet*, I, v, 162), 'Well said, old **mole**! canst work i' th' earth so fast?' And Hotspur in *King Henry IV, Part One*, says how the moldwarp or mole is just one of the boring subjects discussed by Owen Glendower (III, i, 146):

> I cannot choose: sometime he angers me
> With telling me of the **moldwarp** and the ant, ...

This common little animal, which millions of people have never set eyes on and would not recognize if they did, is still called 'mowdiewarp' in many English dialects and 'mowdie' in some Scottish ones.

NEWT AND LIZARD

These are two further contributors to the beastly olla podrida or stew of the Weird Sisters in *Macbeth* (IV, i, 14, 17) – 'eye of **newt,** and toe of frog, . . . **lizard's** leg and howlet's wing'.

'The gilded **newt**', too, is among the odd things that Timon discovers when he is digging for gold (*Timon of Athens*, IV, iii, 182). And Queen Margaret in *King Henry VI, Part Three* (II, ii, 136) tells Richard Plantagenet that he is nothing better than

> . . . a foul mis-shapen stigmatic,
> Mark'd by the Destinies to be avoided,
> As venom toads, or **lizards'** dreadful stings.

NIGHTINGALE AND PHILOMEL

The most succinct and dispassionate account of the mysterious *Titus Andronicus* is probably that of John Masefield in his book called simply *William Shakespeare* (1954):

Written (?)   *Published* (?)   *Source of the Plot* (?)

The Fable. Tamora, Queen of the Goths, whose first-born son is sacrificed by Titus Andronicus, determines to be revenged. She succeeds in her determination. Titus and his daughter Lavinia are mutilated. Two of the Andronici, his sons, are beheaded.

Titus determines to be revenged. He bakes the heads of two of Tamora's sons in a pasty, and serves them up for her to eat. He then stabs her, after stabbing his daughter. He is himself stabbed on the instant; but his surviving son stabs his murderer. Tamora's paramour (the black Aaron) is then sentenced to be buried alive, and the survivors (about half the original cast) move off (as they say) 'to order well the State'.

This is worth close comparison with the Greek mythological

legend of Philomela who was metamorphosed into the Nightingale. The abbreviated account is that of John Lempriere:

Philomela was sister to Procne who had married Tereus, King of Thrace. Procne, ever devoted to her sister, persuaded Tereus to go to Athens and bring back Philomela. On the journey Tereus became enamoured of his sister-in-law. He offered violence to her [*i.e.* violated her], and then cut off her tongue that she might not be able to report his barbarity. He confined her also in a lonely castle. Returning to Thrace he told Procne that her sister had died on the way and that he had paid the last offices to her remains. A year had nearly passed when Procne received secret information that her sister still lived. During her captivity Philomela had described her misfortunes on a piece of tapestry she had woven and had privately conveyed to Procne. The latter hastened to deliver her, and concerted with her on the best way to punish Tereus for his brutality and perfidy. She murdered her son Itylus, who was in the sixth year of his age, and served him up as food to her husband. Tereus, in the midst of his repast, called for Itylus. Whereupon Procne told him the nature of his banquet, and threw her son's decapitated head on the table to prove it. Tereus was about to slay both sisters with his sword when he was transformed by the gods into a hoopoe, Philomela into a nightingale, and Procne into a swallow.

The circumstances and the details are very different. But yet the two legends have rape and mutilation on one side of the ghastly story and unconscious cannibalism on the other. The mutilation of Lavinia is even more severe than that of Philomela since she is deprived not only of her virginity and her tongue but also of both her hands at the wrist. (All who saw the great Peter Brook production of this strange masterpiece of cruelty must remember the piteousness of Vivien Leigh as Lavinia spelling out the legend of her woes with a staff held between her handless arms. This had something of the piercing melancholy of the song of the nightingale.) Shakespeare could easily have read Philomela's story in

Ovid or Seneca (two poets he mentions in his plays more than once). But it has been left to today's scholarship to point out that the plot of *Titus Andronicus* derives directly and almost certainly from the *Thyestes* of Seneca. Professor Peter Alexander declares this in his *Shakespeare* (1964) and gives great credit to Professor Terence Spencer of the Shakespeare Institute at Edgbaston.

The play is very early, and seems to have been composed not long after the poems. It is therefore not surprising to find references to the legend of Philomela, notably in *The Rape of Lucrece* (lines 1128-1129) where Lucrece herself says to the nightingale:

> Come, **Philomel**, that sing'st of ravishment,
> Make thy sad grove in my dishevell'd hair: ...

For the rest Romeo and Juliet have their love-intoxicated argument as to whether the bird that seems to comment on them be the lark or the nightingale. And the latter word or bird is a pet-name for Cleopatra used by Antony at the arrogant height of their mutual rapture (*Antony and Cleopatra*, IV, viii, 20):

> ... My **nightingale**,
> We have beat them to their beds. What, girl! though gray
> Do something mingle with our younger brown, yet ha' we
> A brain that nourishes our nerves, and can
> Get goal for goal of youth.

OSPREY AND OSTRICH

There is a single traceable reference to the Osprey (*Pandion haliaetus*), and but one also to the Ostrich (*Struthio camelus*).

The first is in high praise of Coriolanus, spoken by Aufidius, general of the Volscians, to his Lieutenant (*Coriolanus*, IV, vii, 33):

> I think he'll be to Rome
> As is the **osprey** to the fish, who takes it
> By sovereignty of nature.

The second is in a threat made by the rebel Jack Cade to a Kentish gentleman, Alexander Iden, who means him no harm (*King Henry VI, Part Two*, IV, x, 27): 'Ah, villain, thou wilt betray me, and get a thousand crowns of the king by carrying my head to him! but I'll make thee eat iron like an **ostrich**, and swallow my sword like a great pin, ere thou and I part.'

OTTER, WEASEL, FERRET

'What beast! why, an **otter**. – An **otter**, Sir John! why an **otter**? – Why, she's neither fish nor flesh; a man knows not where to have her.' Falstaff and Prince Hal are discussing Mistress Quickly to her face (*King Henry IV, Part One*, III, iii, 130).

In the same play Lady Percy says to her hot-headed husband, Hotspur (II, iii, 79):

> Out, you mad-headed ape!
> A **weasel** hath not such a deal of spleen
> As you are tost with.

In *King Henry V* (I, ii, 169) Westmoreland utters a calumny on Scotland's fighting habits (especially against the English):

> For once the eagle England being in prey,
> To her unguarded nest the **weasel** Scot
> Comes sneaking, and so sucks her princely eggs;
> Playing the mouse in absence of the cat,
> To spoil and havoc more than she can eat.

In *Cymbeline* (III, iv, 160) Pisanio tells Imogen that if she is successfully to masquerade as a boy she must be

> Ready in gibes, quick-answer'd, saucy, and
> As quarrelous as the **weasel**; ...

And Jaques in *As You Like It* (II, v, 11) between the two stanzas of a song of the greenwood tree, sung by Amiens, declares, 'I can suck melancholy out of a song, as a **weasel** sucks eggs.'

And the Ferret is used, only adjectivally, in *Julius Caesar* (I, ii, 182) in a marvellously vivid allusion to Cicero during a colloquy between Brutus and Cassius:

> ... look you, Cassius,
> The angry spot doth glow on Caesar's brow,
> And all the rest look like a chidden train:
> Calpurnia's cheek is pale; and Cicero
> Looks with such **ferret** and such fiery eyes
> As we have seen him in the Capitol,
> Being crost in conference by some senator.

OWL

Though there are owls of great variety of size and colour in Britain alone, Shakespeare mentions only the (Common or Barn) Owl and the Screech Owl.

The mad Ophelia (*Hamlet*, IV, v, 41) closely follows up the maddest of all her sentences with one full of the most reasonable philosophy: 'They say the **owl** was a baker's daughter. Lord, we know what we are, but know not what we may be.'

But it is the bird's association with death and the supernatural which seems most to haunt the poet. Lady Macbeth, even while waiting for her husband to enter and say he has done the deed, hears the cry of an owl (*Macbeth*, II, ii, 2):

> Hark! Peace!
> It was the **owl** that shriekt, the fatal bellman,
> Which gives the stern'st good-night.

The 'fatal bellman', usually passed over or loosely explained as 'night watchman', is much more satisfyingly noted in the New Penguin edition: 'The owl, as the bird of death, is compared to the bellman sent to give "stern'st good-night" to condemned prisoners the night before their execution.' King Duncan is the condemned prisoner.

Before Bordeaux the French General directly addresses the English Lord Talbot in *King Henry VI, Part One* (iv, ii, 15):

> Thou ominous and fearful **owl** of death,
> Our nation's terror, and their bloody scourge! ...

Queen Tamora thus describes the evil-stricken wood where her worst longings are glutted (*Titus Andronicus*, ii, iii, 96):

> Here never shines the sun; here nothing breeds,
> Unless the nightly **owl** or fatal raven: ...

And even Queen Titania (*A Midsummer Night's Dream*, ii, ii, 5) orders some elves to keep the disturbing owl well away from her lullaby:

> ... some, keep back
> The clamorous **owl**, that nightly hoots and wonders
> At our quaint spirits. Sing me now asleep.

The word 'clamorous' almost suggests the lingering and faltering last notes of the night bird that seems loth to end her sinister howl.

For the Screech Owl one need go no further than *King Henry VI, Part Two*, where the witch, Margery Jourdain, prepares to conjure up spirits before Bolingbroke who remarks in anticipation (i, iv, 17):

Deep night, dark night, the silent of the night,
The time of night when Troy was set on fire;
The time when **screech-owls** cry, and ban-dogs howl,
And spirits walk, and ghosts break up their graves, ...

And later, within the same play (III, ii, 327), Suffolk adds to a long list of horrors and menaces the culminating line, 'And boding **screech-owls** make the consort full!'

OYSTER

Some few allusions to the Oyster are fleeting, and are anyhow dwarfed and minimized by the superb interchange between Cleopatra and her male attendant, Alexas, who has brought news of Antony and a gift from him (*Antony and Cleopatra*, I, v, 34):

ALEXAS: Sovereign of Egypt, hail!
CLEOPATRA: How much unlike art thou Mark Antony!
  Yet, coming from him, that great medicine hath
  With his tinct gilded thee.
  How goes it with my brave Mark Antony?
ALEXAS: Last thing he did, dear queen,
  He kist – the last of many doubled kisses –
  This orient pearl: his speech sticks in my heart.
CLEOPATRA: Mine ear must pluck it thence.
ALEXAS: 'Good friend,' quoth he,
  'Say, the firm Roman to great Egypt sends
  This treasure of an **oyster**; at whose foot,
  To mend the petty present, I will piece
  Her opulent throne with kingdoms; all the east,
  Say thou, shall call her mistress.' So he nodded,
  And soberly did mount an arm-gaunt [arm-girt? arrogant?]
    steed,
  Who neigh'd so high, that what I would have spoke
  Was beastly dumb'd by him.

PADDOCK AND PUTTOCK

See under FROGS AND TOADS, also under HEDGEHOG.

Hamlet imperiously tells the Queen that his madness is but feigned, and that she must tell her husband so (*Hamlet*, III, iv, 190):

> ... 'twere good you let him know;
> For who, that's but a queen, fair, sober, wise,
> Would from a **paddock**, from a bat, a gib [= cat],
> Such dear concernings hide!

King Cymbeline asks his daughter Imogen why she chose Posthumus for a husband and not his own grotesque stepson, Cloten, and gets the answer (*Cymbeline*, I, i, 139): 'I chose an eagle, and did avoid a **puttock**.' And the sour, bitter, and voluble Thersites in *Troilus and Cressida* tells us how he would willingly be any kind of beast rather than be the cuckold Menelaus (v, i, 59): 'To be a dog, a mule, a cat, a fitchew, a toad, a lizard, an owl, a **puttock**, or a herring without a roe, I would not care; but to be Menelaus! I would conspire against destiny ...'

PARROT AND PEACOCK

Neither the Parrot (*Psittacus*) nor the Peacock (*Pavo*) can inspire Shakespeare to his most felicitous style of writing. Of the former, Alexander Pope wrote: 'A very little wit is valued in a woman, as we are pleased with a few words spoken plain by a parrot.' Of the latter, William Cowper has the phrase: 'The self-applauding bird, the peacock.' Shakespeare has nothing so happy about either bird.

Mimicry, which is the parrot's special gift, combined with

the ability to imitate human speech, gets hardly a mention from Shakespeare. He comes closest to it when, in *The Merchant of Venice* (III, v, 43), young Lorenzo, the most patient of blades, grows a trifle impatient with that particularly foolish Fool, Launcelot Gobbo, and says: 'How every fool can play upon the word! I think the best grace of wit will shortly turn into silence, and discourse grow commendable in none only but **parrots**.'

Ostentation, which is the peacock's special trait, has one especial mention in *Troilus and Cressida* (III, iii, 250) where the sneering Thersites has a scalding speech on the strutting Ajax, who is preparing for a combat with Hector. It begins: 'Why, he stalks up and down like a **peacock**, – a stride and a stand: ...' One likes to think that this may have suggested a title to Sean O'Casey for his play about the Dublin housewife, Juno Boyle, and her vainglorious husband. Whatever the source of *Juno and the Paycock*, his early play was an inspiration like its title.

Twenty-two words of verse, almost the obscurest in the whole of *Hamlet* (III, ii, 302) conclude with the very odd word 'pajock'. Presumably this is a variant of the word 'peacock'. Presumably the stanza itself, apparently improvised by Hamlet in the excitement following the Play Scene, has an inner significance:

> For thou dost know, O Damon dear,
> This realm dismantled was
> Of Jove himself; and now reigns here
> A very, very – **pajock**.

Presumably Horatio – with his comment, 'You might have rhymed' – is being a very elementary literary critic. Presumably Hamlet's stanza is but composed of wild and whirling words – with 'pajock' the wildest of them. Presumably Editor Hudson is being something better than naïve when he comments:

216

'Editors have been greatly in the dark as to the reason of the word's being used here.'

PARTRIDGE, PHEASANT, WOODCOCK

Of these three game birds, the Partridge (*Perdix cinerca*) seems to be mentioned only once, the Pheasant (*Phasianus colchicus*) also once only, and the Woodcock (*Scolopax rusticula*) nine or ten times in all.

The Partridge is already killed, and cooked, but not eaten. For it appears momentarily and allusively in a speech of raillery from Beatrice to Benedick in *Much Ado About Nothing*, when each is pretending not to recognize the other at the masked ball (II, i, 140). She says of Benedick: 'He'll but break a comparison or two on me; which, peradventure, not mark'd, or not laugh'd at, strikes him into melancholy; and then there's a **partridge** wing saved, for the fool will eat no supper that night.'

The Pheasant is also ready for eating. It comes a shade surprisingly into a conversation in *The Winter's Tale* (IV, iv, 746):

AUTOLYCUS: I am courtier cap-a-pe; and one that will either push on or pluck back thy business there: whereupon I command thee to open thy affair.

SHEPHERD: My business, sir, is to the king.

AUTOLYCUS: What advocate hast thou to him?

SHEPHERD: I know not, an't like you.

CLOWN: Advocate's the court-word for a **pheasant**: say you have none.

SHEPHERD: None, sir; I have no **pheasant**, cock nor hen.

A brace of pheasants continues to this day to be a court-word for advocate in some country circles.

'Now is the **woodcock** near the gin,' says Fabian when

Malvolio is about to pick up the letter supposed to have been written by Olivia in *Twelfth Night* (II, v, 85). 'Springes to catch **woodcocks**,' says Polonius to Ophelia about Hamlet's trickery (*Hamlet*, I, iii, 115). 'As a **woodcock** to mine own springe, Osric; I am justly kill'd with mine own treachery,' says Hamlet himself (v, ii, 305). But these are all mere figures of speech. And we welcome Dumaine in *Love's Labour's Lost* (IV, iii, 80) with his 'Four **woodcocks** in a dish', until we look into the matter and discover that that too is a figure of speech and that the four 'woodcocks' are the comedy's four heroines.

PELICAN AND GULL

The Pelican is a favourite subject for jocose limericks, being an easy word to rhyme with impunity and mild daring. But the same bird is also a symbol in Christian art, and an emblem of Christ giving his blood for others. Hence some lines by John Skelton, who comes half-way in time between Chaucer and Shakespeare, which are more poignant by far than anything thing on the same subject by the latter king of poets:

> Then sayd the pellycane,
> When my byrdis be slayne
> With my bloude I them reuyue [= revive],
> Scripture doth record
> The same dyd Our Lord,
> And rose from death to lyue.

All this mysticism arose from the same bird's practice of transferring macerated food to its young from the large bag or pouch under its bill. One has seen certain varieties of domestic pigeon – notably the pouters – feeding their young in this way from their inflated crops. But they have not been sanctified for it, as has the Pelican.

This must explain why King Lear says, '' Twas this flesh begot Those **pelican** daughters' (*King Lear*, III, iv, 75). It also goes some way towards explaining why Laertes proposes to Claudius to 'ope his arms' to the friends of the dead Polonius (*Hamlet*, IV, v, 145):

> And, like the kind life-rendering **pelican**,
> Repast them with my blood.

though Laertes usually gets cut here by the director for saying anything so odd. So, usually, does the dying John of Gaunt for saying to Richard II (*King Richard II*, II, i, 126):

> That blood already, like the **pelican**,
> Hast thou tapt out, and drunkenly caroused: ...

The word Gull in Shakespeare is used, usually, in the sense of a knave or a fool. But the web-footed bird of the same name (*Larus canus*) is obviously meant by the Earl of Worcester in his elaborate speech to King Henry (*King Henry IV*, *Part One*, V, i, 59) which goes on and on like this:

> And, being fed by us, you used us so
> As that ungentle **gull**, the cuckoo's bird,
> Useth the sparrow, did oppress our nest;
> Grew by our feeding to so great a bulk,
> That even our love durst not come near your sight ...

We may be tempted here to interrupt with a line of Pope, 'And ten low words oft creep in one dull line'!

And there is a similar sort of mixed-up ornithology in *Timon of Athens* (II, i, 27) at the point where a Senator is telling Caphis, a creditor's servant, how to proffer his master's bill:

> Get you gone:
> Put on a most importunate aspect,
> A visage of demand; for, I do fear,
> When every feather sticks in his own wing,

Lord Timon will be left a naked **gull**,
Which flashes now a phœnix. Get you gone.

The remainder of the little scene is not perhaps Shakespeare at his very best:

CAPHIS: I go, sir.
SENATOR: Take the bonds along with you,
  And have the dates incompt.
CAPHIS: I will, sir.
SENATOR: Go.   [*Exeunt*

PHŒNIX

The obscurest and wildest of wildfowl is the Phœnix, almost wholly mythical but Egyptian in origin. It is said to appear in Egypt every 500 years, though the intervals greatly vary in different accounts. It is said also to set itself on fire but to be re-born in the flames. But even this characteristic has various differing versions. It is said to have resembled the plover, but it is also said to have resembled that **very different bird**, the eagle.

The Phœnix is one of the two avian characters in Shakespeare's most unintelligible poem, the other being the Turtle Dove. Everyone who owns a one-volume Shakespeare has read this poem, *The Phœnix and the Turtle* – at least once but probably never again. It is gnomic and mystical – two words by which scholars usually mean unintelligible. One looks in vain for any explanation or interpretation of this poem in the great Shakespearean scholars of the past. Hazlitt eschews it and Coleridge dodges it. So one consults two of the best Shakespearean scholars who are still with us – Ivor Brown and George Rylands. The former in his great book, *Shakespeare*, refers to it, only in an aside, as 'the mysterious, metaphysical, and supposedly Shakespearean poem, *The Phœnix and the Turtle*'. The latter, after praising 'the manifestations of the passions of love' in all its forms throughout Shakespeare, adds this (in his splendid essay, *Shakespeare the Poet*): 'But in *The Phœnix and the Turtle* Shakespeare celebrates love of yet another kind, selfless, sexless, "interinanimating", as Donne puts it – not the marriage of two minds but the union of two souls:

> So they loved, as love in twain
> Had the essence but in one;
> Two distincts, division none:
> Number there in love was slain.

Shakespeare's own adventure in the metaphysical style [Mr Rylands goes on] combines at once the quality of a proposition in Euclid and of a piece of music. It is pure, abstract, symbolical and complete.' But it is also unintelligible! (One surmises, to be strictly fair, that '*own* adventure' is a misprint for '*one* adventure'.)

The Phœnix is a mysterious apparition at its every mention in the plays. When in *The Tempest* the invisible Prospero conjures up a banquet for his shipwrecked visitors (III, iii, 20) we have this interchange:

ALONSO: Give us kind keepers, heavens! – What were these?
SEBASTIAN: A living drollery. Now I will believe
  That there are unicorns; that in Arabia
  There is one tree, the **phœnix'** throne; one **phœnix**
  At this hour reigning there.

And when at the end of *King Henry VIII* the Archbishop of Canterbury utters lengthy blessings upon the babe who is to grow up into the great Queen Elizabeth, he has this passage (v, iv, 36):

WSAM–H

221

God shall be truly known; and those about her
From her shall read the perfect ways of honour,
And by those claim their greatness, not by blood.
Nor shall this peace sleep with her: but as when
The bird of wonder dies, the maiden **phœnix**,
Her ashes new create another heir,
As great in admiration as herself; ...

For another reference see the quotation from *Timon of Athens* under PELICAN AND GULL.

The Phœnix is also the name of a hotel in Ephesus in *The Comedy of Errors*; and of a ship mentioned in *Twelfth Night* (v, i, 59).

PIGS, HOGS AND SWINE

'Where hast thou been, sister?' asks one Witch of another in *Macbeth* (I, iii, 2), and gets the horrid answer: 'Killing **swine**.'

It is the most sinister of several references to the beast (under this collective name), just as Cordelia's is the most tender (*King Lear*, IV, vii, 38):

> ... and wast thou fain, poor father,
> To hovel thee with **swine**, and rogues forlorn,
> In short and musty straw? Alack, alack!

The hog, well qualified, is one of the terms of abuse to which Queen Margaret can lend her rasping tongue when face to face with Gloster in *King Richard III* (I, iii, 229): 'Thou elvish-markt, abortive, rooting **hog**!'

The hog is only one of the guises which Puck proposes to assume in order to chase and tease the Athenian workmen (*A Midsummer Night's Dream*, III, i, 106):

Sometime a horse I'll be, sometime a hound,
  A **hog**, a headless bear, sometime a fire,
And neigh, and bark, and grunt, and roar, and burn,
  Like horse, hound, **hog**, bear, fire, at every turn.

Shylock, in his own way illustrating the theory that there is
no accounting for tastes, remarks (*The Merchant of Venice*, IV,
i, 47): 'Some men there are love not a gaping **pig**.' Fluellen,
being Welsh, pronounces the word 'big' as 'pig' and gets
himself into a pretty tangle from which he is extricated by
Gower who, being English, corrects him. This exchange is in
King Henry V (IV, vii, 13):

FLUELLEN: ... What call you the town's name where Alexander
the Pig was porn?
GOWER: Alexander the Great.
FLUELLEN: Why, I pray you, is not pig great? the pig, or the great,
or the mighty, or the huge, or the magnanimous, are all one
reckonings, save the phrase is a little variations.
GOWER: I think Alexander the Great was born in Macedon: ...

Good playing can make this funny. But strongly unfunny is
the scene in *Titus Andronicus* (IV, ii, 146) where Aaron the
Moor stabs his black baby's Nurse with the mocking comment: 'Weke, weke! So cries a **pig** prepared to th' spit.'

PORPENTINE

Such is the now obsolete spelling of the Porcupine ('a rodent
quadruped of the genus *Hystrix*') which bristles through
several of the plays.

Thus the Ghost tells Hamlet (I, v, 18) that a full account of
his harrowing story would have the effect of making

       Thy knotted and combined locks to part,
       And each particular hair to stand an end,
       Like quills upon the fretful **porpentine**: ...

The Duke of York in *King Henry VI, Part Two* (III, i, 360) tells us something of the earlier history of Jack Cade, the rebel:

> In Ireland have I seen this stubborn Cade
> Oppose himself against a troop of kerns,
> And fought so long, till that his thighs with darts
> Were almost like a sharp-quill'd **porpentine**.

Finally the word is used as a mere term of abuse by Ajax to Thersites. This is in *Troilus and Cressida* (II, i, 24) – and it may be said here that the actor Stephen Murray made the bitterest Thersites in recollection:

AJAX: The proclamation!
THERSITES: Thou art proclaim'd a fool, I think.
AJAX: Do not, **porpentine**, do not: my fingers itch.
THERSITES: I would thou didst itch from head to foot, and I had the scratching of thee; I would make thee the loathsom'st scab in Greece.

The Porpentine was also the name of the inn at Ephesus used by various characters in *The Comedy of Errors*.

QUAIL

The Quail (*Coturnix communis*) is closely allied in family to the partridge and is similarly a much-appreciated game bird at table. That arch-gastronomer and master of English, M. André Simon, recommended it wrapped in vine-leaves which had already been soaked in cognac, and then roasted and served with a gravy made of skinned and de-seeded grapes and more cognac. Such trifles, washed down with the appropriate wine, kept that great man alive and well till he was much over ninety.

Shakespeare is not in the least concerned with the quail as provender for epicures. Thersites in *Troilus and Cressida* (v, i, 50), a master of bitter scorn and misanthropy, has what appears to be a good word for Agamemnon when he begins his tirade: 'Here's Agamemnon, an honest fellow enough, and one that loves **quails**: . . .' But he then proceeds in his more usual vein of virulent abuse.

The one other reference to quails is in *Antony and Cleopatra* (ii, iii, 33) where Antony, parting from his wife Octavia, and an Egyptian soothsayer, has a curious and revealing little soliloquy which reveals (1) that quails were sometimes used instead of cocks in cock-fighting sports and (2) that Antony was already wearying of the very idea of matrimony and longing for his Cleopatra:

> . . . Be it art or hap,
> He hath spoken true: the very dice obey him;
> And, in our sports, my better cunning faints
> Under his chance: if we draw lots, he speeds;
> His cocks do win the battle still of mine,
> When it is all to nought; and his **quails** ever
> Beat mine, inhoopt, at odds. I will to Egypt:
> And though I make this marriage for my peace,
> I' the East my pleasure lies.

Here, as in many another place, Shakespeare's verse is closely parallel to Plutarch's prose.

RABBITS AND CONIES

Cony is simply the old name for the Rabbit, and is still used in the Statutes and in Heraldry. But the frequent phrase 'cony-catcher' or 'cony-catching' simply means 'cheat' or 'cheating', 'deceive' or 'deceiver'. Thus Slender in *The Merry Wives of*

Windsor (I, i, 120) has no rabbits in mind when he says to Falstaff:

Marry, sir, I have matter in my head against you: and against your **cony-catching** rascals, Bardolph, Nym, and Pistol; they carried me to the tavern and made me drunk, and afterwards picked my pocket.

But Rosalind, in the guise of Ganymede, clearly has the rabbit in mind when she is thus accosted by Orlando in the Forest of Arden (*As You Like It*, III, ii, 339):

ORLANDO: Where dwell you, pretty youth? . . . Are you native of this place?
ROSALIND: As the **cony**, that you see dwell where she is kindled.

Rabbits under their own name bound or abound elsewhere, at least figuratively. The voluble page called Moth imagines his master Don Armado singing a love song (*Love's Labour's Lost*, III, i, 17) 'with your hat penthouse-like, o'er the shop of your eyes; with your arms crossed on your thin-belly doublet, like a **rabbit** on a spit; . . .'

Bardolph applies the word to the Page as a mere term of abuse in *King Henry IV, Part Two* (II, ii, 84): 'Away, you whoreson upright **rabbit**, away!'

In *The Taming of the Shrew* (IV, iv, 98) Biondello says to Lucentio: 'I knew a wench married in an afternoon as she went to the garden for parsley to stuff a **rabbit**; and so may you, sir: and so, adieu, sir.'

Rabbit is *Lepus cuniculus* and it is said to be able to breed seven times in a year.

RATS

Among major English poets only Robert Browning, in his celebrated *Pied Piper*, has successfully coped with Rats with that good humour and wit which alone can neutralize the nastiness of the subject.

Shakespeare knows all about the nastiness. Mad Tom in *King Lear* (III, iv, 136) says that he 'swallows the old **rat** and the ditch-dog', and tells us a line or two later that 'mice and **rats**, and such small deer, Have been Tom's food for seven long year'. But as usual the Witches in *Macbeth* beat all others in sheer horribleness. The First Witch will follow the sailor (whose wife has offended her) to Aleppo (I, iii, 9):

> And, like a **rat** without a tail,
> I'll do, I'll do, and I'll do.

But what will the fiend-like hag *do*? A deed without a name?

Nor is Claudio's observation to Lucio in *Measure for Measure* (I, ii, 126) exactly uplifting or jolly:

> Our natures do pursue,
> Like **rats** that ravin down their proper bane,
> A thirsty evil; and when we drink we die.

No, the Rat (*Mus decumanus*) is, so to speak, Robert Browning's pigeon. The poem was dedicated to William Charles Macready, eldest son of the great English actor of the same name. It was written in 1842 to amuse the little boy who was on a sick-bed. This dedicatee is directly addressed in the last four lines which contain the moral of the tale. The last couplet is said to rhyme abominably by children – and their parents – who have not the sense to emphasize the two words 'from' (as here). This done, they rhyme most engagingly:

> So, Willy, let me and you be wipers
> Of scores out with all men, especially pipers!
> And whether they pipe us *from* **rats** or *from* mice,
> If we've promised them aught, let us keep our promise!

RAVEN, ROOK, CHOUGH

The Raven (*Corvus corax*) is automatically enrolled among the birds of evil by Lady Macbeth on hearing that the King of Scotland is at hand (*Macbeth*, I, v, 39):

> The **raven** himself is hoarse
> That croaks the fatal entrance of Duncan
> Under my battlements.

For a blistering curse on both Prospero and Ariel (*The Tempest*, I, ii, 321) Caliban mentions his own mother, the foul witch Sycorax:

> As wicked dew as e'er my mother brush'd
> With **raven's** feather from unwholesome fen
> Drop on you both!

Thersites in *Troilus and Cressida*, himself a habitual croaker, exclaims (v, ii, 191): 'Would I could meet that rogue Diomed! I would croak like a **raven**; I would bode, I would bode.'

The Queen of the Goths in *Titus Andronicus* (II, iii, 96) says of her blighted and baleful forest:

> Here never shines the sun; here nothing breeds,
> Unless the nightly owl or fatal **raven**: . . .

Othello compares to the raven his memory of that handkerchief (IV, i, 20):

> O, it comes o'er my memory,
> As doth the **raven** o'er the infected house,
> Boding to all, . . .

and Hamlet harangues the villain in the middle of the Play Scene (III, ii, 270): 'Begin, murderer; pox, leave thy damnable faces, and begin. Come: the croaking **raven** doth bellow for revenge.'

These are but six of three times as many ravens that croak darkly throughout the plays. The Rook (*Corvus frugilegus*) is not nearly so much in evidence, though some odd variants of its name occur in some magic places. Thus in *King Henry VI, Part Three*, the King tells Gloster, in the long speech in the course of which the latter stabs him dead, that among the many weird happenings at Gloster's birth (v, vi, 47), 'The **raven rooked** her on the chimney's top.' And Macbeth – yet again Macbeth – has his infinitely sinister (III, ii, 49):

> Light thickens; and the crow
> Makes wing to th' **rooky** wood: ...

Of references to that other member of the crow family, the Chough, one is very seldom heard in the theatre, being in a longish speech by a minor character called First French Lord who must nevertheless seem to be speaking cogently about any international conference of this present or any other century (*All's Well That Ends Well*, IV, i, 16):

> ... therefore we must every one be a man of his own fancy, not to know what we speak one to another; so we seem to know, is to know straight our purpose; **choughs'** language, gabble enough, and good enough. As for you, interpreter, you must seem very politic.

The other reference to choughs, and to rooks likewise, is in Macbeth's searing speech to his Lady at the end of the Banquet Scene when their guests – together with Banquo's Ghost – have all departed (*Macbeth*, III, iv, 122). One clearly remembers the great Macbeth of Olivier here – seen only at Stratford-on-Avon – white with weariness, vibrant-voiced with guilt:

> It will have blood; they say blood will have blood:
> Stones have been known to move, and trees to speak;

Augurs, and understood relations have
By maggot-pies and **choughs** and **rooks** brought forth
The secret'st man of blood.

SALMON AND TROUT

Iago's remark to Desdemona (*Othello*, 11, i, 155) about women
in general:

> She that in wisdom never was so frail
> To change the cod's head for the **salmon's** tail.

is just one of the villain's subtleties, and all the scholars and
editors tend to be dumb about it. But it is a fact that 200 and
more years ago a baked cod's head in a gill of red wine was
esteemed a delicacy in Boston, Mass.

There are only two mentions of the trout and both are
figurative. When Maria in *Twelfth Night* throws down her
mistress's forged letter (11, v, 22) and says 'Here comes the
trout that must be caught with tickling' she is referring to
Malvolio coming down the garden-walk (and referring also,
incidentally, to a primitive form of trout-fishing practised by
paddling little boys to this day).

The mention in *Measure for Measure* (1, ii, 82) is incomparably
less innocent, Pompey being a pimp and Mistress Overdone a
bawd in Old Vienna:

MISTRESS OVERDONE: ... What's the news with you?
POMPEY: Yonder man is carried to prison.
MISTRESS O: Well: what has he done?
POMPEY: A woman.
MISTRESS O: But what's his offence?
POMPEY: Groping for **trouts** in a peculiar river.
MISTRESS O: What, is there a maid with child by him?
POMPEY: No, but there's a woman with maid by him.

Lastly, Fluellen's delicious Welsh comment (*King Henry V*, IV, vii, 32) that there is a river in Macedon and likewise in Monmouth, 'and there is **salmons** in both' must not be omitted.

SCORPIONS

These to Shakespeare were not examples of the arachnid of the genus Scorpio – lobster-like but a bright orange-scarlet in colour, and with a bitter sting in the tail. They were, instead, bogies and bugbears, imaginary doubts and fears.

Thus in *King Henry VI, Part Two*, that mistress of anger and pelting words, Queen Margaret, tells the King amid a downpour of speech (III, ii, 86) that she has heard a voice say unto her:

> . . . 'Seek not a **scorpion's** nest,
> Nor set no footing on this unkind shore.'

In *Cymbeline* (V, v, 43) the physician Cornelius informs the king that his daughter Imogen had been secretly disliked by his infamous and poisonous queen (incidentally, a queen without a name):

> Your daughter, whom she bore in hand to love
> With such integrity, she did confess
> Was as a **scorpion** to her sight; whose life,
> But that her flight prevented it, she had
> Ta'en off by poison.

To which King Cymbeline has an apt observation followed by an absolutely unanswerable question, all in exactly eleven words: 'O most delicate fiend! Who is't can read a woman?'

Much more familiar is the single horripilant line Macbeth addresses to his Lady, even while he is arranging a double murder, 'a deed of dreadful note' involving Banquo and his young son (*Macbeth*, III, ii, 35): 'O, full of **scorpions** is my mind, dear wife!'

SEA-MONSTERS

Shakespeare's two references to a Sea-Monster – a marvellously vague phrase in itself – are respectively general and particular.

The one is instanced by King Lear just before he utters his tremendous curse on his eldest daughter, Goneril. He is full of imprecations and distractions. 'Darkness and devils!' he begins. Then we are made to realize that he is possessed with the thought of flying to his second daughter, Regan. He interrupts himself, begins statements which he leaves unfinished. 'Prepare my horses,' he orders. Then out pours his tremendous utterance (*King Lear*, I, iv, 265):

> Ingratitude, thou marble-hearted fiend,
> More hideous when thou show'st thee in a child
> Than the **sea-monster**!

The particular reference is made by Portia in *The Merchant of Venice* (III, ii, 53) just before Bassanio makes his choice of the three caskets:

> Now he goes,
> With no less presence, but with much more love,
> Than young Alcides, when he did redeem
> The virgin tribute paid by howling Troy
> To the **sea-monster**: I stand for sacrifice;
> The rest aloof are the Dardanian wives,
> With bleared visages, come forth to view
> The issue of th' exploit. Go, Hercules!
> Live thou, I live: with much, much more dismay
> I view the fight than thou that makest the fray.

The story, taken from Ovid, is that of Hesione, daughter of the Trojan king, Laomedon, who offered Hercules six beautiful horses if he would save his daughter and slay the monster. Portia, it must be said, does not make this at all clear. Neither should she have assumed that even an Elizabethan schoolboy (or one of today) would know that Alcides is just another name for Hercules.

SERPENTS AND SNAKES

The *Oxford Dictionary* confirms one in the impression that these two words mean the same thing – one of the 'limbless vertebrates constituting the reptilian order *Ophidia*' – but that by 'serpent' we mean nowadays one of the bigger and more venomous kinds of snake.

Shakespeare has plenty of time for both. There is a mention of the Serpent in each of the long poems of his youth. Venus says to her Adonis at the very outset of her siege (lines 17–18):

> Here come and sit, where never **serpent** hisses,
> And being set, I'll smother thee with kisses; . . .

and Tarquin approaching the sleeping Lucrece for his fell purpose is similarly compared (lines 362–364):

> Who sees the lurking **serpent** steps aside;
> But she, sound sleeping, fearing no such thing,
> Lies at the mercy of his mortal sting.

But the plays themselves are a positive snake-pit or serpent-warren, and one must be selective and particular. We might even concentrate on one great play alone, like *Antony and Cleopatra*, which may be said to seethe with Ophidia. Cleopatra, extolling Antony in his absence, uses such terms as these (I, v, 23):

> The demi-Atlas of this earth, the arm
> And burgonet of men. He's speaking now,
> Or murmuring, 'Where's my **serpent** of old Nile?'
> For so he calls me: now I feed myself
> With most delicious poison: ...

In the following act Cleopatra receives a Messenger from the still-absent Antony (II, v, 36):

MESSENGER: Good madam, hear me.
CLEOPATRA: Well, go to, I will;
    But there's no goodness in thy face: if Antony
    Be free and healthful – so tart a favour
    To trumpet such good tidings! If not well,
    Thou shouldst come like a Fury crown'd with **snakes**,
    Not like a formal man.

Two minutes later the hapless Messenger feels bound to mumble the hapless words, 'He's married, madam,' and takes to his heels on the flash of Cleopatra's knife (II, v, 75):

CHARMIAN: Good madam, keep yourself within yourself:
    The man is innocent.
CLEOPATRA: Some innocents scape not the thunderbolt.
    Melt Egypt into Nile! and kindly creatures
    Turn all to **serpents**! Call the slave again,
    Though I am mad, I will not bite him: call.
CHARMIAN: He is afeard to come.
CLEOPATRA: I will not hurt him.

A minute later the miserable Messenger has to repeat himself (II, v, 88):

MESSENGER: I have done my duty.
CLEOPATRA: Is he married?
    I cannot hate thee worser than I do,
    If thou again say 'Yes'.
MESSENGER: He's married, madam.

CLEOPATRA: The gods confound thee! dost thou hold there still?
MESSENGER: Should I lie, madam?
CLEOPATRA: O, I would thou didst,
So half my Egypt were submerged, and made
A cistern for scalèd **snakes**! Go, get thee hence:
Hadst thou Narcissus in thy face, to me
Thou wouldst appear most ugly. He is married?
MESSENGER: I crave your highness' pardon.
CLEOPATRA: He is married?
MESSENGER: Take no offence that I would not offend you:
To punish me for what you make me do
Seems much unequal: he's married to Octavia.

This is playwriting. And it is very often, in stage production, stupidly cut.

One other great play insists upon not being overlooked in this matter of snakes and serpents. It is the one which has 'fillet of a fenny **snake**' (IV, i, 12) among the ingredients of the grisly brew in the Witches' Cauldron. It is, incidentally, a good test of anyone's knowledge of *Macbeth*, be they students or be they even actors and actresses, to say who utters this particular line, 'Look like the innocent flower, But be the **serpent** under't' (I, v, 67). Is it Macbeth to his wife, or is it Lady Macbeth to her husband?

See also ASPS, ADDERS, VIPERS.

SHARKS

The biological description of the Shark – 'a selachian fish of the sub-order *Squali* of the order *Plagiostomi*' – is, appropriately enough, rather a mouthful. One looks up 'selachian' and finds: 'Of or belonging to the genus *Selache* of sharks; the sharks and their allies.' This is just one of the ways of dictionaries, even the best of them.

The poet probes far more deeply than the lexicologist. When in *Macbeth* (IV, i, 23) we find among the Witches' ingredients the 'maw and gulf of the ravin'd salt-sea **shark**' we realize that the poet is giving in eight words what the mere word-spinner would take at least fifty words to convey: the bottomless gullet and insatiable gorge of the vicious fish itself – the stinging taste of the lashing and hissing element in which the shark lives to eat, and eats to live – and even some of the immediate alarm engendered in the human observer by the savagely disporting and blood-boltered brute.

SHEEP, OLD AND YOUNG

Here Shakespeare is in his native and pastoral element for the nonce.

In *The Tempest* we have Iris telling Ceres of her 'turfy mountains, where live nibbling **sheep**' (IV, i, 62).

In *Troilus and Cressida* (III, iii, 311) Thersites uses the word about Achilles, figuratively and with his accustomed mordancy: 'I had rather be a tick in a **sheep** than such a valiant ignorance.'

In *The Winter's Tale* (IV, iii, 787) Autolycus has the right, healthy phrase for the old Shepherd: 'An old **sheep**-whistling rogue.'

In *The Two Gentlemen of Verona*, that infelicitous play, there are still some few felicities as when Proteus and Speed, the clown, bring to a head their punning duel (I, i, 89):

PROTEUS: The **sheep** for fodder follow the shepherd, the shepherd for food follows not the **sheep**: thou for wages followest thy master, thy master for wages follows not thee: therefore thou art a **sheep**.
SPEED: Such another proof will make me cry 'baa'.

In *As You Like It* (iii, ii, 73) another duel of wits brings out the best in Corin the old shepherd and the worst in Touchstone the jester:

CORIN: Sir, I am a true labourer: I earn that I eat, get that I wear; owe no man hate, envy no man's happiness; glad of other men's good, content with my harm; and the greatest of my pride is, to see my **ewes** graze and my lambs suck.

TOUCHSTONE: This is another simple sin in you; to bring the **ewes** and the **rams** together, and to offer to get your living by the copulation of cattle; to be bawd to a **bell-wether**; and to betray a **she-lamb** of a twelvemonth to a crooked-pated, old, cuckoldly **ram,** out of all reasonable match. If thou be'st not damn'd for this, the devil himself will have no shepherds; I cannot see else how thou shouldst scape.

In *The Merchant of Venice* (i, iii, 80) there is a more or less commercial interchange between Shylock and Antonio which also involves copulation (and this maddeningly means the passage's deletion from school editions of the play):

SHYLOCK: . . . the **ewes,** being rank,
  In th' end of autumn turned to the **rams**;
  And when the work of generation was
  Between these woolly breeders in the act,
  The skilful shepherd peel'd me certain wands, . . .

and so forth. Antonio interrupts the Jew with a perceptive question, and gets an answer which proves Shylock to be a wit as well as a man of the world:

ANTONIO: Was this inserted to make interest good?
  Or is your gold and silver **ewes** and **rams**?
SHYLOCK: I cannot tell: I make it breed as fast: . . .

In *The Winter's Tale* (i, ii, 67) Polixenes describes to Hermione the boyhood he spent with her husband Leontes:

WSAM—I

> We were as twinn'd **lambs** that did frisk i' the sun,
> And bleat the one at the other: what we changed
> Was innocence for innocence; we knew not
> The doctrine of ill-doing, no, nor dream'd
> That any did. . . .

In *Othello* (I, i, 89) we may note Iago's blunt serenade to old Brabantio, Desdemona's father:

> Even now, now, very now, an old black **ram**
> Is tupping your white **ewe**. Arise, arise . . .

And thence we may pass on, for a conclusion, to what the young poet was writing in verse before he was a playwright at all. In *The Rape of Lucrece* (lines 463–464) he permits himself a double meaning in his description of Tarquin's hand on Lucrece's bosom:

> His hand, that yet remains upon her breast, –
> Rude **ram**, to batter such an ivory wall! – . . .

and later in the same poem (lines 677–679) it is, with the nicest mixture of indignation and gusto, that he describes the immediate aftermath of the rape:

> The wolf hath seized his prey, the poor **lamb** cries;
> Till with her own white fleece her voice controll'd
> Entombs her outcry in her lips' sweet fold: . . .

In these and other such devious ways we may let

> . . . sweetest Shakespeare, Fancy's child,
> Warble his native wood-notes wild –

which, somewhat surprisingly, is what another very young poet, John Milton, wrote in *L'Allegro* barely twenty years after Shakespeare's death.

SNAILS

The common types of the true Snail belong to the genus *Helix* (especially *Helix aspersa* or *hortensis*, the common or garden snail, and *Helix pomatia*, the edible variety).

Five of the attributes of the gasteropod which Shakespeare recognizes and illustrates are these: it is sluggish, delicate, retiring, unhurried, unprofitable.

Here, respectively, are the plays and places – *The Comedy of Errors* (II, ii, 193), *Love's Labour's Lost* (IV, iii, 334), *King Lear* (I, v, 27), *As You Like It* (II, vii, 145) and *The Merchant of Venice* (II, v, 46).

And here – again respectively – are the speakers and the utterances:

(1) LUCIANA: 'Dromio, thou drone, thou **snail**, thou slug, thou sot!'

(2) BEROWNE: 'Love's feeling is more soft and sensible / Than are the tender horns of cockled **snails**.'

(3) FOOL (*to Lear*): 'I can tell why a **snail** has a house. . . . Why, to put's head in; not to give it away to his daughters, and leave his horns without a case.'

(4) JAQUES: 'Then the whining schoolboy, with his satchel / And shining morning face, creeping like **snail** / Unwillingly to school.'

(5) SHYLOCK [of Launcelot]: 'The patch is kind enough; but a huge feeder, / **Snail-slow** in profit, and he sleeps by day / More than the wild-cat.'

Incidentally, and as a corollary, Shakespeare in one of his early poems improved, if anything, on the image of Berowne (No. 2 above). He is describing Venus's recoil of terror at seeing Adonis gored by the wild boar (lines 1033–1038):

Or as the **snail,** whose tender horns being hit,
Shrinks backward in his shelly cave with pain,
And there, all smother'd up, in shade doth sit,
Long after fearing to creep forth again;
    So at his bloody view her eyes are fled
    Into the deep-dark cabins of her head.

SPARROWS, FINCHES, ROBINS

From a swarm of Sparrows and Finches and other such little daytime birds, one must be content to pick and choose only such as Shakespeare makes particularly odd or attractive.

The best-known sparrow occurs in Hamlet's grave colloquy with Horatio just before death parts them at the end of the play (v, ii, 215):

HORATIO: If your mind dislike any thing, obey it: I will forestall their repair hither, and say you are not fit.
HAMLET: Not a whit, we defy augury: there's a special providence in the fall of a **sparrow.** If it be now, 'tis not to come; if it be not to come, it will be now; if it be not now, yet it will come: the readiness is all: since no man knows aught of what he leaves, what is 't to leave betimes? Let be.

In his comment on this passage Granville Barker uses the rare word 'fatidic', meaning 'gifted with the power of prophecy'. He writes: 'Hamlet's fatidic speech definitely alarms Horatio, who makes a move as if to stop the match after all – in which he is checked by that curt, commanding "Let be".' The two words are omitted in many editions and are indeed not in the Folio. But the best Hamlet of our middle-century, Gielgud, made them both curt and commanding last time he played the part.

In a little scene in the Masque of Ceres in *The Tempest* the gods are charmingly shown to be capable of perfectly human behaviour (IV, i, 98):

> Mars's hot minion is return'd again;
> Her waspish-headed son has broke his arrows,
> Swears he will shoot no more, but play with **sparrows,**
> And be a boy right out.

But editors do not by any means always agree that the reference is to Venus and Cupid, or that it is to Paphos her birthplace that the goddess has returned.

There is a mention of a hedge-sparrow by the Fool in *King Lear* (see under CUCKOOS); and of a bunting in *All's Well That Ends Well* (II, v, 7) where the contemptuous Lafeu says to Bertram about the flamboyant Parolles, 'I took this lark for a **bunting.**'

As for finches, Thersites in *Troilus and Cressida* calls Patroclus 'Finch-egg!' which is a very mild term of abuse for Thersites; and Bottom the Weaver includes an indeterminate finch in one of his snatches of song (*A Midsummer Night's Dream*, III, i, 129):

> The **finch,** the **sparrow,** and the lark,
> The plain-song cuckoo gray, ...

The Robin or robin-redbreast seems to have but a single mention in Shakespeare in Speed's witty list of the attributes of any true lover in *The Two Gentlemen of Verona* (II, i, 16):

> You have learn'd ... to wreathe your arms, like a malecontent; to relish a love-song, like a **robin-redbreast**; to walk alone, like one that had the pestilence; to sigh, like a school-boy that had lost his A B C; ...

But Shakespeare's contemporary, John Webster, makes much more magical use of the robin in the first four lines of the Dirge in *The White Devil*:

241

Call for the **robin-redbreast** and the wren,
Since o'er shady groves they hover,
And with leaves and flowers do cover
The friendless bodies of unburied men.

There is no more beautiful Dirge in the language – with the exception of 'Fear no more the heat o' the sun' in *Cymbeline*.

SPIDERS AND SPINNERS

A watchman Fairy before Titania's bower sings to keep Spiders and Spinners well away (*A Midsummer Night's Dream*, II, ii, 20):

Weaving **spiders**, come not here;
Hence, you long-legg'd **spinners**, hence!

And Mercutio, in his dazzling impromptu about Queen Mab and her chariot, tells us of 'her wagon-spokes made of long **spinners'** legs' (*Romeo and Juliet*, I, iv, 59). So much for fairies and spiders!

Leontes, King of Sicilia, in *The Winter's Tale* has ten lines which show his tortuous thought when suspecting the conduct of his wife with his old friend, Polixenes, King of Bohemia. The lines contain a quite horrendous figure of a spider in a drinking glass (II, i, 36):

How blest am I
In my just censure, in my true opinion!
Alack, for lesser knowledge! how accurst
In being so blest! There may be in the cup
A **spider** steept, and one may drink, depart,
And yet partake no venom; for his knowledge
Is not infected: but if one present
Th' abhorr'd ingredient to his eye, make known
How he hath drunk, he cracks his gorge, his sides,
With violent hefts: I have drunk, and seen the **spider**.

A spider in a bottle is almost as evil a thing, even when used figuratively. In *King Richard III* that arch-mistress of malediction, Queen Margaret (widow of Henry VI), tells Queen Elizabeth (wife of Edward IV) that she need waste no sympathy on Gloster (I, iii, 242):

> Poor painted queen, vain flourish of my fortune!
> Why strew'st thou sugar on that bottled **spider**,
> Whose deadly web ensnareth thee about?
> Fool, fool! thou whett'st a knife to kill thyself.
> The day will come that thou shalt wish for me,
> To help thee curse that poisonous bunch-backt toad.

The day *does* come, nearly three acts later, when Queen Elizabeth says to Queen Margaret (IV, iv, 79):

> O, thou didst prophesy the time would come
> That I should wish for thee to help me curse
> That bottled **spider**, that foul bunch-backt toad!

This Elizabeth is no one's favourite, but she here proves she has a good memory for a curse. She also has a line in this same play (I, iii, 110) which must always raise a smile in any good audience: 'Small joy have I in being England's queen!'

SQUIRREL

That unusually endearing rodent, the Squirrel (*Sciurus vulgaris*), has little to do in Shakespeare.

A very minor mystery in *The Two Gentlemen of Verona* is why the clown Launce should mention to Proteus 'the other **squirrel**' (IV, iv, 58) when his talk, before and after this, is all of dogs, i.e. of his dog Crab and the rest of doggery:

The other **squirrel** was stolen from me by the hangman boys in the market-place: and then I offer'd her [Silvia] mine own, who is a dog as big as ten of yours, and therefore the gift the greater.

The other references are faëry matters. Mercutio tells us that Queen Mab's chariot was 'an empty hazel-nut, made by the joiner **squirrel**' (*Romeo and Juliet*, I, iv, 67); and Titania makes a charming offer to Bottom, to be executed by a remarkably daring fairy (*A Midsummer Night's Dream*, IV, i, 36):

> TITANIA: I have a venturous fairy that shall seek
> The **squirrel's** hoard, and fetch thee hence new nuts.
> BOTTOM: I had rather have a handful or two of dried peas.
> But, I pray you, let none of your people stir me:
> I have an exposition of sleep come upon me.
> TITANIA: Sleep thou, and I will wind thee in my arms.
> Fairies, be gone, and be all ways away.

Ralph Richardson's sleepy Nick Bottom was memorable here as in many other places.

STARLING

The Starling (*Sturnus vulgaris*) occurs – to the best of one's researches – only in one place in Shakespeare. But this is an advantage over a considerable number of British birds which do not occur there at all. These include such poetic-sounding birds as the bittern and the heron, the magpie, the linnet, and the kingfisher. Tits and terns are no less absent.

The Starling is brought in only because of its propensity to talk almost like a raven, if not nearly so well as a parrot. This is in *King Henry IV, Part One*, where Hotspur ('whipt and scourged with rods, Nettled, and stung with pismires' – his own self-description) is talking about – so far as one can make out whom he is talking about – Bolingbroke (I, iii, 219):

> He said he would not ransom Mortimer;
> Forbad my tongue to speak of Mortimer;
> But I will find him when he lies asleep,
> And in his ear I'll holla 'Mortimer!'
> Nay,
> I'll have a **starling** shall be taught to speak
> Nothing but 'Mortimer', and give it him,
> To keep his anger still in motion.

There is nothing else whatever about this darkling bird that trembles as it sings. Nothing, for example, about its amazing gregariousness so that a whole multitude or murmuration of starlings may be seen, as if of one accord, swooping to the eaves or roofs of public buildings in big cities. It would also seem to be a bird of exceptional good taste since the public buildings – especially in Birmingham, Liverpool and London – are actual picture galleries. This is one's own not particularly avian observation.

SWALLOW AND MARTLET

King Duncan, on the morning of the very day he is murdered in his sleep, has his famous and highly agreeable greeting to the castle in which he is to meet his doom (*Macbeth*, I, vi, I):

> This castle hath a pleasant seat; the air
> Nimbly and sweetly recommends itself
> Unto our gentle senses.

Whereupon Banquo continues in the same vein:

> This guest of summer,
> The temple-haunting **martlet**, does approve,
> By his lov'd mansionry, that the heavens' breath
> Smells wooingly here: no jutty, frieze,
> Buttress, nor coign of vantage, but this bird

Hath made his pendent bed and procreant cradle:
Where they most breed and haunt, I have observed
The air is delicate.

And then enters Lady Macbeth with her fulsome welcoming phrases.

This genial conversation is of the highest dramatic value, coming as it does between a direct hatching of regicide between host and hostess and the elaborate falsity of the lady's actual welcome. And across the conversation, as it were, flies the 'temple-haunting **martlet**' or eave-loving swallow like a symbol of peace.

The *Oxford Dictionary* says of the martlet that it is the swift (*Cypselus apus*), and of the swallow (*Hirundo rustica*) that it is not quite the same thing. It says further of the swift that it is, or was, 'formerly often confused with the swallow'. Why 'formerly'? Both fly too fleetly for any but the ornithologist to detect the difference.

Perhaps the Prince of Arragon in *The Merchant of Venice* is just temporizing not very meaningfully before Portia's caskets when he says that the fond eye 'like the **martlet**, builds in the weather on the outward wall', and perhaps it may be assumed that he is too exercised to say what he means (II, ix, 27).

Antony's friend, Scarus, has a very striking line about Cleopatra in the sea-fight (*Antony and Cleopatra*, IV, xii, 3):

> **Swallows** have built
> In Cleopatra's sails their nests: the augurers
> Say they know not, they cannot tell; look grimly,
> And dare not speak their knowledge.

just before Antony comes in to tell us all:

> All is lost;
> This foul Egyptian hath betrayed me: . . .

Richmond in *King Richard III* (v, ii, 22) approaches Bosworth
Field with the resonant lines:

> All for our vantage. Then, in God's name, march:
> True hope is swift, and flies with **swallows'** wings;
> Kings it makes gods, and meaner creatures kings.

And Perdita reminds us that the swallow is the harbinger of
summer rather than of spring in her wondrous lines in *The
Winter's Tale* (iv, iii, 118):

> Daffodils
> That come before the **swallow** dares, and take
> The winds of March with beauty; ...

SWAN AND CYGNETS

Two lovely allusions in the early poem, *The Rape of Lucrece*,
could easily be overlooked among the references in the dramas.
One is a platitude, but a very striking one (lines 1009–1012):

> The crow may bathe his coal-black wings in mire,
> And unperceived fly with the filth away;
> But if the like the snow-white **swan** desire,
> The stain upon his silver down will stay.

And Lucrece is referring to her own violated state when she
says (lines 1611–1612):

> And now this pale **swan** in her watery nest
> Begins the sad dirge of her certain ending: ...

The curious charm of the very word 'cygnet' is brought out
in all Shakespeare's allusions to the baby swan. Prince Henry
in *King John* (v, vii, 21) has a trembling and beautiful image
just before the king, his father, is carried in, poisoned and
dying, in his chair:

> I am the **cygnet** to this pale faint swan,
> Who chants a doleful hymn to his own death,
> And from the organ-pipe of frailty sings
> His soul and body to their lasting rest.

In the very first scene of *Troilus and Cressida* the shaky hero tells Pandarus of the white wonder of his Cressida's hand 'to whose soft seizure the **cygnet's** down is harsh' (I, i, 57). And at the end of *King Henry VI, Part One* (v, iii, 55) Suffolk leads in Queen Margaret as his prisoner and says:

> Thou art allotted to be ta'en by me:
> So doth the **swan** her downy **cygnets** save,
> Keeping them prisoner underneath her wings.

Emilia in *Othello* (v, ii, 245), stabbed in the back by her own husband, has an extraordinarily moving little death scene in which she echoes her dead mistress's song of 'Willow':

> What did thy song bode, lady?
> Hark, canst thou hear me? I will play the **swan**,
> And die in music: [*Singing*] 'Willow, willow, willow.'

And Celia stoutly defends her friendship to Rosalind before her own father, the usurping Duke Frederick, in *As You Like It* (I, iii, 69):

> . . . if she be a traitor,
> Why, so am I; we still have slept together,
> Rose at an instant, learn'd, play'd, eat together;
> And wheresoe'er we went, like Juno's **swans**,
> Still we went coupled and inseparable.

Who was it who first described Shakespeare himself as 'Sweet Swan of Avon'? Most people would guess – and guess rightly – that it was Ben Jonson, but few are familiar with the poem it occurs in, or where it was first printed. The occasion was the First Folio of Shakespeare's plays which appeared in

1623, just seven years after the poet's death. Ben Jonson's was perhaps the best of a prefatory sheaf of poems in the Master's praise. To say that it was the best is not very high praise, since – as so often happens on these occasions – the writers merely tried to outvie one another in laudation. Ben Jonson's poem had the title:

> *To the Memory of My Beloved, The Author,*
> *Mr William Shakespeare*
> *And what he hath left us*

and its last ten lines run thus:

> *Sweet swan of Avon! what a sight it were*
> *To see thee in our waters yet appeare,*
> *And make those flights upon the bankes of Thames,*
> *That so did take Eliza, and our James!*
> *But stay, I see thee in the hemisphere*
> *Advanc'd and made a constellation there!*
> *Shine forth, thou starre of poets, and with rage*
> *Or influence chide, or cheere, the drooping stage;*
> *Which, since thy flight from hence, hath mourn'd like night,*
> *And despaires day, but for thy volume's light.*

The poem, as a whole, is no better than it should have been.

THINGS AND SHAPES

Both of these words, when used in a certain way, can have an odd and somehow scaring effect of strangeness. It may be because of their lack of outline. A Shape, in this sense, has no shape at all; and a Thing, so used, can be something unimaginable.

Hamlet has scarcely opened (i, i, 21) when Horatio, referring to the reported apparition of the dead king, says to Bernardo,

'What, has this **thing** appear'd again to-night?' and gets the reply, 'I have seen nothing.' There is in Horatio's question some scorn and some scepticism, but there is also a hint of fearfulness in the very word 'thing'.

It can be the same with the very word 'shape' or 'shapes'. When in *King Henry IV, Part One*, that possessed Welshman, Owen Glendower, describes the circumstances of his birth to Hotspur (III, i, 12):

> . . . at my nativity
> The front of heaven was full of fiery **shapes**,
> Of burning cressets; and at my birth
> The frame and huge foundation of the earth
> Shaked like a coward.

he is heeded by Hotspur with very rational and abusive scorn. But we in the audience are awed by Glendower's 'shapes', much more so than by his burning cressets and earth tremors.

But it is not necessary to explore beyond *The Tempest* to find instances of this peculiarly subtle use of both the words. Sometimes within the same scene, e.g.

(1) Prospero describing the death of the witch Sycorax to Ariel:

PROSPERO: Then was this island –
Save for the son that she did litter here,
A freckled whelp, hag-born – not honour'd with
A human shape.
ARIEL: Yes, Caliban, her son.
PROSPERO: Dull **thing**, I say so; . . . (I, ii, 281)

(2) Prospero ordering Ariel to disguise himself as a sea-nymph:

> . . . invisible
> To every eyeball else. Go take this **shape**,
> And hither come in't: go; hence with diligence!
> (I, ii, 302)

(3) Prospero to Caliban:

> I pitied thee,
> Took pains to make thee speak, taught thee each hour
> One thing or other: when thou didst not, savage,
> Know thine own meaning, but wouldst gabble like
> A **thing** most brutish, I endow'd thy purposes
> With words that made them known.
>
> (I, ii, 353)

(4) Miranda to Prospero (on seeing Ferdinand for the first time):

> I might call him
> A **thing** divine; for nothing natural
> I ever saw so noble.
>
> (I, ii, 418)

(5) Prospero to Miranda (on her view of Ferdinand):

> Thou think'st there are no more such **shapes** as he,
> Having seen but him and Caliban: foolish wench!
> To the most of men this is a Caliban,
> And they to him are angels.
>
> (I, ii, 479)

But one's own favourite use of the word 'shapes' occurs later in the same play among the stage directions (III, iii, 21, 87). The play was first printed in the First Folio, seven years after his death, and some scholars think that the directions are not from Shakespeare's own hand. If this be so, the hand was worthy of the task. The directions are thus printed and spelt in the First Folio itself:

Solemne and strange Musicke: and Prosper on the top (invisible): Enter severall strange **shapes**, bringing in a Banket [so spelt]; and dance about it with gentle actions of salutations, and inviting the King, Ec. to eate, they depart. . . .

Thunder and Lightning. Enter Ariell (like a Harpey); claps his wings upon the Table, and with a quient [*sic*] device the Banquet vanishes. . . .

He [Ariel] vanishes in Thunder: then to soft Musicke. Enter the **shapes** againe, and daunce (with mockes and mowes) and carrying out the Table.

The isle is full of Shapes and Things, as well as noises.

THRUSH, THROSTLE, JAY

Portia is passably witty to Nerissa about the long list of her suitors at Belmont, and when she comes to the French lord, Monsieur Le Bon, she says he is too many men wrapped up in one (I, ii, 57):

God made him, and therefore let him pass for a man. .... he is every man in no man; if a **throstle** sing, he falls straight a-capering; he will fence with his own shadow: if I should marry him, I should marry twenty husbands. ...

The two other references to the song-thrush or throstle (*Turdus musicus*) are both, appropriately enough, in songs – one, unremarkable, sung by Bottom in *A Midsummer Night's Dream* (III, i, 126), the other, very remarkable indeed, sung by Autolycus in *The Winter's Tale* (IV, ii, 10). The first is a little ditty which includes 'the **throstle** with his note so true' among a carolling company which includes also the ousel or blackbird, the wren, the finch, the sparrow, the lark, and the cuckoo. But the Autolycus lyric of twenty lines beginning 'When daffodils begin to peer' is – at least as to the first four of the six stanzas – one of the great Songs of Spring.

It is only necessary to realize that 'pugging' probably means aching, and to know with certainty that 'aunts' are 'doxies' and not relatives, to appreciate that here is magic. The first of the lines quoted have true and still heart-of-the-country feeling: the second and fifth and sixth are a dawn chorus in words; the third and fourth have a characteristic inconsequence; and the seventh and eighth have a sheer bucolic bliss:

> The white sheet bleaching on the hedge,
>   With hey! the sweet birds, O, how they sing!
> Doth set my pugging tooth on edge;
>   For a quart of ale is a dish for a king.

> The lark, that tirra-lirra chants,
>   With hey! with hey! the **thrush** and the **jay**,
> Are summer songs for me and my aunts,
>   While we lie tumbling in the hay.

The jay (*Garrulus glandarius*) is coupled with the thrush for no good ornithological reason, but solely because Autolycus couples them in the best of his songs just quoted, 'With hey! with hey! the **thrush** and the **jay**.'

Among the other desirable delights of his desert island Caliban offers his new men-gods, Trinculo and Stephano, is to 'show thee a **jay's** nest' (II, ii, 176). And Mistress Ford in *The Merry Wives of Windsor* (III, iii, 35), seeing the approach of Falstaff with an anticipative leer on his face, says, 'We'll use this unwholesome humidity, this gross watery pumpion [=water melon or pumpkin]; we'll teach him to know turtles from **jays**.' Whereupon editor Ridley of the New Temple Shakespeare very helpfully tells us that 'doves are the type of constancy, as jays of flightiness'.

TIGERS

In such a play as *The Two Gentlemen of Verona* it is a quite unusual flight of fancy when Proteus says apropos of Orpheus (III, ii, 77):

WSAM—K

For Orpheus' lute was strung with poets' sinews,
Whose golden touch could soften steel and stones,
Make **tigers** tame, and huge leviathans
Forsake unsounded deeps to dance on sands.

There are many other allusions to the tiger (*Felis tigris*) and some of the best are in some of the least familiar places. Thus Menenius says of Coriolanus (*Coriolanus*, v, iv, 28), 'There is no more mercy in him than there is milk in a male **tiger**; that shall our poor city find.' And Romeo (*Romeo and Juliet*, v, iii, 32), in a desperate speech to his servant while he is breaking into the Capulet Monument (and in some wild and whirling words which are usually cut in performance), says:

> ... hence, be gone:
> But if thou, jealous, dost return to pry
> In what I further shall intend to do,
> By heaven, I will tear thee joint by joint,
> And strew this hungry churchyard with thy limbs:
> The time and my intents are savage-wild;
> More fierce and more inexorable far
> Than empty **tigers** or the roaring sea.

Whereupon the servant Balthazar, quitting his master as though he were an empty tiger in person, summarily leaves with the parting line, 'I will be gone, sir, and not trouble you.' Balthazar, as we say today, beats it.

The Tiger is also the name of an Ephesian inn in *The Comedy of Errors*. It is likewise the name of a ship mentioned in *Twelfth Night* (v, i, 60) as being boarded on an occasion by Antonio, the sea-captain friend of Sebastian; and of another ship mentioned by the First Witch in *Macbeth* (I, iii, 7) who chased 'the master o' th' **Tiger**' in order to 'drain him dry as hay'.

TORTOISE AND TURTLE

Both are four-footed reptiles of the order *Chelonia* – the former slow-paced, land-lubberly, and inedible; the latter aquatic and providing a uniquely delicious soup with the grace of a little added sherry.

It is said of the seedy Apothecary in *Romeo and Juliet* (v, i, 42) that 'in his needy shop a **tortoise** hung'. And Prospero uses the same word figuratively in *The Tempest* (i, ii, 317) to Ariel when we might say 'slow-coach', as here, 'Come, thou **tortoise**, when?'

Wherever Shakespeare uses the word 'turtle' he means the dove; but if in his baffling poem *The Phœnix and the Turtle* he meant the reptile and not the dove, the poem could hardly mean less than it does. See under PHŒNIX.

UNICORN

The invaluable Dr Brewer tells us what we may easily have forgotten – that two Unicorns flanked the Royal Arms of Scotland before the Union of the Crowns, and that James VI of Scotland, when he went south to be James I of England, took with him one of the Unicorns. With this he supplanted the Red Dragon which, as representing Wales, had been one of the supporters of the English shield, the other being the Lion.

Dr Brewer further sends us to Edmund Spenser in whose *Faerie Queene* (Book II, Canto 5, Lines 1–2) we may read:

> Like as a Lyon, whose imperiall powre
> A prowd rebellious **Unicorne** defies . . .

and gather that the animosity which existed between the lion and unicorn (cf. the still-surviving nursery rhyme about the couple fighting 'all round the town') is allegorical to that which existed between England and Scotland.

Shakespeare has his references. In *The Tempest* (III, iii, 22) when 'severall strange Shapes' bring in a banquet and lay it before the shipwrecked noblemen, one of the latter, Sebastian, says, 'A living drollery. Now I will believe that there are **unicorns**.' Again, Timon of Athens says to Apemantus (*Timon of Athens*, IV, iii, 335), 'Wert thou the **unicorn**, pride and wrath would confound thee, and make thine own self the conquest of thy fury.' And again, Decius Brutus tells us of Julius Caesar (*Julius Caesar*, II, i, 203):

> . . . he loves to hear
> That **unicorns** may be betray'd with trees,
> And bears with glasses, elephants with holes,
> Lions with toils, and men with flatterers: . . .

But that is all. One turns eagerly to the poems, especially to *Venus and Adonis*, hoping to chase a single Unicorn. But all in vain.

VULTURE

'Let **vultures** gripe thy guts!' says Pistol in *The Merry Wives of Windsor* (I, iii, 82); and 'Let **vultures** vile seize on his lungs also!' says Pistol again in *King Henry IV, Part Two* (V, iv, 139). In both cases he is probably quoting from some forgotten gory melodrama.

'There cannot be that **vulture** in you to devour so many . . . ,' says Macduff to Malcolm, who has been declaring himself even less fit than Macbeth for kingship (*Macbeth*, IV, iii, 73). And King Lear tells his second daughter, Regan, about the monstrousness of his first daughter, Goneril (*King Lear*,

II, iv, 134), 'O Regan, she hath tied Sharp-toothed unkindness, like a **vulture**, here.' And the old king points to his heart.

Even the *Oxford Dictionary* seems to stand a little in awe of this unlovable bird. Telling us it is one of the 'large birds of prey of the order *Raptores*', it goes on to say that these 'feed almost entirely upon carrion and have the head and neck altogether or almost featherless'.

The Vulture watches us from afar in desert places. It has calculation in both its eyes. It hates us living and it loves us dead.

WHALE AND LEVIATHAN

Shakespeare seems oddly far-fetched, or momentarily out of his depth, when referring to this monstrous Cetacean by either of its English appellations. When Henry V before Harfleur refers to the leviathan he achieves only a stilted figure (*King Henry V*, III, iii, 24):

> We may as bootless spend our vain command
> Upon th' enragèd soldiers in their spoil,
> As send precepts to the **leviathan**
> To come ashore.

Oberon is positively being *outré* when he tells Puck (*A Midsummer Night's Dream*, II, i, 173) to make haste in these terms:

> Fetch me this herb; and be thou here again
> Ere the **leviathan** can swim a league.

And Puck is very much more natural and felicitous in his reply, 'I'll put a girdle round about the earth in forty minutes.'

Shakespeare's himself again when, in *The Two Gentlemen of Verona* (III, ii, 80), he tells us how Orpheus with his lute could

> Make tigers tame, and huge **leviathans**
> Forsake unsounded deeps to dance on sands.

But see under TIGER.

It is 'the belching **whale**' which threatens to swallow up the babe Marina in her infant craft (*Pericles, Prince of Tyre*, III, i, 62). Again, troops fly or die in *Troilus and Cressida* (v, v, 22) like 'scalèd sculls [which may mean schools of fish] before the belching **whale**'. In *The Merry Wives of Windsor* (II, i, 63) Mistress Ford tells us of a tempest which threw a whale ashore at Windsor 'with so many tuns of oil in his belly'. But that one turned out to be merely Sir John Falstaff.

WILD BOAR

One is obliged to the late André Simon's *Concise Encyclopaedia of Gastronomy* for this concise piece of information about the Wild Boar (*Sus scrofa*) : 'The wild hog of Continental Europe, southern Asia and North Africa is believed to have provided the original stock from which all races of domestic swine have been raised. In England the gastronomic reputation of the wild boar stands on its *head* which was made into a fine Brawn, and was also used as a table decoration and a tavern sign. [E.g. The Boar's Head Tavern in Eastcheap throughout *King Henry IV, Part One* and *Part Two*.] In France the Wild Boar (*Sanglier*) is still hunted in many parts of the country, and the flesh of the young (*Marcassin*) is highly esteemed as a table delicacy.'

'Eight **wild-boars** roasted whole at a breakfast, and but twelve persons there; is this true?' asks Maecenas of Enobarbus in *Antony and Cleopatra* (II, ii, 183) of entertainment in Egypt.

But most of the other references in the plays are figurative and non-gastronomical. Petruchio, coming to woo his Shrew, asks (*The Taming of the Shrew*, I, ii, 199):

> Have I not in my time heard lions roar?
> Have I not heard the sea, puf'd up with winds,
> Rage like an angry **boar** chafed with sweat?

Aaron the Moor (*Titus Andronicus*, IV, ii, 138) calls himself when roused to rage a 'chafed **boar**'. It is said of Alcibiades in *Timon of Athens* (V, i, 166) that 'like a **boar** too savage, [he] doth root up his country's peace'. Richmond in *King Richard III* (V, ii, 7) is referring to Gloster (whose crest the boar was) when he says:

> The wretched, bloody, and usurping **boar**,
> That spoil'd your summer fields and fruitful vines,
> Swills your warm blood like wash, and makes his trough
> In your embowell'd bosoms, this foul swine
> Lies now even in the centre of this isle,
> Near to the town of Leicester, as we learn:
> From Tamworth thither is but one day's march. . . .

These are but a few of the more striking of the wild boar's appearances in the plays.

But it is in the succulent long poem of *Venus and Adonis* that this raging beast has his happiest hunting ground. He is, in fact, that panting tale's tertiary character. There he is plain 'boar' and his wildness is taken for granted. But in the course of the poem he is variously called 'angry-chafing', 'blunt', 'foul', and 'urchin-snouted'.

WOLF

In a mountainous waste in Wales, where he is exiled with his brother and father, Arviragus in *Cymbeline* passes these random remarks (III, iii, 35):

> What should we speak of
> When we are old as you? when we shall hear
> The rain and wind beat dark December, how,
> In this our pinching cave, shall we discourse
> The freezing hours away? We have seen nothing:

> We are beastly; subtle as the fox for prey;
> Like warlike as the **wolf** for what we eat:
> Our valour is to chase what flies; our cage
> We make a quire, as doth the prison'd bird,
> And sing our bondage freely.

To which old Belisarius answers: 'How you speak!' And we echo: 'Passing well!' and repeat the passage by heart to anyone who tries to argue that *Cymbeline* is an ill-written play as well as an ill-constructed one.

But the immediate point is the line about the Wolf whose wild voracity among the animals is as great as that of the vulture and the cormorant among the birds. Shakespeare notes this attribute in other places. 'If thou wert the **wolf**, thy greediness would afflict thee, and oft thou shouldst hazard thy life for thy dinner,' says Timon of Athens to Apemantus (*Timon of Athens*, IV, iii, 333). And an unnamed Gentleman in *King Lear* (III, i, 4) has a magnificent speech (which is usually cut as the Gentleman himself is) in answer to Kent's simple question: 'Where's the king?':

> Contending with the fretful elements;
> Bids the wind blow the earth into the sea,
> Or swell the curled waters 'bove the main,
> That things might change or cease; tears his white hair,
> Which the impetuous blasts, with eyeless rage,
> Catch in their fury, and make nothing of;
> Strives in his little world of man to out-scorn
> The to-and-fro-conflicting wind and rain.
> This night, wherein the cub-drawn bear would couch,
> The lion and the belly-pinched **wolf**
> Keep their fur dry, unbonneted he runs,
> And bids what *will* take *all*.

Ariel is told by Prospero of the sound he made when he was imprisoned within a cloven pine (*The Tempest*, I, ii, 287): 'Thy groans did make **wolves** howl.' The Constable of France says of the English soldiery before Agincourt that 'they will eat like **wolves,** and fight like devils' (*King Henry V*, III, vii, 149). Other allusions to the wolf are plentiful. Yet nowhere does Shakespeare so well catch the beast's utterly ruthless savagery as John Webster does in the Dirge (already quoted) where various animals and birds are summoned to cover 'the friend-less bodies of unburied men', and the ten lines end with the couplet:

> But keep the **wolf** far thence, that's foe to men,
> For with his nails he'll dig them up again.

WORM AND GLOW-WORM

Allusions to the Worm (or *Lumbricus*: 'a slender, creeping, naked, limbless animal') are too numerous to be reckoned. But for its particular mention one recalls the performance of two of our major actors in some of their best parts. 'Let's talk of graves, of **worms,** and epitaphs,' said Gielgud's Richard II, almost exultant in his sorrow at his own deposition (*Richard II*, III, ii, 146). And the same actor's Hamlet put a sly and bitter humour into his explanation of what had happened to Polonius in the end: 'A certain convocation of politic **worms** are e'en at him' (*Hamlet*, IV, iii, 21).

Similarly and vividly one recalls Olivier's Mercutio very angry indeed at being stabbed and having to die: 'A plague o' both your houses! They have made **worms'**-meat of me' (*Romeo and Juliet*, III, i, 109). And, still more brilliantly, the same actor's Hotspur who died stammering over his last word which was 'worms' (*King Henry IV, Part One*, V, iv, 83):

HOTSPUR: O, I could prophesy,
But that the earthy and cold hand of death
Lies on my tongue: no, Percy, thou art dust,
And food for –   [*Dies*

PRINCE HAL: For **worms**, brave Percy: fare thee well, great heart!

On this last unforgotten and unforgettable occasion Hotspur reached the word and Prince Hal, so to speak, helped him out with it. Whether the great actor or his director first thought of this, it was enormously affecting, an inspiration.

References to the Glow-worm are few but invariably happy. Pericles himself has a charming simile (*Pericles, Prince of Tyre*, II, iii, 43): 'Like a **glow-worm** in the night, / The which hath fire in darkness, none in light.' Titania tells her fairies how to provide night-tapers (*A Midsummer Night's Dream*, III, i, 169). They must crop the waxen thighs of humble-bees 'and light them at the fiery **glow-worm's** eyes'.

Sir Hugh Evans arranging the rout in Windsor Forest at the end of *The Merry Wives of Windsor* (v, v, 79) declares: 'And twenty **glow-worms** shall our lanterns be.' And the Ghost has a marvellous way of telling Hamlet that he scents the morning air (*Hamlet*, I, v, 89):

> The **glow-worm** shows the matin to be near,
> And 'gins to pale his uneffectual fire:
> Adieu, adieu, adieu! remember me.

Incidentally, the glow-worm (*Lampyris noctiluca*) is not a worm at all, but a beetle – the only tolerable one.

WREN

The Wren (*Troglodites parvulus*) is not only the smallest of British birds, but it lays a greater number of eggs in one season than any bigger British bird. All the same, when Sir Toby Belch says of his approaching Maria (*Twelfth Night*, III, ii, 65): 'Look, where the youngest **wren** of nine comes', it is exceedingly doubtful if he is referring to the tiny bird's big egg-production. No one knows what he means exactly, and most scholars are therefore utterly silent about it. All except Scholar Hudson in the Windsor Shakespeare who comes away with the statement: 'The expression seems to have been proverbial; the wren generally laying nine or ten eggs, and the last hatched being the smallest of the brood.' Well, well!

Bottom the Weaver sings of 'the **wren** with little quill' – by which he means its musical piping (*A Midsummer Night's Dream*, III, i, 127). And King Lear in his brain-storm declares the little bird as guilty of the joy of life as any other living creature (*King Lear*, IV, vi, 113):

> The **wren** goes to't, and the small gilded fly
> Does lecher in my sight.

In another flight of fancy Gloster in *King Richard III* (I, iii, 70) goes so far as to compare the wren with the eagle:

> I cannot tell: the world is grown so bad,
> That **wrens** may prey where eagles dare not perch:
> Since every Jack became a gentleman,
> There's many a gentle person made a Jack.

But this, of course, is characteristic irony.

The true quality of the Wren is in the combination of its minuteness and its courage. Lady Macduff in *Macbeth* (IV, ii, 9) has a marvellous metaphor for this:

> . . . for the poor **wren**,
> The most diminutive of birds, will fight –
> Her young ones in her nest – against the owl.

Here one has placed the ablative-absolute clause – 'her young ones in her nest' – between dashes, deliberately. For every Lady Macduff we have ever seen or heard utters the whole sentence in a single breath. She thus makes arrant nonsense of a peculiarly beautiful image.

Still more beautiful is the plea for pity made by Imogen in *Cymbeline* (IV, ii, 302). It is a plea to the gods because Imogen has just recovered from a dead faint to find herself lying beside the headless and bleeding corpse of the rogue Cloten which is half buried in flowers:

> Good faith,
> I tremble still with fear: but if there be
> Yet left in heaven as small a drop of pity
> As a **wren's eye**, fear'd gods, a part of it!

A wren's eye!

The scene is all but unplayable in the theatre – in its bizarre mixture of the grotesque and the horrible. Here one would recommend one of the best of all theatre-books, *Ellen Terry and Bernard Shaw: a Correspondence*, for a thorough and witty discussion as to whether *Cymbeline* itself is actable or not. This discussion runs to fully thirty pages in all, and reveals how Ellen Terry's Imogen in the Lyceum revival of 1896 was obliged to cut the 'wren's eye' passage at rehearsal, and how she felt obliged to restore it on the first night and throughout the play's run. The same letters are valuable also for the way in which they communicate what must have been Ellen Terry's adorableness in the part. In her own reminiscences, *The Story of My Life* (another treasure of a theatre-book), she herself calls Imogen 'the only *inspired* performance of these later years'; and she describes the Imogen costume designed by Alma Tadema as 'one of the loveliest dresses that I ever wore'. Her photograph in that dress – with her head thrown back, a garland in her hair, and the fingers of her left hand pressed to her lips – is just about one's favourite picture of any actress in any part. Almost better than anything in *Cymbeline*, some lines from John Keats's *Ode on Melancholy* fit this picture to perfection:

> She dwells with Beauty – Beauty that must die;
> And Joy, whose hand is ever at his lips
> Bidding adieu; . . .

A wren's eye! It seems right that a book which ranges in subject between whales and Caliban, between dragons and beetles and other fearful wildfowl, should conclude with a mention of one of the smallest visible things in the whole of Nature or of Shakespeare.

PART THREE

Plants and Flowers

CONTENTS

Contents

ACONITE

The aconite is a poisonous plant of the Buttercup Family (= Ranunculaceae); and a narcotic drug formed from it and used in pharmacy is called aconitum. It is this latter which is Shakespeare's only and indirect reference to the plant itself. This occurs in *King Henry IV, Part Two*, in the scene (Act IV, Scene 4) where the King expresses his concern for the wildness of his heir, Prince Hal. The latter is absent, though two of his younger brothers are present. Of these two brothers one, Prince Humphrey of Gloucester, may be judged from the start as being neither mischievous nor a sneak:

KING: Humphrey, my son of Gloucester,
  Where is the prince your brother?
GLOUCESTER: I think he's gone to hunt, my lord, at Windsor.
KING: And how accompanied?
GLOUCESTER: I do not know, my lord.
KING: Is not his brother, Thomas of Clarence, with him?
GLOUCESTER: No, my good lord, he is in presence here.

Clarence, therefore, comes forward with his very first and perfunctory line: 'What would my lord and father?' And Henry IV – who has as much to say as his sons have little – thereupon launches on the relevant long speech which culminates in a mention of aconitum. After twenty-two lines we come to:

> And thou shalt prove a shelter to thy friends,
> A hoop of gold to bind thy brothers in,
> That the united vessel of their blood,
> Mingled with venom of suggestion
> (As, force perforce, the age will pour it in)

271

Shall never leak, though it do work as strong
As **aconitum** or rash gunpowder.

To all of this, Clarence has the single line to utter: 'I shall observe him with all care and love'. The part consists of 23 lines, one of which is probably the feeblest bit of stagecraft in the whole of Shakespeare: 'Let us withdraw into the other room.' It is true that Laurence Olivier, making at 17 his first London appearance in Shakespeare, doubled Clarence with Snare, one of the two sheriff's-officers who arrest Falstaff in Act II. But Snare has even fewer opportunities to make his mark since he has only 15 words to utter. Olivier's name was mentioned by a stage-paper which mentioned everybody else. But they got his first name wrong, spelling it with a *w*!

ALMONDS

To most of us the almond is something between a nut and a fruit. But to the Oxford Dictionary it is (somewhat Johnsonianly) 'the kernel of a drupe, the produce of the almond tree of which there are two kinds, the sweet and the bitter'. This method of definition simply sends us exploring further to discover that a 'drupe' is in its turn 'a stone fruit, a fleshy or pulpy fruit enclosing a stone or nut having a kernel, as the olive, plum, cherry'. (The word 'almond' itself is Middle English, the origin being the Old French *almande*, the still older French *alemandle*, and the Latin *amygdala*).

The dictionary gives two pleasing examples of the word as used by great English writers – (1) Dryden: 'Mark well the flowering Almonds in the Wood' and (2) Ruskin: 'Balls, or rather almonds, of purple marble.'

But Shakespeare's solitary use of the word is figurative, occurring in that rather equivocal play *Troilus and Cressida* at the very end of Act v Scene 2 when the railing Thersites is left alone after the departure of Troilus and Aeneas and Ulysses, and has a brief but intensely characteristic soliloquy in prose:

Would I could meet that rogue Diomed! I would croak like a raven; I would bode, I would bode. Patroclus would give me any thing for the intelligence of this whore; the parrot will not do more for an **almond** than he for a commodious drab. Lechery, lechery! Still wars and lechery! Nothing else holds fashion. A burning devil take them.

APPLES

Shakespeare unlike some lesser poets did not, on the whole, find the apple inspiring, either singly or in combination. He tends to consider it prosaically or proverbially, rather than as a poetical fruit or tree.

Later poets have been much more lyrical. Andrew Marvell, being rather mystical in his own Garden, could exclaim:

> What wondrous life is this I lead –
> Ripe apples drop about my head!

and at once we can hear their delicate thud as they fall. Keats could imagine his Autumn conspiring with the maturing sun 'to bend with apples the moss'd cottage-trees'. R. L. Stevenson enters with fine assurance – and one touch of genius – into the imagination of the little boy when he writes:

> The friendly cow, all red and white,
>   I love with all my heart:
> She gives me cream with all her might,
>   To eat with apple-tart.

From this it is a far cry to ages long ago, when one of the Greek dramatic poets achieved a wonderful single line that is a great poem in itself (or at least inspired his translator, Gilbert Murray, to express his single line in eight effulgent words):

The apple trees, the singing, and the gold.

After which even Shakespeare – on the subject of apples, at least – is an anti-climax. There are some fifteen references in the plays, but few are remarkable enough to quote. 'Faith, as you say, there's small choice in rotten **apples**' – Hortensio to Gremio in *The Taming of the Shrew* (i, i, 139) – has the taste and tone of an actual proverb.

'An **apple**, cleft in two, is not more twin,' says the sea-captain Antonio in *Twelfth Night* (v, i, 230) when he meets his beloved Sebastian along with the latter's sister, Viola. We hear several times of Falstaff's dislike of apple-johns, which are old and shrivelled fruits though still sound at heart (*King Henry IV, Part Two*, II, iv). The sight of Shylock reminds Antonio (*The Merchant of Venice*, I, iii, 100–102) that

> An evil soul producing holy witness
> Is like a villain with a smiling cheek –
> A goodly **apple** rotten at the heart . . .

And the self-important Porter in the penultimate scene of *King Henry VIII* has a prose castigation of the London apprentices, which wonderfully communicates a sharp sense of what Elizabethan play audiences were like: 'These are the youths that thunder at a playhouse, and fight for bitten **apples** . . .'

But there are no other apples that matter in the whole of Shakespeare. He does not appear even to have heard of it as being the 'forbidden fruit' of the Garden of Eden. He leaves that not unimportant apple to Thomas Otway who concluded the third act of *The Orphan* (1680) thus strikingly if not quite Shakespeareanly:

Woman,
Destructive, damnable, deceitful woman!
Woman to man first as a blessing given,
When innocence and love were in their prime!
Happy awhile in Paradise they lay,
But quickly woman longed to go astray;
Some foolish new adventure needs must prove,
And the first devil she saw, she changed her love;
To his temptations lewdly she inclined
Her soul, and for an apple damned mankind.

The word 'apple' is Old English and has no known European root. To the botanist it is *Pyrus Malus.*

APRICOTS

The word occurs only twice in Shakespeare, and on both occasions in the plural and in its rather engaging old spelling, 'apricock'. The Oxford Dictionary defines it as 'a stone-fruit allied to the plum, of an orange colour, roundish-oval shape, and delicious flavour'. This is well enough, though the fruit's colour is not orange, any more than it is gold or yellow. It is – apricot. The word has been traced to the Portuguese *albricoque* but may have an Arabian root. The botanical name (used as early as 1573) is *Prunus Armeniaca.*

Titania, enamoured of Bottom the Weaver turned Ass, orders her elves to treat him well:

Be kind and courteous to this gentleman,
Hop in his walks, and gambol in his eyes,
Feed him with **apricocks**, and dewberries,
With purple grapes, green figs, and mulberries . . .
(*A Midsummer Night's Dream*, III, i, 158–61)

And in *King Richard II* the Head Gardener, in the Duke of

275

York's garden at Langley, gives instructions to his two sub-
gardeners:

> Go, bind thou up yon dangling **apricocks**,
> Which, like unruly children, make their sire
> Stoop with oppression of their prodigal weight . . .

and proceeds to other comparisons with the garden and the
state of England. These are overheard by Richard's Queen
and her attendant ladies. Seeing the gardeners drawing near,
the ladies had concealed themselves behind trees, the Queen
observing: 'My wretchedness unto a row of pins. They'll talk
of state.' And talk of state they did.

Reverting to the colour of the ripe apricot, it may best be
identified with that of the edible fungus Chantarelle (Can-
tharellus Cibarius) which is not uncommon in late autumn in
the few remaining wild woods of Buckinghamshire. This
fungus, after being plucked an hour or two and carried home
to the kitchen, emits – one will swear – a faint odour of
the fruit whose colour it bears. Edward Bunyard in his
succulent book on fruit, *The Anatomy of Dessert*, does not
appear to have noticed this fact, which is all the odder because he is or was a genuine gastronomer. He writes: 'At its
best the Apricot has a certain Eastern lusciousness, a touch of
the exotic which comes strangely into our homely country.'
And he writers further and still more characteristically:

'The peculiarly rich flavour of this delicious fruit demands
some care in the selection of its accompanying wine. Port is
too stout and self-reliant, a dry sherry accords well, but best of
all, I think, a rich Sauterne. An Yquem, or, for the indigent, a
Coutet or a Suduirant, makes admirable harmony. But if a
gracious Titania is present to say

> Be kind and courteous to this gentleman,
> Feed him with **apricocks** and dewberries,

many would be willing, with a graceful gesture, to waive the question of wine.'

ASPEN

The **aspen** (*Populus Tremula*) is a small tree belonging to the large family of the willows (*Salicaceae*). It is characterized by the tremulousness of its leaves which, being borne on exceptionally long and flattened stalks, move on the slightest breeze and so give the little tree a shivering appearance. Shakespeare uses the word aspen only twice, and in both cases adjectivally and as a simile. Once in comedy, once in tragedy.

Doll Tearsheet observes that Hostess Quickly is shaking with indignant rage, and the latter replies: 'Do I? yea, in very truth, do I, an 'twere an **aspen** leaf. I cannot abide swaggerers.' (*King Henry IV Part Two*, II, iv, 103). By 'swaggerers' Hostess Quickly appears to mean, in the old sense, people who talk boastfully.

The plight of Lavinia is vastly more piteous. She is the daughter of Titus Andronicus and she has just been deflowered and mutilated by the two sons of his enemy, Tamora, the Queen of the Goths. In this dire condition she is found wandering distractedly by her uncle Marcus who remembers how her missing hands could 'tremble like **aspen** leaves upon a lute'.

Commenting upon this direful passage in *Titus Andronicus* (II, iv, 44) the learned editors of the Arden Shakespeare point out that the aspen simile occurs in literature long before Shakespeare: 'This comparison is found as early as Chaucer, *Troilus and Crisseyde* (III, 1200).' Duteously one searches this out, and finds a description of Cressida trembling in the arms of Troilus: 'Right as an aspes leaf she gan to quake', and the 'glossarial index' to Professor Skeat's edition tells us that 'asp' in Chaucer means an aspen tree. But one may go further in Chaucer and fare even better. A line describing one of the Canterbury Pilgrims – 'Lyk an aspes leaf he quook for ire' – is more expressive still for a man quaking with anger.

Incidentally, the scholars still fight shy of the question as to how much of Chaucer was known by Shakespeare, who has no mention anywhere of the earlier poet's existence or of his works. It could just possibly be that the scholars have no idea!

BARLEY

Shakespeare has two interesting references to barley. The first is in the sixteen-line address of Iris to Ceres in the masque in *The Tempest* (IV, i, 60) beginning:

> Ceres, most bounteous lady, thy rich leas
> Of wheat, rye, **barley**, vetches, oats, and pease ...

This in a lovely scene which is almost invariably thrown away on actresses who are too immature to give utterance to its richly mature imagery.

The second is in the French King's palace – in *King Henry V* (III, v) – where the high nobles express themselves as longing to fight the English invaders and so be rid of them. The Duke of Bourbon threatens, if they remain unfought, to sell his dukedom and 'buy a slobbery and a dirty farm, in that nook-shotten isle of Albion'. It sounds extremely contemptuous, 'nook-shotten'. But the scholars mainly agree that the compound adjective can mean no more than 'characterized by a highly-irregular and much-indented coast-line'. Then the High Constable of France takes over from the Duke of Bourbon and in the same swaggering vein:

> Dieu de batailles! where have they this mettle?

Is not their climate foggy, raw, and dull,
On whom, as in despite, the sun looks pale,
Killing their fruit with frowns? Can sodden water,
A drench for sur-reined jades, their **barley-broth**,
Decoct their cold blood to such valiant heat?
And shall our quick blood, spirited with wine,
Seem frosty? O, for honour of our land . . .

'Sur-reined' simply means over-ridden. But it is 'barley-broth' that gives us pause for all sorts of reasons. So many editors just give so many categorical definitions of the phrase as meaning ale or soup. Professor Dover Wilson admits dubiety, but comes to a rather muddled conclusion: 'The wine-drinking Frenchman's idea of beer, which, like the mash given to overdriven horses, is largely composed of malt'. The out-of-date editor Henry Hudson is as up-to-date and likely as any of his successors: 'Barley-broth is probably meant as a Frenchman's sneer at English ale or beer.'

Howsoever these things be, 'barley bree' in the language of Robert Burns was probably the most potent of beers, the one for which 'Willie brew'd a peck o' maut', and so gave us one of the world's supreme drinking songs though there be only twenty lines of it. The essence of the song is in its refrain:

We are na fou', we're no that fou',
  But just a drappie in our ee;
The cock may craw, the day may daw,
And aye we'll taste the barley bree.

BERRIES

The berry or berries, of a sort unspecified, get mention on half a dozen occasions, always interestingly and even picturesquely.

WSP—B

> When thou camest first,
> Thou strok'st me, and made much of me; wouldst give me
> Water with **berries** in't . . .

says Caliban to Prospero (*The Tempest* I, ii, 334) about the days
when to Prospero the monster seemed no more than a harmless slave. And later the monster suggests some of the many
things he may do for his new masters, Trinculo and Stephano,
if they will do him the honour of letting him serve them
(II, ii, 159):

> I'll show thee the best springs; I'll pluck thee **berries**;
> I'll fish for thee . . .

In a play much less familiar, the blackamoor Aaron en-
visages berries as part of the diet for the black baby which
Tamora, Queen of the Goths, has borne to him (*Titus
Andronicus*, IV, ii, 178–9):

> I'll make you feed on **berries** and on roots,
> And feast on curds and whey, and suck the goat . . .

In *Antony and Cleopatra* (I, iv, 62–8) Octavius Caesar tells us
how Antony in his soldiering days, and before his enslavement
to Cleopatra, was unfastidious in his appetite and would gladly
eat the wildest of wild fruit – 'the roughest **berry** on the
rudest hedge'. Moreover he would browse 'the barks of trees'
in snowbound country, or in the Alps would eat 'strange
flesh which some would die to look on', washing down such
non-delicacies with

> The stale of horses, and the gilded puddle
> Which beasts would cough at . . .

But not Mark Antony!
The one fine passage in which the berry is introduced as a
simile or figure of speech occurs in *A Midsummer Night's*

Dream when Helena is explaining at some length how she and her friend Hermia had hitherto been inseparable (III, ii, 208–12):

> So we grew together
> Like to a double cherry, seeming parted,
> But yet an union in partition,
> Two lovely **berries** moulded on one stem ...

Thereafter Helena involves herself in a heraldic simile which is too involved even for the scholars. But thereafter Helena is usually cut anyhow! Otherwise we should in the theatre be murmuring – like Hamlet's mother at the Player Queen – 'The lady doth protest too much, methinks'. This is how Helena goes on, when she is allowed to do so:

> So, with two seeming bodies, but one heart,
> Two of the first, like coats in heraldry,
> Due but to one, and crownèd with one crest.
> And will you rend our ancient love asunder,
> To join with men in scorning your poor friend?

BIRCH

The Oxford Dictionary defining the birch declares the word itself to be an Indo-Germanic tree-name. It also gives a charming quotation from Turner: 'BYRCHE SERVETH FOR BETYNGE OF STUBBORNE BOYES.' This was one William Turner (1520–68) who was in his time a physician, a botanist, a Fellow of Pembroke at Cambridge, and the Dean of Wells.

It is somewhat saddening to find that Shakespeare's single reference is much more to the twigs of the tree, and their punitive powers, than to the tree itself. The Duke in *Measure*

for Measure is discoursing to Friar Thomas about the sorry state
of Vienna (I, iii, 20):

> We have strict statutes and most biting laws, –
> The needful bits and curbs to headstrong steeds, –
> Which for this fourteen years we have let sleep;
> Even like an o'ergrown lion in a cave,
> That goes not out to prey. Now, as fond fathers,
> Having bound up the threatening twigs of **birch**,
> Only to stick it in their children's sight
> For terror, not to use, do find in time
> The rod more mock'd than fear'd; so our decrees,
> Dead to infliction, to themselves are dead;
> And liberty plucks justice by the nose,
> The baby beats the nurse, and quite athwart
> Goes all decorum.

It is a worthy description of a permissive society! But it tells
us nothing whatever about the birch (*Betula*) – 'most shy and
ladylike of trees' (as J. R. Lowell called it). To see birch trees
in the background of a book – their small leaves quivering,
their white bark shining – one must go as far afield as the
Sportsman's Sketches of Ivan Turgenev. They do not exist in
Shakespeare.

BLACKBERRIES OR BRAMBLES

The blackberry – (*Rubus Fruticosus*) it is called – though it is
pale green when unripe, almost a cherry-red when ripening,
and black only when it is fully ripe and eatable. It must surely
be Great Britain's most plentiful wild fruit, and it is therefore
much used for the making of jams and jellies, especially in
Scotland. The word bramble is another name for it, although
the Dictionary assures us that this may be used of any rough

prickly herb, 'especially the blackberry', but not exclusively the blackberry.

It is a little odd, therefore, that Shakespeare refers to blackberries only thrice, and then not literally but as a symbol of plenteousness, etc. Odder still that he uses the alternative word 'bramble' only once in his plays, though one may easily imagine that brambles scratched the legs of such wood-wanderers as Rosalind and Celia and Imogen and Perdita. He has one mention in his narrative poems of 'brambles' in the plural. This happens in Venus's description of the wild boar which she is trying to dissuade Adonis from hunting and thus endangering himself (lines 625–30):

> His brawny sides, with hairy bristles arm'd,
> Are better proof than thy spear's point can enter;
> His short thick neck cannot be easily harm'd;
> Being ireful, on the lion he will venture:
> The thorny **brambles** and embracing bushes,
> As fearful of him, part: through whom he rushes.

The one dramatic mention of brambles (again in the plural) occurs in *As You Like It* (III, ii, 377) when Rosalind describes Orlando's habits to his very self: 'There is a man haunts the forest, that abuses our young plants with carving Rosalind on their barks; hangs odes upon hawthorns, and elegies on **brambles**.' (Edith Evans's Rosalind used to make this speech the very ecstasy of make-believe and by-play).

The three blackberry references are less important and less vivid. Two of them occur in the same play and the same scene – Act II Scene iv of *King Henry IV, Part One*. First, Falstaff says to Prince Hal and Pointz: 'Give you a reason on compulsion! if reasons were as plenty as **blackberries**, I would give no man a reason upon compulsion, I.' A few minutes later Falstaff is whimsically pretending to Prince Hal to be the King, his father: 'If, then, thou be son to me, here lies the point: Why, being son to me, art thou so pointed at? Shall the blessed Sun of heaven prove a micher, and eat **blackberries**? A question not to be ask'd.' This is obscure, and for all the editions and editors of my acquaintance it is a question not to be answered! Instead they rush to explain that 'to mich' (the same as the Scottish 'to mooch') is to act or behave furtively, or – quite simply – to steal.

The third reference in the plays occurs in a soliloquy, in the contumelious ravings of the hard-bitten cynic Thersites (in Act v Scene iv of *Troilus and Cressida*). And here the allusion is to the berry's wildness, prevalence, and consequent cheapness: 'The policy of these crafty sneering rascals – that stale old mouse-eaten dry cheese, Nestor, and that same dog-fox, Ulysses – is not proved worth a **blackberry**.'

But to find any description of the fruit itself – of its curious intractability, for example – we must look not in Shakespeare but in the writings of the late and revered André Simon. That prince of modern gastronomers points out that the blackberry 'is as difficult to check in woods and hedges as it is to coax in gardens'. It is he, also, who tells us when it is best to eat: 'Blackberries are not necessarily ripe when black; they must be soft, as well as black, and detached without bruising. Then, and then only, are blackberries sweet and juicy and probably the best of all bush berries.'

BRANCH AND BOUGH

These two words occur fairly often, but nearly always figuratively and metaphorically. Even the Head Gardener at the heart of *King Richard II* is purely botanical only in the first place. He tells his under-gardeners to carry on with their pruning, and when he proceeds to let his tongue 'tang arguments of state' (like Malvolio) his boys, knowing him of old, are probably out of earshot, though the Queen and her Ladies overhear him to his confusion. It is true that one boy, presumably the eldest, answers the old man in kind and asks why do any gardening at all:

> When our sea-wallèd garden, the whole land,
> Is full of weeds; her fairest flowers choked up,
> Her fruit-trees all unpruned, her hedges ruin'd,
> Her knots disorder'd, and her wholesome herbs
> Swarming with caterpillars?

For this the apprentice is abruptly told to hold his peace, in so many words. And a few lines later the Head Gardener moralizes on the very act of pruning:

> All superfluous **branches**
> We lop away, that bearing **boughs** may live:
> Had *he* done so, himself had borne the crown,
> Which waste of idle hours hath quite thrown down.

Other Shakespearean mentions are fleeting. Ariel, in the last act of *The Tempest*, sings of his ambition to live like the bee 'under the blossom that hangs on the **bough**'. And Orlando in search of food (*As You Like it*, Act II Scene vii) comes upon the exiled Duke and his comrades 'under the shade of melancholy **boughs**'.

Much more evocative is the opening of one of the most striking and stricken of all the Sonnets (No. 73):

> That time of year thou mayst in me behold
> When yellow leaves, or none, or few do hang
> Upon those **boughs** which shake against the cold –

and then continues with that famous line that so magically conveys the sadness of still autumn:

> Bare ruin'd choirs, where late the sweet birds sang.

BUDS

A great and moving poem in itself is the third line of Shakespeare's Sonnet No. 18:

> Rough winds do shake the darling **buds** of May

The word 'bud' is endearing, like the names of other young and tender things in nature – 'chick' and 'duckling', for example, and 'kitten' and 'cub' and 'foal'. Yet Shakespeare makes surprisingly little of the word in other places – even in its purely literal significance – the rudiment of a branch, cluster of leaves, or blossom.

Three times over in one play, *The Two Gentlemen of Verona*, the *bud* is diseased – three times in one scene, oddly enough (I, i, 8 44–50): 'as in the sweetest **bud**, the eating canker dwells'. And: 'as the most forward **bud** is eaten by the canker ere it blow'. And: 'blasting in the **bud**, losing his verdure even in the prime'. Titania, in *A Midsummer Night's Dream*, appoints her fairies on various tasks: 'Some to kill cankers in the musk-rose **buds.**' (II, ii, 3). Viola, in more famous lines, tells her Duke of her imaginary sister (*Twelfth Night*, II, iv, 114):

> She never told her love,
> But let concealment, like a worm i' the **bud**,
> Feed on her damask cheek.

And Cleopatra has a very striking image which one has never known any stage Cleopatra to deliver really tellingly, uttered when a messenger from Antony arrives without due ceremony (III, xiii, 40):

> See, my women!
> Against the blown rose may they stop their nose
> That kneel'd unto the **buds**.

Elsewhere in English literature most of the poets seem curiously insusceptible to the charm of the little word, though one continually astonishing prose-playwright makes persistent use of it as a pet name. This is William Wycherley, and the character who uses it is the sex-starved Mrs Pinchwife, the Country Wife, who uses it to her aged and jealous husband *sans cesse*, and with a charm that is a strong part of her outrageous character. Her very first utterance to him in the comedy is: 'O my dear, dear **bud**, welcome home! Why dost thou look so fropish? Who has nangered thee?' At the very height of the disgraceful action she says to him: 'O Lord, O Lord, you are such a passionate man, **bud**!' And her very last remark to him is: 'Yes, indeed, **bud**.'

But this, of course, is prose, and the plainest, homeliest prose. Shakespeare nowhere uses the word as a pet name. It is as though, in his youth, he was content to have given it its apotheosis, in the purely botanical sense, in the great sonnet (No. 18) that begins:

> Shall I compare thee to a summer's day?
> Thou art more lovely and more temperate:
> Rough winds do shake the darling **buds** of May,
> And summer's lease hath all too short a date . . .

Juliet, bidding Romeo goodnight, is no less exquisite (II, ii, 121):

> This **bud** of love, by summer's ripening breath,
> May prove a beauteous flower when next we meet.

BURDOCKS AND DOCKS

These are coarse and rank blooms that sometimes occur in the chaplets that wander-witted Shakespearean characters, like

Lear and Ophelia, tend to put around their brows or their shoulders. Burdock is one such, and it is an extreme example of variation in the various editions of the text. In most (but not all) modern editions it occurs spelt thus, and is usually (but not always) in the plural. These are the lines which Cordelia utters when her distraught father is reported as having been seen (*King Lear* IV, iv, 1–6):

> Alack, 'tis he: why, he was met even now
> As mad as the vex'd sea; singing aloud;
> Crown'd with rank fumiter and furrow-weeds,
> With **burdocks**, hemlock, nettles, cuckoo-flowers,
> Darnel, and all the idle weeds that grow
> In our sustaining corn.

Who first decided upon the variant of 'burdock' or 'burdocks', and why did he so? The word in the First and Second Quartos is 'hor-docks'; in the First Folio it is 'hardokes'; in a George Steevens edition (of 1805) it is 'harlocks', but is given a footnote: 'A typographical error for "charlock" or wild mustard.'

The Oxford Dictionary says that 'hardock' is 'some coarse weed, probably burdock'; that harlock is 'some flower not identified – it cannot well be either "hardock" or "charlock".' A certain impatience with the complacency of editors makes one echo Sam Weller saying to the Judge: 'That depends upon the taste and fancy of the speller, my Lord.' Can Shakespearean editing in such cases be a similar matter of taste and fancy?

Plain docks, the unspecified sort, occur twice elsewhere in Shakespeare – and on both occasions as an individual specimen in a kind of wild untended garden. Thus in *The Tempest* two somewhat tedious characters discuss between them what might be grown on the island on which they are shipwrecked.

'Had I plantation of this isle, my lord . . .' says old Gonzalo, and the two interrupt him, Antonio to say that he (Gonzalo) would 'sow it with nettle-seed', and Sebastian adds: 'Or **docks**, or mallows' (II, i, 141). More interesting and pertinent by far is the Duke of Burgundy in *King Henry V* (v, ii, 50), complaining bitterly and at length, that war has laid waste the crops and gardens of his fair land so that

> The even mead . . .
> Wanting the scythe, all uncorrected, rank,
> Conceives by idleness, and nothing teems
> But hateful **docks**, rough thistles, kecksies, burs,
> Losing both beauty and utility.

The kecksy is a very old dialect word for a hollow stem, or a plant with such a stem.

It is a little sad that Shakespeare has nowhere any mention of the dandelion either by itself or in combination with the burdock. That old-fashioned drink, dandelion and burdock, said to be an infusion of these two herbs, is still to be purchased – though it grows rarer with the years – in little village shops in South Wales and a few other parts of Britain, mostly in the north. Old herbalists recommend, as a sure cure for dropsy, an ounce of dried burdock-root if it be added to two pints of boiling water which must then be boiled down to one pint in all.

BURNET

The burnet is any plant belonging to the genera Sanguisorba and Poterium (natural order, Rosaceae), as the Great or Common Burnet, the Lesser or Salad Burnet. The dictionary mentions also the Burnet Rose and defines it as the 'Scotch Rose' (*Rosa Spinosissima*), and one remembers it in an Ayrshire childhood as a creamy-white variant of the dog-rose with a much richer fragrance.

But Shakespeare mentions an unspecified or unparticularized burnet – and that only once. It is in the Duke of Burgundy's catalogue in *King Henry V* (v, ii, 45–9), where it is ranked among the refined sort of weeds as distinct from the coarser sort that includes the docks:

> The even mead, that erst brought sweetly forth
> The freckled cowslip, **burnet**, and green clover,
> Wanting the scythe, all uncorrected, rank,
> Conceives by idleness, and nothing teems,
> But hateful docks . . .

BUSH AND BRAKE

Both words have so many meanings that it would be as well to concentrate on the purely vegetative. Even so, both are ill-defined. A bush is something halfway between a plant and a tree, and a brake is a clump of bushes, brushwood, or briers.

Both are much in evidence in *A Midsummer Night's Dream*. Peter Quince, both as director and as property man, says that Moonshine might best be represented by one who must come in with 'a **bush** of thorns and a lanthorn' (III, i, 61). Puck follows the scared players 'thorough bog, thorough **bush**, thorough brier' (III, i, 110). Theseus tells us how the poet and lover tends to give rein to imagination: 'How easy is a **bush** supposed a bear!' (v, i, 22). Demetrius threatens to desert Helena in the wild woods (II, i, 227–8):

> I'll run from thee and hide me in the **brakes**,
> And leave thee to the mercy of wild beasts.

It is a brake that is used for wings or dressing-room by the Athenian Thespians. Thus Quince says to his leading man: 'Pyramus, you begin: when you have spoken your speech, enter into that **brake** – and so every one according to his cue' (III, i, 69–71). And it was in that same brake that Puck caught Pyramus and made an Ass of him (III, ii, 15).

In a much less familiar play, Part III of *King Henry VI*, two keepers in a chase in the north of England propose to lie in wait for deer: 'Under this thick-grown **brake** we'll shroud ourselves' (III, i, 1). And the King in the same play voices Shakespeare's sympathy for wingèd creatures in fear and trouble (v, vi, 13–14):

> The bird that hath been limèd in a **bush**,
> With trembling wings misdoubteth every **bush**.

A line uttered by Tamora, Queen of the Goths, is one of the few gleams of light in that dark satanic play, *Titus Andronicus* (II, iii, 12): 'The birds chant melody on every **bush**.'

Bushes, naturally enough, abound in the Forest of Arden. Touchstone, in *As You Like It*, is just about to say to his unblushing bride:

> Come, sweet Audrey,
> We must be married, or we must live in bawdry

when his philosopher-friend Jaques gives him good counsel: 'Will you, being a man of your breeding, be married under a **bush** like a beggar?' (III, iii, 78). And it is another bush, in another part of the forest, which harbours the two improbable animals, a reptile and a lioness, which occasion so complete a change – astonishing even in Shakespeare – in the character of Oliver, Orlando's elder brother. He describes this quite incredible double-incident to Rosalind and Celia, in the third person, too, to make the incredible business preposterous as well. One thought so at the age of twelve, and one thinks so still (IV, iii, 106–120):

> A wretched raggèd man o'ergrown with hair,
> Lay sleeping on his back; about his neck
> A green and gilded snake had wreathed itself,
> Who with her head nimble in threats approached
> The opening of his mouth; but suddenly
> Seeing Orlando, it unlinked itself,
> And with indented glides did slip away
> Into a **bush**: under which **bush**'s shade
> A lioness, with·udders all drawn dry,
> Lay couching, head on ground, with catlike watch,
> When that the sleeping man should stir; for 'tis
> The royal disposition of that beast
> To prey on nothing that doth seem as dead;
> This seen, Orlando did approach the man,
> And found it was his brother, his elder brother.

What sort of a man is he who can so describe how he was all but swallowed by a snake and all but mauled by a desiccated lioness? Surely there must be high scorn and laughter in Rosalind's first rejoinder: 'But, to Orlando: did he leave him there, Food to the sucked and hungry lioness?' However, Oliver produces the napkin stained with Orlando's blood; Rosalind faints clean away; and Arden's itself again.

CAMOMILE

The camomile is a plant of the order Compositae, which means of the daisy family. In botanical jargon, it is 'a plant the head of whose flower is made up of many florets sessile on a common receptacle, and surrounded by a common involucre of bracts'. It is also *Anthemis Nobilis*, a creeping herb with downy leaves and flowers white in the ray and yellow in the disk.

Shakespeare in his sole mention of the camomile tells us, in a single line, much about its nature but nothing about its appearance. This is in *King Henry IV*, *Part One* (II, iv, 380 *et seq.*) where Falstaff is talking to Prince Hal in the style and manner of his father, the King:

'Harry, I do not only marvel where thou spendest thy time, but also how thou art accompanied: for though the **camomile**, the more it is trodden on, the faster it grows, yet youth, the more it is wasted, the sooner it wears. That thou art my son, I have partly thy mother's word, partly my own opinion; but chiefly a villainous trick of thine eye, and a foolish hanging of thy nether lip, that doth warrant me. If, then, thou be son to me, here lies the point: Why, being son to me, art thou so pointed at?' And so on, in gorgeous fooling.

Those who saw our last great Falstaff – Sir Ralph Richardson away back in 1944 – must often wonder why he has never consented or been cajoled into recording his performance. A richer fulfilment of the part is not in living memory. Sir Ralph came mighty close to Leigh Hunt's ideal of Falstaff: 'Above all things witty and festive, unable to admit care or to give it, making his moral enormities appear as natural and jovial a part of him as his fat; in short, a perpetual feast to himself and to his beholders.' But then Leigh Hunt went on to say that he had never beheld his ideal Falstaff on the boards.

CARNATIONS

This word carnation is, oddly enough, primarily a colour in Shakespeare, though the colour is clearly that which may belong to the flower itself, a bright rosy pink or flesh-colour.

''A could never abide **carnation**; 'twas a colour he never liked,' says Mistress Pistol rather cryptically of Falstaff at his death and when she, presumably, had laid him out. There are plenty of persons who consider pink to be a displeasing colour, especially in its more shocking shades. And it is conceivable that the Hostess is declaring the dead Falstaff to have been one such, in this famous little scene in *King Henry V* (II, iii). But it is important to note that the Hostess's remark is a non-sequitur arising from her misunderstanding of the Boy's remark immediately preceding her own, to the effect that Falstaff in dying had declared women to be 'devils incarnate'. Those who saw the Olivier film version of the play will easily recall seeing the great veteran comedian George Robey, as Falstaff, dying in mime while these verbal exchanges were made.

The one place where Shakespeare mentions the carnation, alternating it with its older name of gillivor or gillyflower, is in *The Winter's Tale* just before Perdita's illustrious set-piece about flowers of spring. (This is in Act IV, Scene iii, though in some editions Scene iv). Her interlocutor is Polixenes, who is unaware that the girl is the long-lost daughter of his friend Leontes.

> PER.:   Sir, the year growing ancient –
> Not yet on summer's death, nor on the birth
> Of trembling winter, the fairest flowers o' the season
> Are our **carnations** and streak'd gillivors,
> Which some call nature's bastards: of that kind
> Our rustic garden's barren; and I care not
> To get slips of them.
> POL.:   Wherefore, gentle maiden,
> Do you neglect them?
> PER.:   For I have heard it said
> There is an art which in their piedness shares

With great creating nature.
POL.:   Say there be;
Yet nature is made better by no mean,
But nature makes that mean . . .
PER.:   So it is.
POL.: Then make your garden rich in gillyvors,
And do not call them bastards.
PER.:   I'll not put
The dibble in earth to set one slip of them;
No more than were I painted I would wish
This youth should say 'twere well, and only therefore
Desire to breed by me.

But the whole uncut passage is so abstruse in its reasoning
that the scholars tend to ignore it, characteristically, as re-
quiring no reasoning. Its conclusion would seem to make even
the admired Perdita seem pert and forward, until she arrives
at her list of more congenial flowers in the course of the same
scene.

One editor, M. R. Ridley, of the New Temple Edition,
faces up to the abstruse argument about nature and art, and
about the flowers of winter and spring. But his note itself
would seem to require further elucidation: 'Perdita's trouble
is that she disliked the autumn (middle-aged) flowers which
would suit them, and so has to approximate with winter
flowers. Both carnations and gillyflowers were traditionally
connected with wantonness.'

More relevant and immensely more helpful than any of the
editors is the late Dr Caroline Spurgeon in her astonishing
book, *Shakespeare's Imagery* (1935): 'He has a great number of
images drawn from grafting – a new process in his time – and
was clearly immensely interested in its possibilities and
results, being led to wonder, with Polixenes (*The Winter's Tale*,
IV, iv, 79–97), if such marvels of control and improvement

WSP–C

may be achieved by scientific cross-breeding in plants and flowers, why not also in the human race?'

CEDAR

That dignified tree, the cedar (*Pinus Cedrus*), is mentioned a round dozen of times by Shakespeare and more than once used as a symbol of ancient and lofty lineage. Thus Gloster in *King Richard III* (I, iii, 263–5) exclaims:

> I was born so high,
> Our aery buildeth in the **cedar**'s top,
> And dallies with the wind, and scorns the sun –

lines that have proved the undoing of more than one ordinarily born actor who has depicted Richard as a mere demon of melodrama.

Titus says to his brother, the tribune in *Titus Andronicus* (IV, iii, 45–8):

> Marcus, we are but shrubs, no **cedars** we,
> No big-boned men fram'd of the Cyclops' size;
> But metal, Marcus, steel to the very back . . .

Archbishop Cranmer in the presence of the Princess Elizabeth foresees some future ruler of England in *King Henry VIII* (v, v, 52–5):

> He shall flourish,
> And, like a mountain **cedar**, reach his branches
> To all the plains about him. Our children's children
> Shall see this, and bless heaven.

Dumain in *Love's Labour's Lost* (IV, iii, 86) thinks of his mistress's character as well as her carriage when he calls her 'as

upright as the **cedar**'. The soothsayer utters words of sooth
to the ancient king at the end of *Cymbeline* when he says
(v, v, 454–8):

> The lofty **cedar**, royal Cymbeline,
> Personates thee: and thy lopp'd branches point
> Thy two sons forth; who, by Belarius, stol'n,
> For many years thought dead, are now reviv'd,
> To the most majestic **cedar** join'd, whose issue
> Promises Britain peace and plenty.

(He also does his best to tidy up Shakespeare's worst last act).

In *King Henry VI, Part Two* the Earl of Warwick goes nobly
into battle with the words (v, ii, 204–7):

> This day I'll wear aloft my burgonet,
> As on a mountain top the **cedar** shows
> That keeps his leaves in spite of any storm,
> Even to affright thee with the view thereof.

In *King Henry VI, Part Three* another Earl of Warwick goes
no less nobly into another battle knowing he will not return
(v, ii, 8–12):

> My blood, my want of strength, my sick heart shows,
> That I must yield my body to the earth,
> And, by my fall, the conquest to my foe,
> Thus yields the **cedar** to the axe's edge,
> Whose arms gave shelter to the princely eagle.

Prospero (in *The Tempest*, v, i, 46–8) gives, among the
instances of his 'so potent art' as a magician, this example:

> ... the strong-based promontory
> Have I made shake, and by the spurs pluck'd up
> The pine and **cedar** ...

And, finally, there is Coriolanus saying very superbly to his

mother Volumnia when he finds her on her knees at his feet
(*Coriolanus*, v, iii, 56–62):

> What's this?
> Your knees to me? to your corrected son?
> Then let the pebbles on the hungry beach
> Fillip the stars; then, let the mutinous winds
> Strike the proud **cedars** gainst the fiery sun;
> Murdering impossibility, to make
> What cannot be, slight work.

Then, what was it that was 'like the sough of the wind
through cedars'? It was the voice of Edmund Kean's Othello
in the play's third act, according to William Hazlitt.

CHAPLETS, GARLANDS, NOSEGAYS

The Clown in the pastoral heart of the play (*The Winter's Tale*,
IV, iii, 44) tells us that his sister has made 'four-and-twenty
nosegays for the shearers'.

Titania tells Oberon that his quarrel with her is seriously
affecting the weather and the seasons:

> '. . . hoary-headed frosts
> Fall in the fresh lap of the crimson rose,
> And on old Hiems' thin and icy crown
> An odorous **chaplet** of sweet summer buds
> Is, as in mockery, set; the spring, the summer,
> The childing autumn, angry winter, change
> Their wonted liveries; and the mazèd world
> By their increase now knows not which is which . . .'

(*A Midsummer Night's Dream*, II, i, 107–14) *Hiems* is winter,
and *childing* signifies fruitful.

Silvia is hailed in another play's famous song, sweetly set by Schubert in course of time:

> She excels each mortal thing
> Upon the dull earth dwelling;
> To her let us **garlands** bring.
>
> (*Two Gentlemen of Verona*, IV, ii, 50–2)

Richard Crookback threatens to storm a princess into matrimony:

> Bound with triumphant **garlands** will I come
> And lead thy daughter to a conqueror's bed ...
>
> (*King Richard III*, IV, iv, 339–40)

Ophelia's suicide is described by Queen Gertrude in a kind of unhappy ecstasy:

> There is a willow grows aslant a brook,
> That shows his hoar leaves in the glassy stream:
> There with fantastic **garlands** did she make
> Of crow-flowers, nettles, daisies, and long purples,
> That liberal shepherds give a grosser name,
> But our cold maids do dead men's fingers call them.
>
> (*Hamlet*, IV, vii, 167–72)

And Sir Hugh Evans, a Welsh parson in Windsor, cures himself of woe and worry by singing an old song of Christopher Marlowe – that 'dead shepherd' whom Shakespeare quotes more than once:

> There shall I make thee beds of roses,
> And a thousand fragrant **posies** ...
> By shallow rivers to whose falls
> Melodious birds sing madrigals.
>
> (*The Merry Wives of Windsor*, III, i, 18–19)

CHERRIES

Shakespeare uses this word cherry with a curious persistence (and with a marked variety of meanings) throughout *A Midsummer Night's Dream*. Thus young Demetrius in the forest, waking from the sleep during which Puck has poured a love-philtre into his eyes, is reminded of this fruit on first seeing the soft lips of Helena (III, ii, 140):

> O, how ripe in show
> Thy lips, those kissing **cherries**, tempting grow!

A little later on, in the same scene, Helena reproaches her friend Hermia for drifting away from her when they had always been inseparable (III, ii, 208–11):

> So we grew together,
> Like to a double **cherry**, seeming parted;
> But yet an union in partition,
> Two lovely berries moulded on one stem.

Much later on, in the grotesque play within the play, Francis Flute, who was chosen to play the heroine Thisbe, was clearly much more at ease in mending bellows (his profession) than in learning his lines. He addresses Wall well enough though already with some hint of extemporizing (v, i, 186–9):

> O wall, how often hast thou heard my moans,
> For parting my fair Pyramus and me,
> My **cherry** lips have often kiss'd thy stones;
> Thy stones with lime and hair knit up in thee.

But in her death scene this Thisbe is word-imperfect to the very verge of disaster (v, i, 318–24):

These lily lips,
This **cherry** nose,
These yellow cowslip cheeks
Are gone, are gone;
Lovers make moan;
His eyes were green – as leeks.

In very different vein is the reference in *King John*. This is
usually dismissed by critics as 'a dull play with some marvellous things in it', and one of the marvellous things (both as
poetry and as psychology) is surely the scene in which Prince
Arthur is teased into the shedding of tears by his mocking and
wrangling women-relatives. This scene has had insufficient
praise from the literary critics, and hardly any at all from the
dramatic critics. And one gives it here, though **cherry** comes
into it only as symbolizing something trivial and worthless
(II, i, 159–82):

QUEEN ELINOR: Come to thy grandam, child.
CONSTANCE: Do, child, go to it' grandam, child;
  Give grandam kingdom, and it' grandam will
  Give it a plum, a **cherry**, and a fig,
  There's a good grandam.
ARTHUR: Good my mother, peace!
  I would that I were low laid in my grave;
  I am not worth this coil that's made for me.
QUEEN ELINOR: His mother shames him so, poor boy, he weeps.
CONSTANCE: Now shame upon you, whether she does or no!
  His grandam's wrongs, and not his mother's shames,
  Draw those heaven-moving pearls from his poor eyes,
  Which heaven shall take in nature of a fee;
  Ay, with these crystal beads shall heaven be brib'd
  To do him justice, and revenge on you.
QUEEN ELINOR: Thou monstrous slanderer of heaven and earth!
CONSTANCE: Thou monstrous injurer of heaven and earth!
  Call me not slanderer; thou and thine usurp

The dominations, royalties and rights
Of this oppress'd boy; this is thy eld'st son's son,
Unfortunate in nothing but in thee;
Thy sins are visited in this poor child,
The canon of the law is laid on him,
Being but the second generation
Removèd from thy sin-conceiving womb.
KING JOHN: Bedlam, have done.

Bedlam? The reading is seldom queried. But one prefers 'beldam' which is, after all, what Macbeth called the Witches (III, v, 2) on one occasion.

In the endlessly lush narrative poem of *Venus and Adonis* (lines 1099–104) the goddess has her delectable description of how her beautiful youth was admired by the fishes and the birds:

When he beheld his shadow in the brook,
The fishes spread on it their golden gills;
When he was by, the birds such pleasure took,
That some would sing, some other in their bills
    Would bring him mulberries and ripe-red **cherries**;
    He fed them with his sight, they him with berries.

It is like the painting of Piero di Cosimo and of Jean Renoir in their so different ages. It is sensuality's very self in verse. It is Shakespeare in his teens.

CLOVE AND COLOQUINTIDA

Botanically a clove is a flower-bud, and coloquintida is the spongey and very bitter pulp of a gourd-like fruit. More particularly, the clove is the dried flower-bud of *Caryophyllus Aromaticus* and is much used as a pungent aromatic spice. (Time was when an apple pie was not a complete thing without its cloves.) And coloquintida, or colocynth, is the Bitter Apple (*Citrullus Colocynthis*) with this decidedly bitter pulp that has its uses as a purgative drug.

The only reference to a clove in Shakespeare is slight. It crops up in a would-be witty passage in *Love's Labour's Lost* and is promptly snuffed out in a feeble pun (v, ii, 649–53). The passage is one of the innumerable interruptions to a pageant of *The Nine Worthies* which is being staged by three unworthy actors – the Spaniard Don Armado, Moth his page, and Sir Nathaniel the schoolmaster. Don Armado delivers no more than a line and a half of the part of Hector when he is interrupted:

> ARMADO: The armipotent Mars, of lances the almighty,
>   Gave Hector a gift, –
> DUMAIN: A gilt nutmeg.
> BIRON: A lemon.
> LONGAVILLE: Stuck with **cloves**.
> DUMAIN: No, cloven.
> ARMADO: Peace! –
>   The armipotent Mars, of lances the almighty, etc. etc.

Armado's rebuke in the single word 'Peace!' is superb and justified.

The only reference in Shakespeare to coloquintida is, on the other hand, far from slight or trivial (*Othello*, I, iii). Spoken to Roderigo, it is an early intimation of Iago's evil purpose with regard to Desdemona's chances of lasting bliss: 'These Moors are changeable in their wills . . . the food that to him now is as luscious as locusts shall be to him shortly as bitter as **coloquintida.** She must change for youth: when she is sated with his body, she will find the error of her choice . . .'

COWSLIPS

'In a **cowslip**'s bell I lie,' sings Ariel in *The Tempest* (v, i, 89), reminding us that the sprite was no bigger than a fairy. 'The **cowslips** tall her pensioners be,' says the Fairy who encounters Puck, and tells him of Titania; adding a moment later:

> I must go seek some dewdrops here,
> And hang a pearl in every **cowslip**'s ear

(*A Midsummer Night's Dream*, II, i, 10 and 14–15)

The outdoor-minded Burgundy in *King Henry V* notes that 'the freckled **cowslip**, burnet, and green clover' used to prosper in the meads of France in time of peace (v, ii, 49). But the indoor-minded Iachimo in *Cymbeline* (II, ii, 37–42) is reminded of the same flower only by a feature on the left breast of the sleeping Imogen:

> On her left breast
> A mole cinque-spotted, like the crimson drops
> I' the bottom of a **cowslip**; here's a voucher
> Stronger than ever law could make; this secret
> Will force him think I have pick'd the lock, and ta'en
> The treasure of her honour.

It is all the less pleasant to have to record that the cowslip – this well-loved member of the Primulaceae, this favoured flower of little children as well as of Shakespeare's fairies – has a name of quite base and lowly origin. The direct source of the word is the Old English *cú-slyppe* which signifies 'cow-slobber' and – however one may hesitate to make the divulgement – 'cow-dung'. The Scottish version of the latter, 'cooclap', has at the very least an onomatopoetic quality.

CUCKOO-BUDS AND CUCKOO-FLOWERS

Several common-or-garden flowers receive from Shakespeare only what we may call catalogue mention: they occur – and are given no more than their names – in those lists that certain characters detail on occasion.

Thus Perdita, near the end of her particular and justly celebrated flower-piece, merely mentions 'bold oxlips and the crown imperial – Lilies of all kinds, the flower-de-luce being one'. (*The Winter's Tale*, IV, iv, 126–7).

Cordelia tells us her distracted old father wore 'hemlock, nettles, **cuckoo-flowers**, darnel, and all the idle weeds that grow in our sustaining corn' (*King Lear*, IV, iv, 4–6).

One of the few pleasant features of the equivocal (and un-named) Queen in *Cymbeline* is her behest to a servant: 'The violets, cowslips, and the primroses, Bear to my closet' (I, v, 84–5).

The 'fantastic garlands' that the demented Ophelia fashioned for herself included 'crow-flowers, nettles, daisies, and long purples . . .' (*Hamlet*, IV, vii, 169).

And the Song of Spring at the end of *Love's Labour's Lost* (v, ii, 884–8) could hardly be more vernal in its opening:

> When daisies pied, and violets blue,
> And lady-smocks all silver white
> And **cuckoo-buds** of yellow hue
> Do paint the meadows with delight.

Buttercups (which are 'cuckoo-buds of yellow hue') do still paint the meadows with delight in the mile or so between Stratford-on-Avon and the village of Shottery; and it is impossible in a summer dawn, when there are no tourists or professors around, not to yield wholeheartedly to the fancy that a great young poet, with such a song in his heart and on his lips, went wooing in that direction nearly four hundred years ago.

CYPRESS

The cypress tree not being indigenous to Britain it is quite possible that Shakespeare never set eyes on one. The word cypress itself does not appear to stir him to lyrical ecstasy. He leaves to lesser and later poets the celebration of this sad, straight pointer up to heaven. To Byron who addressed it thus in *The Giaour:*

> Dark tree, still sad when others' grief is fled,
> The only constant mourner o'er the dead.

To Tennyson in his high hall-garden:

> Now sleeps the crimson petal, now the white;
> Nor waves the cypress in the palace walk . . .

To Matthew Arnold addressing some mystical maidens:

> Pluck, pluck cypress, O pale maidens:
> Dusk, O dusk the hall with yew!

To Poe in one poem, *Ulalume,* whose title is a poem in itself:

> Here once, through an alley Titanic
> Of cypress, I roamed with my soul –
> Of cypress, with Psyche, my Soul.

But to Shakespeare this is only the tree from whose hard black wood coffins are made, and whose twigs are used for funeral sprays. The Duke of Suffolk in *King Henry VI, Part Two* (III, ii, 321-4) includes it in his curse upon his enemies:

Poison be their drink!
Gall, worse than gall, the daintiest that they taste!
Their sweetest shade, a grove of **cypress** trees!
Their chiefest prospect, murdering basilisks!

And, far better known, Feste the Clown in *Twelfth Night* (ii, iv, 51–2) has his sorrowful song:

Come away, come away, death,
And in sad **cypress** let me be laid ...

But here again it is the coffin that is in the song-writer's thoughts, not the tree.

DAFFODILS

It is odd that this golden favourite among flowers is mentioned only twice by Shakespeare, and both in the same act of the same play, though by two very different characters. Autolycus in *The Winter's Tale* (iv, ii, 1–2) begins one of his characteristic songs – irresponsibility's very self – with the three lines:

When **daffodils** begin to peer, –
With hey! the doxy over the dale, –
Why, then comes in the sweet o' the year ...

And Perdita (iv, iii, 118–20) magically conjures the flower's essence in a clause of only sixteen words:

golden **daffodils**,
That come before the swallow dares, and take
The winds of March with beauty ...

Critical comment is hushed into silence.

The derivation of the word 'daffodil' itself is mysterious and unsatisfactory.

DAISIES

It is yet another instance of the poet's genius to have his mad
Ophelia proffer a single daisy to her brother, and then go on
immediately to give a plain and lacerating hint of the reason
for her condition: 'There's a **daisy**, I would give you some
violets, but they wither'd all when my father died ...'
(*Hamlet*, IV, v, 181). There is mention of daisies again at
Ophelia's drowning and in the Spring Song at the end of
Love's Labour's Lost (See under CUCKOO-BUDS AND
CUCKOO-FLOWERS).

Much less familiar is the occurrence of the daisy in a simile
concerning the white hand of Lucrece as it lay exposed on her
bed-cover in the eye of the guilty Tarquin (*The Rape of Lucrece*,
lines 393–5).

> Without the bed her other fair hand was,
> On the green coverlet; whose perfect white
> Show'd like an April **daisy** on the grass ...

And the rare adjectival form of the word occurs in
Cymbeline (IV, ii, 400–2) when the Roman captain proposes to
dig a grave for the youth who is dead or presumed dead:

> The boy hath taught us manly duties; let us
> Find out the prettiest **daisied** plot we can,
> And make him with our pikes and partisans
> A grave ...

DARNEL

A form of the Italian Rye-Grass, said to be now 'a rare casual'.
Shakespeare's Joan of Arc (or 'La Pucelle' in *King Henry VI*,

Part One) tells an assembly of noblemen that this weed has contaminated the corn (III, ii, 41–4):

> Good morrow, gallants, want you corn for bread?
> I think the Duke of Burgundy will fast
> Before he'll buy again at such a rate:
> 'Twas full of **darnel**; do you like the taste?

and for her impudence is called by the Duke 'vile fiend and shameless courtezan' and 'hag of all despite'.

The much more botanical-minded Duke of Burgundy in *King Henry V* (v, ii, 45) includes darnel among the weeds which have turned rank the fair land of France:

> ... her fallow leas,
> The **darnel**, hemlock, and rank fumitory
> Doth root upon ...

(But see also BURDOCKS AND DOCKS).

EGLANTINE

When – in *A Midsummer Night's Dream* – the King of the Fairies tells us that he knows a flowery bank in the forest (II, i, 251–2):

> Quite over-canopied with luscious **woodbine**,
> With sweet musk-roses, and with **eglantine** ...

he is guilty of a kind of hendiadys which – the dictionary assures us – is a rhetorical figure in which two different words are used for one object, for example, last will and testament. For no ordinary dictionary – as distinct from a specialized botanical one – differentiates between those two forms of fragrant sweet-brier!

That much more difficult play, *Cymbeline*, has the only other mention of eglantine in Shakespeare – occurring where the tortuous-tongued youth, Arviragus, is telling us of the various flowers with which he proposes to sweeten the sad grave of Imogen. He includes (iv, ii, 224):

> The leaf of **eglantine**, whom not to slander,
> Outsweeten'd not thy breath ...

ELDER

Shakespeare's few references to this low-growing, creamy-blossomed tree (*Sambucus*) are all unexpectedly sinister. In *Titus Andronicus* (ii, iv, 270–2) that ignoble Roman, Saturninus, reads aloud a letter to the effect that his brother Bassianus has been murdered and buried near a spot where he is reading:

> Look for thy reward
> Among the nettles at the **elder-tree**
> Which overshades the mouth of that same pit
> Where we decreed to bury Bassianus.

In *Love's Labour's Lost* (v, ii, 602) we have Biron interrupting the inset play of *The Nine Worthies* to point out that Judas (Maccabaeus not Iscariot) was 'hanged on an **elder**'.

And in *Cymbeline* we again have the tortuous-minded Arviragus coming away with a cryptic remark to his brother Guiderius (iv, ii, 59–61):

> Grow, patience!
> And let the stinking **elder**, grief, untwine
> His perishing root with the increasing vine!

No scholar of our acquaintance even tries to explain this

intricate language. But the supposed father of the young men, Belarius, puts a stop to the dialogue with the crystal-clear next line: 'It is great morning. Come, away!'

ELM

Shakespeare's two most striking references to the elm (*Ulmus Campestris*) both concern its habit of intertwining itself with other more or less parasitic, or at least climbing, plants. In these cases the intertwiners are the vine and the ivy.

Thus in *The Comedy of Errors* (II, ii, 170–7) Adriana, mistaking Antipholus of Syracuse for her husband (his twin-brother, Antipholus of Ephesus), declares:

> Come, I will fasten on this sleeve of thine:
> Thou art an **elm**, my husband, – I a vine
> Whose weakness married to thy stronger state,
> Makes me with thy strength to communicate:
> If aught possess thee from me, it is dross,
> Usurping ivy, brier, or idle moss;
> Who, all for want of pruning, with intrusion
> Infect thy sap, and live on thy confusion.

Thus, also, in *A Midsummer Night's Dream* (IV, i, 39–44) Titania, Queen of the Fairies, entwines herself with Bottom the Weaver turned into an Ass, and does so with a kind of pre-eminent single-mindedness, saying:

> Fairies be gone, and be a while away –
> Sleep thou, and I will wind thee in my arms:
> So doth the woodbine the sweet honeysuckle
> Gently entwist; the female ivy so
> Enrings the barky fingers of the **elm**.
> O, how I love thee! how I dote on thee! –

WSP–D

which is immediately followed by the stage direction, *They Sleep.*

FENNEL

'There's **fennel** for you, and columbines,' says Ophelia in her scene of madness, and is here generally supposed to be addressing King Claudius since both plants are supposed – without much warrant – to be 'significant of cajolery and ingratitude'. Thus, anyhow, one old editor, Henry Hudson. Newer editors tend to avoid the issue, seeming to consider 'the Language of Flowers' a piece of Victorian nonsense, when it is really something very much older.

Fennel is mentioned elsewhere as an esculent and not a herb (for it is known and appreciated today as a flavouring for sauces, fish, and soups). Thus Falstaff, in a wildly exuberant speech at the height of his revels in the Eastcheap tavern in *King Henry IV, Part Two* (II, iv, 220–30), has this speech which would require at least its own length in explanatory footnotes. It is Falstaff's answer to Doll Tearsheet's question as to why Prince Hal so accords with Poins:

Because their legs are both of a bigness; and 'a plays at quoits well; and eats conger and **fennel**; and drinks off candles' ends for flap-dragons; and rides the wild mare with the boys; and jumps upon joint-stools ...

Hudson quotes George Steevens as saying that 'conger with fennel was formerly regarded as a provocative'. (Provocative of what?) Then he quotes another old scholar called Robert Nares, who wrote around 1822: 'Fennel was generally considered as an inflammatory herb; and therefore, to eat conger and fennel was to eat two high and hot things together, which was esteemed an act of libertinism.' It is the kind of scholarship which takes us not very far, if indeed any distance at all.

FERN-SEED

Botanists insist upon the word 'spore' being used for the seed of the Cryptogamia (i.e. ferns, mosses, algae, lichens and fungi). Yet the rest of the world has never taken to the word 'spore' and positively revels in the word seed used indiscriminately and in all its senses. A 'spore', by dictionary definition, is 'one of the minute reproductive bodies characteristic of flowerless plants'.

So minute that it has been persistently said throughout the centuries to be invisible! That this is nonsense – at least in the case of ferns – can be proved by the simplest experiment of placing a fern-leaf (for example of bracken or of the common Male Fern) face downwards on a sheet of white paper. In an hour or so, if the fern-leaf is lifted, it will be found to have deposited considerable traces of a powder which has the consistency of fine tobacco-snuff. This is fern-seed – or, as the botanists insist on saying, the spore of the fern.

Not only was fern-seed said to be invisible: it was even said to make invisible any person who carried any in his pockets! This is a superstition out of the Dark Ages and, like most other examples of superstition, superlatively illogical. Yet this lack of logic has infected even the scholars, or those who really ought to be wiser than most of the rest of us.

In *King Henry IV, Part One* there occurs Shakespeare's single but deeply interesting reference to fern-seed and its alleged qualities (II, i, 85–94). This is in an involved scene between Gadshill and a mysterious character called 'Chamberlain' who is not in the list of the play's dramatis personae:

GADSHILL: . . . We steal as in a castle, cock-sure; we have the receipt of **fern-seed**, we walk invisible.

CHAMBERLAIN: Nay, by my faith, I think you are more beholden to the night than to **fern-seed** for your walking invisible.

GADSHILL: Give me thy hand: thou shalt have a share in our purchase, as I am a true man.

CHAMBERLAIN: Nay, rather let me have it as you are a false thief.

GADSHILL: Go to; Homo is a common name to all men. Bid the other bring my gelding out of the stable. Farewell, you muddy knave.

It is a by no means easy passage in which almost every other word calls out for a note or a gloss. But, concentrating only upon the fern-seed, let us see what a rigmarole six accepted scholars have achieved, forbearing all comment except to note that Dr Johnson himself proves to be not above cribbing from an ancient herbalist-writer when driven to do so by 'pure ignorance':

(1) Dover Wilson (1946): Fern-seed. Being invisible itself, this was supposed, according to the primitive logic that governed the old science, to confer invisibility upon those who carried it. It could be found on Midsummer Eve (St John's Eve) at which time alone it was visible.

(2) M. R. Ridley (1937): Fern-seed – the traditional medicine for invisibility.

(3) Henry Hudson (*c.* 1910): Fern-seed was of old thought to have the power of rendering invisible those who carried it. So in Ben Jonson's *New Inn* (1, i): 'Because indeed I had no medicine, sir, to go invisible; no fern-seed in my pocket.' I suspect the key to the mystery lies partly in this, that ferns do not propagate by seeds, but by spores, which are invisible.

(4) George Steevens (1805): The ancients, who often paid more attention to received opinions than to the evidence of their senses, believed that fern bore no seed. Our ancestors imagined that this plant produced seed which was invisible. Hence, from

314

an extraordinary mode of reasoning, founded on the fantastic doctrine of signatures, they concluded that they who possessed this secret of wearing this seed about them would become invisible.

(5) Dr Samuel Johnson (1765): Fern is one of those plants which have their seed on the back of the leaf so small as to escape the sight. Those who perceived that fern was propagated by semination and yet could never see the seed were much at a loss for a solution of the difficulty; and as wonder always endeavours to augment itself they ascribed to fern-seed many strange properties; some of which the rustick virgins have not yet forgotten or exploded.

(6) John Gerard in his *Herball* (1597): The Ferne is one of those plants which have their seede on the back of the leaf, so small as to escape the sighte. Those who perceived that ferne was propagated by semination, and yet could never see the seede, were much at a losse for a solution of the difficultie.

All sorts of readers – 'rustick virgins' included – should relish a comparison and collation of these last two quotations.

FIGS

It is certainly somewhat odd – though probably a mere coincidence – that the fig should have two widely apart mentions within the same play, *Antony and Cleopatra*, and yet should have hardly any other mention elsewhere in the works. In Act I, Scene ii, line 32 Cleopatra's maid, Charmian, is told by the soothsayer that she shall outlive the lady whom she serves, and gaily answers: 'O excellent! I love long life better than **figs**.' One scholar, Ridley, comments on this that the odd phrase is probably of proverbial origin, although 'there is surely intended an ironic forecast of the basket of figs in Act v'. This is borne to Cleopatra by a peasant and it contains the asp which is to cause her death. He carries in the basket, and he is announced by one of Cleopatra's guard (v, ii, 234–6):

> Here is a rural fellow,
> That will not be denied your highness' presence;
> He brings you **figs**.

A few minutes later, at Cleopatra's death, the same guardsman sees the wound and has a marvellous comment which, as often as not, is cut in stage performance (v, ii, 350–2):

> This is an aspic's trail, and these **fig leaves**
> Have slime upon them, such as the aspic leaves
> Upon the caves of Nile.

Charmian, meanwhile, has just perished by the same deadly means.

In a very different play and mood the inclusion of figs is not to be overlooked in the macédoine of fruits which Titania offers to her bucolic Weaver (*A Midsummer Night's Dream*, III, i, 160–1):

> Feed him with apricocks, and dewberries,
> With purple grapes, green **figs**, and mulberries.

FLOWERS IN GENERAL

We find flowers, in general and unspecified, flourishing in plenty throughout Shakespeare. Here are half a dozen choice and less familiar instances.

We find in *The Merry Wives of Windsor* (v, v, 70) 'in emerald tufts, **flowers** purple, blue, and white.' And two lines further on we are told that 'fairies use **flowers** for their charactery'.

We find in *Titus Andronicus* (ii, iii, 198–201) a sudden mention of flowers – like fresh air out of a charnel-house – when one of the sons of Titus falls into a pit in the forest to be murdered there:

> What subtle hole is this,
> Whose mouth is cover'd with rude-growing briers,
> Upon whose leaves are drops of new-shed blood
> As fresh as morning dew distill'd on **flowers**?

We find them in *Cymbeline* (iv, ii, 296–8) strewn on the headless body of Cloten which Imogen has very nearly lain down beside:

> O gods and goddesses!
> These **flowers** are like the pleasures of the world;
> This bloody man, the care on't. I hope I dream . . .

And in *Romeo and Juliet* (v, iii, 12) where the County Paris breathes his lovely line over the dead Juliet he was to have married:

> Sweet **flower**, with **flowers** thy bridal bed I strew.

And even in the poems, as distinct from the plays, we find Lucrece – in her dishonoured plight – giving us a variation on a theme more than once expressed in the Sonnets (*Rape of Lucrece*, lines 869–72):

> Unruly blasts wait on the tender Spring;
> Unwholesome weeds take root with precious **flowers**;
> The adder hisses where the sweet birds sing;
> What virtue breeds iniquity devours . . .

FURZE, GORSE, BROOM

Ariel tells Prospero how he led the shipwrecked lordlings through 'tooth'd briers, sharp furzes, pricking goss (= gorse), and thorns which enter'd their frail shins'. (*The Tempest*, IV, i, 180). In the same play Gonzalo, in the very process of being shipwrecked, declares: 'Now would I give a thousand furlongs of sea for an acre of barren ground; long heath, brown **furze**, any thing; the wills above be done; but I would fain die a dry death.' (I, i, 63–6). In the mythological masque in the same play (IV, i, 66) Iris has an exquisite speech to Ceres with a reference to her broom-groves

> Whose shadow the dismissèd bachelor loves,
> Being lass-lorn

All these are references to various forms of the *Planta Genista* which was the emblem of, and originated the name of, the Plantagenet family which ruled England for 250 years – from King Henry II in 1154 to King Richard II in 1399. The word 'Plantagenet' has the rumble of history in it – just as has Westmorland and Northumberland. And Shakespeare never tires of repeating its four sonorous syllables throughout his historical plays.

Yet only once does he give a hint that he might have known the broom to have been this great family's emblem. Nor is it even very certain. It is in *King Henry VI, Part Three* (I, i, 49–50) where Warwick the King-Maker declares:

> I'll plant Plantagenet, root him up who dares –
> Resolve thee, Richard; claim the English crown.

318

GRAPES

Whether wine inspired Shakespeare we shall never know. But certain it is that the grape, which is, of course, wine's originator, did little to sharpen his wit or his fancy.

Touchstone in his little scene with William (the country fellow who loves Audrey) has one of the most vapid of all his observations and it is apropos of the grape (*As You Like It*, v, i, 31–6):

TOUCHSTONE: ... The heathen philosopher, when he had a desire to eat a **grape**, would open his lips when he put it into his mouth, meaning thereby that **grapes** were made to eat, and lips to open. You do love this maid?
WILLIAM: I do, sir.
TOUCHSTONE: Give me your hand. Art thou learned?
WILLIAM: No, sir.

(That great actor, Charles Laughton, used to say long before he conquered London that Touchstone was the one Shakespeare part he most longed to play. He never did, and what could even he have made of it? On the other hand William, which hardly seems a part at all, was once turned into a wondrous and unforgettable blank by another beginner – away back in 1936 – who was later to become Sir Alec Guinness).

That tedious old courtier, Lafeu, in *All's Well That Ends Well*, has two inscrutable sallies about the grape (II, i, 73, and II, iii, 105). Iago says cryptically of Desdemona: 'The wine she drinks is made of **grapes**' (*Othello*, II, i, 254). Coriolanus is described by Menenius: 'The tartness of his face sours ripe **grapes** (*Coriolanus*, v, iv, 15). Timon tells the bandits to 'go, suck the subtle blood of the **grape**' (*Timon of Athens*, IV, iii,

430). Antony with his captains sings to Bacchus: 'With thy **grapes** our hairs be crown'd!' (*Antony and Cleopatra*, II, vii, 116).

But it is only in one of Cleopatra's great speeches before her death (V, ii, 280–2) that the grape in Shakespeare has anything like poetic justice done to it:

> Give me my robe, put on my crown, I have
> Immortal longings in me. Now no more
> The juice of Egypt's **grape** shall moist this lip.

GRASS

In the case of so common a topic as grass one picks out the more striking phrases from the less familiar references in Shakespeare. Some are striking enough to be much better known than they are. Thus amid the chattering and bickering of the shipwrecked nobles in *The Tempest* old Gonzalo suddenly says a word in the island's favour: 'How lush and lusty the **grass** looks! How green!' (II, i, 50).

In *A Midsummer Night's Dream* (I, i, 211) young Lysander quite magically talks of the moon 'decking, with liquid pearl, the bladed **grass**'.

In *King Henry V* (I, i, 65) the Bishop of Ely describes how Prince Hal's wildness 'grew like the summer **grass**, fastest by night'.

In *King Richard II* (III, iii, 100) the king prophesies that Bolingbroke may change the complexion of England's peace:

> To scarlet indignation, and bedew
> Her pastures' **grass** with faithful English blood.

In *King Henry VI, Part Two* (III, ii, 337) Suffolk tells **of a** mountain-top 'where biting cold would never let **grass** grow'.

In *Timon of Athens* (IV, iii, 425) the bandits protest to Timon:

> We cannot live on **grass,** on berries, water,
> As beasts, and birds, and fishes.

In *Titus Andronicus* (IV, iv, 70–1) the Emperor Saturninus receives some bad news very dramatically:

> These tidings nip me, and I hang the head
> As flowers with frost, or **grass** beat down with storms.

And *Hamlet* himself (III, ii, 358) gives us an old proverb – or at least half of an old proverb – on the subject: 'While the **grass** grows – the proverb is something musty.' The proverb should conclude: '. . . oft starves the silly steed'.

HAREBELLS

The boy Arviragus in *Cymbeline* (IV, ii, 222), addressing the supposed-dead Imogen, said that among the flowers he strewed on her she should not lack 'the azur'd **harebell**, like thy veins'. It is Shakespeare's sole mention of the harebell (*Campanula Rotundifolia*) which is light blue and 'azur'd', and an autumn flower on grassy banks (in Britain at least). This has nothing in common (excepting blueness) with that other 'bluebell', the wild hyacinth (*Endymion Non-scriptus*) which is blue-velvet and grows in May and June, preferring woodlands. But there are many Scots, including grown-ups, who lay claim to both flowers as being the Bluebells of Scotland. No one country can have it both ways – unless, of course, it be Scotland.

HARVEST AND AUTUMN

'The teeming **autumn**, big with rich increase' (Sonnet No. 80) inspired Shakespeare more than did any other season. It drew splendid far-flung similes from him. Like Hotspur's about his certain lord so neat and trim:

> Fresh as a bridegroom, and his chin new reap'd
> Show'd like a stubble-land at **harvest** home
> > (*King Henry IV, Part One*, I, iii, 34–5)

Or like Petruchio's about Katharina:

> For I will board her, though she chide as loud
> As thunder when the clouds in **autumn** crack
> > (*The Taming of the Shrew*, I, ii, 94–5)

Or like Volumnia's about her son:

> .... his bloody brow
> With his mailed hand then wiping, forth he goes,
> Like to a **harvest-man**, that's tasked to mow
> Or all, or lose his hire   (*Coriolanus*, I, iii, 34–7)

But he is richer still, and even more evocative, when he paints the happy autumn fields directly (through Iris in *The Tempest*, IV, i, 134–8):

> You sunburnt sicklemen, of **August** weary,
> Come hither from the furrow, and be merry,
> Make holiday; your rye-straw hats put on,
> And these fresh nymphs encounter every one
> In country footing.

HAWTHORN AND MAY

Rosalind asks Orlando who can be the young man who 'hangs odes upon **hawthorns**, and elegies on brambles' in the Forest of Arden. It is, of course, himself, and the subject of the verses is, of course, herself (*As You Like It*, III, ii, 353).

Quince says to his troupe of very amateur actors: 'This green plot shall be our stage, this **hawthorn-brake** our tiring-house' (*A Midsummer Night's Dream*, III, i, 4). Helena in the same play has the happy vernal phrase: 'When wheat is green, when **hawthorn-buds** appear'.

Falstaff wooing Mistress Ford has a marvellous simile for girlish young men: 'I cannot coz and say thou art this and that, like a many of these lisping **hawthorn-buds**, that come like women in men's apparel . . .' (*Merry Wives*, III, iii, 77).

Edgar (in *King Lear*, III, iv, 47) utters one of the most icy-cold lines in the whole of English poetry: 'Through the sharp **hawthorn** blows the cold wind.' (But this would appear to be a line from an old forgotten song, not by Shakespeare.)

'May' is an old English word for 'hawthorn-blossom', first used in 1584 when Shakespeare was twenty. *Hamlet* (III, iii, 80), trying to kill his uncle at prayer, exclaims (though he is usually cut here in the theatre):

> He took my father grossly, full of bread,
> With all his crimes broad blown, as flush as **May**.

The passage gets at least three notes and glosses from the scholars and editors. But to none does it seem ever to have occurred that the May referred to may not be the month but hawthorn-blossom. It is just a possibility.

HAY AND STRAW

When Bottom, turned Ass, wearies of charming but in-substantial fruits and berries, he says to his enamoured Titania: 'Methinks I have a great desire to a bottle of **hay**; good **hay**, sweet **hay,** hath no fellow.' ('Bottle' is an old word for 'bundle'). (*A Midsummer Night's Dream*, IV, i, 32-5).

There is more hay – doubtless a stack full – at the end of one of Autolycus's magically irresponsible songs in *The Winter's Tale* (IV, iii, 9–12):

> The lark that tirra-lirra chants,
> > With heigh! with hey! the thrush and the jay!
> Are summer songs for me and my aunts,
> > While we lie tumbling in the **hay.**

(And here we should note that 'aunts' is an old word for 'doxies' or 'lights-o'-love').

King Edward IV setting off for Coventry to depose King Henry VI speaks like a wise farmer (*King Henry VI, Part Three*, IV, viii, 60–1):

> The sun shines hot, and if we use delay,
> Cold biting winter mars our hoped-for **hay.**

The First Witch in *Macbeth* (I, iii, 18) could hardly be more sinister when she tells us how she was refused roast chestnuts by a sailor's wife, and how she will be revenged upon the sailor: 'I will drain him dry as **hay.'**

And of the twenty-odd mentions of straw in Shakespeare, by far the most notable is that in *Measure for Measure*, where Pompey (an old bawd's servant) announces to Abhorson (an executioner) the emergence from his prison cell of Barnardine (described in the cast as 'a dissolute prisoner'): 'He is coming, sir, he is coming; I hear his **straw** rustle.' (IV, iii, 34). What an entrance line for any kind of actor!

HAZELS AND FILBERTS

The filbert being the cultivated or garden form of the hazel (*Corylus Avellana*) it is a little odd that the filbert-tree should occur in Shakespeare only on Prospero's desert island. But there it is (*The Tempest*, II, ii, 170)! Caliban trying to please Trinculo the jester – who is his new man-god – shows him where wild food is to be found on the island: 'I'll bring thee to clustering **filberts** . . .'

Mercutio has a curious predilection for mentioning the hazel. In his Queen Mab scherzo, the chariot of the fairies' midwife is 'an empty **hazel**-nut' (I, iv, 68); and in a later scene of the same play (*Romeo and Juliet*) he teases Benvolio for being so touchy and quarrelsome, an odd case of a pot calling a kettle black. The comparatively calm Benvolio is a copper kettle if ever there was one (III, i, 20): 'Thou wilt quarrel with a man for cracking nuts, having no other reason but because thou hast **hazel** eyes; what eye, but such an eye, would spy out such a quarrel?'

The word recurs figuratively among the mock-compliments which Petruchio bestows on his angry Katharina, praising her mildness and sweetness, in despite of her bitter temper (*The Taming of the Shrew*, II, i, 248–50):

> O slanderous world! Kate like the **hazel**-twig
> Is straight and slender, and as brown in hue
> As **hazel**-nuts, and sweeter than the kernels.

HEBENON

Ever since it was first used by Christopher Marlowe there has been much argument about the etymology of the word hebenon. Can it be henbane, a poisonous English weed of the Nightshade Family (*Solonaceae*)? Or can it be ebon or ebony? Or can the word come from *eibenbaum*, which is the German word for yew? Henbane seems, on the whole, the likeliest origin. A handy guide to the wild flowers of Britain makes this sound just like a very nasty old man: 'A stout, evil-looking, evil-smelling biennial.'

It is, anyhow, a word with sinister associations. It is used in Shakespeare only by the Ghost of Hamlet's father (I, v, 70) who describes to Hamlet how –

> Sleeping within my orchard,
> My custom always of the afternoon,
> Upon my sécure hour thy uncle stole
> With juice of cursed **hebenon** in a vial,
> And in the porches of my ear did pour
> The leperous distilment . . .

HONEYSUCKLE AND WOODBINE

When the loyal Paulina in *The Winter's Tale* uses the word 'honey-mouthed' she means 'soft-speaking to the point of insincerity' (thus: 'If I prove **honey-mouthed**, let my tongue blister' – II, ii, 33). This – we guess without authority – is what Mistress Quickly means by her unprecedented use of honey-suckle as an adjective when she hauls up Falstaff before the Lord Chief Justice for debt and dishonourable action in *King Henry IV, Part Two* (II, i, 46). And by 'honey-seed' she must mean pretty much the same thing: sheer temper makes her coin such words, to such a degree has indignation sharpened her tongue: 'Ah, thou **honey-suckle** villain . . . Ah, thou **honey-seed** rogue, thou art a **honey-seed**, a man-queller, and a woman-queller.'

In a scene of high comedy in *Much Ado About Nothing*, Beatrice 'like a lapwing, runs close by the ground' to hear the other ladies singing Benedick's praise. She does so in a bower:

> Where **honeysuckles**, ripen'd by the sun,
> Forbid the sun to enter (III, i, 7)

A few lines later we hear that Beatrice has all this time been 'couched in the **woodbine** coverture'. Obviously woodbine is synonymous with honeysuckle.

How comes it then that Titania (in *A Midsummer Night's Dream*, IV, i, 42) says of herself embracing Bottom the Weaver:

> So doth the **woodbine** and the sweet **honeysuckle**
> Gently entwist.

One editor somewhat weakly exclaims: 'Something is clearly wrong here.' No more than that! But the New Cambridge editors ingeniously – surely over-ingeniously? – demonstrate that the reading 'bindweed' is more plausible. It would seem that the compositor absent-mindedly – and thinking of the bindweed (*Convolvulus*) in his own garden at home! – printed 'woodbine' for 'bindweed'.

HYSSOP

This bushy and aromatic plant, hyssop, has strong Biblical connections. It was used in Jewish ceremonial rites. 'Purge me with hyssop and I shall be clean,' says the Psalmist.

Shakespeare's sole allusion to it occurs in Iago's prose harangue to Roderigo on the subject of virtue (*Othello*, I, iii, 320):

Virtue? A fig! 'tis in ourselves that we are thus, or thus; our bodies are gardens, to the which our wills are gardeners, so that if we will plant nettles, or sow lettuce, set **hyssop**, and weed up thyme; supply it with one gender of herbs, or distract it with many; either to have it

WSP–E

sterile with idleness, or manured with industry, why, the power, and corrigible authority of this, lies in our wills. If the balance of our lives had not one scale of reason to poise another of sensuality, the blood and baseness of our natures would conduct us to most preposterous conclusions; but we have reason to cool our raging motions, our carnal stings, our unbitted lusts; whereof I take this, that you call love, to be a sect or scion.

To all of which the foolish Roderigo – whom Iago himself has just called 'silly gentleman' – has no rejoinder whatever, excepting the three wretched words: 'It cannot be.' Such evidences of Iago's ranging intellectuality are too often and too much cut in the theatre, with the result that the character becomes a mere melodramatic and meaningless villain. He is a very complex villain, by no means a simple one.

IVY

Prospero, in his pleonastic narration to Miranda of how his brother had usurped his kingdom way back home long ago, thus describes the usurper (*The Tempest*, I, ii, 86):

> The **ivy** which hid my princely trunk,
> And sucked my verdure out on't

But here Shakespeare – or at least Prospero – libels the ivy which is not a parasite, like the dodder or the mistletoe, but merely uses a tree or a wall as a physical support, and has roots of its own in the earth.

He also, rather surprisingly, suggests it as fodder for strayed sheep, as when the Old Shepherd in *The Winter's Tale* speculates on the whereabouts of two which are missing from his flock: 'If anywhere I have them, 'tis by the seaside, browzing of **ivy**' (III, iii, 66).

Titania's comparison of herself with the clinging ivy that 'enrings the barky fingers of the elm' is already commented upon under ELM.

LAVENDER

The particularly Old English flowering herb, lavender, is mentioned in *The Winter's Tale* and nowhere else in Shakespeare. It has a mere mention, but it has the very first place in Perdita's celebrated floral catalogue (IV, iv, 104) that begins:

> Here's flowers for you;
> Hot **lavender**, mints, savory, marjoram . . .

But the curious adjective 'hot' gives many of the scholars pause. M. R. Ridley of the New Temple Edition says: 'Mysterious – no one has explained why lavender should be hot,' and goes on to tell us: 'The New Cambridge editors suggest goat in the sense of wild (*cf.* goat-marjoram), but they do not explain why the lavender should be wild when everything else is from Perdita's garden.' But this is surely hair-splitting. The word may genuinely be 'hot' in the old sense of pungent or acrid (first found in 1548, six years before Shakespeare was born).

LEAVES IN GENERAL

The leaves in autumn or the fall seem to fascinate Shakespeare far more than their unfurling buds in the spring, or their pride

of summer greenness. We need go no further than the Sonnets
to read how:

> That time of year thou mayst in me behold
> When yellow **leaves**, or none, or few do hang ...
>
> (No. 73)

Or how:

> When lofty trees I see barren of **leaves,**
> Which erst from heat did canopy the herd,
> And summer's green, all girded up in sheaves,
> Borne on the bier with white and bristly beard ...
>
> (No. 12)

Or how:

> Never-resting time leads summer on
> To hideous winter and confines him there;
> Sap checked with frost, and lusty **leaves** quite gone,
> Beauty o'ersnowed, and bareness everywhere ...
>
> (No. 5)

Or how:

> With thee away, the very birds are mute;
> Or, if they sing, 'tis with so dull a cheer
> That **leaves** look pale, dreading the winter's near.
>
> (No. 97)

LEEK

To this day the prosaic leek is the national emblem of Wales
despite efforts, increasing in recent years, to give that honour
to the immeasurably more poetical daffodil.

In *A Midsummer Night's Dream* (v, i, 342), and in its comic
tragedy within the fairy comedy, the dying Thisbe, over the

body of the dead Pyramus, is merely being desperate for a rhyme for 'cheeks' when she tells us – prosaically rather than lyrically – that 'his eyes were green – as **leeks**'.

Every other mention of the leek in Shakespeare – and there are at least a dozen – concern that intensely comical and marvellously drawn Welsh soldier, Fluellen, in *King Henry V*. (The part was unforgettably well played by Mervyn Johns in a production of the play in 1936 at The Ring in Blackfriars, one of the Second World War's casualties). In a charming snatch of conversation the King, on the field of battle in France, tells Fluellen of his own Welshness (IV, vii, 108):

FLUELLEN: . . . I do believe your majesty takes no scorn to wear the **leek** upon Saint Tavy's day.
HENRY: I wear it for a memorable honour;
For I am Welsh, you know, good countryman.

And the later scene of quarrelling between Fluellen and that flaunting English braggart, Pistol, has so many 'pribbles and prabbles' about leek-wearing and leek-eating that one would have to be a Welsh-born Shakespearean fully to understand it (V, i, 1–87).

Elsewhere in the same play Fluellen has a Welsh rhapsody which astonishingly catches and entraps the inconsequence of Welsh fooling pretending to take itself seriously. He is speaking to the English officer, Gower (IV, vii, 20–38):

I think it is in Macedon where Alexander is born. I tell you, captain, if you look in the maps of the world, I warrant you shall find, in the comparisons between Macedon and Monmouth, that the situations, look you, is both alike. There is a river in Macedon, and there is also moreover a river at Monmouth. It is called Wye at Monmouth; but it is out of my prains what is the name of the other river. But 'tis all one, 'tis alike as my fingers is to my fingers; and there is salmons in both . . .

The actor, Mervyn Johns, spoke the last six words with quite unforgettable emphasis and Welsh perfection.

LILIES

Shakespeare in his poems, just as much as in his plays, uses the lily as a symbol of whiteness. Venus (in *Venus and Adonis*), in her unavailing wrestling matches with Adonis, is compared to 'a **lily** prisoned in a gaol of snow' at one point (line 362). At another point, when he struggles to be free from her embrace 'she locks her **lily** fingers one in one' (line 228). And in the Sonnets there occurs the strange and striking line: '**Lilies** that fester smell far worse than weeds.' (No 94).

In the plays the flower springs up in all the expected places. Just as 'hot lavender' comes first in Perdita's catalogue of blossoms, so the lily comes last – '**lilies** of all kinds, the flower-de-luce being one' (*The Winter's Tale*, IV, iv, 134).

It springs up in the unexpected places also. Launce the clown in *Two Gentlemen of Verona* throws down his staff to represent his own sister: 'She is white as a **lily**, and as small as a wand.' And Constance in *King John* (II, i, 53) tells the infant Arthur:

> Of Nature's gifts thou mayst with **lilies** boast,
> And with the half-blown rose . . .

In heraldic references in Shakespeare the lily is usually the fleur-de-lis or flower-de-luce.

MALT

(See also under BARLEY). In one of his long speeches that bristle with verbal and phraseological difficulties, Gadshill (a follower of Falstaff of whom we know very little except that he was 'well-in-flesh' like the Knight he followed) talks of 'mad mustachio purple-hued **malt-worms**' (*King Henry IV, Part One*, II, i, 65–85).

One scholar-editor (Ridley) says unhelpfully of the whole speech: 'I can see no reason for the spate of conjectural emendations: Gadshill is deliberately playing with and coining words.' So we have to go back to another scholar-editor (Hudson) to find that the particular phrase quoted may mean: 'Such as had their faces made red with drinking ale' – as red as Bardolph's celebrated nose.

In *Part Two* of the same play (II, iv, 322) Falstaff himself says of Bardolph that 'his face is Lucifer's privy-kitchen where he doth nothing but roast **malt-worms**' – where the meaning would seem to be very similar.

Hardly less unsatisfying is the use of 'malt-horse' as a term of abuse. Thus Dromio of Syracuse (in *The Comedy of Errors*, III, i, 32): 'Mome [or numskull], **malt-horse**, capon, cox-comb, idiot, patch !' And Petruchio says to his servant Grumio: 'You peasant swain, you whoreson **malt-horse** drudge' (*The Taming of the Shrew*, IV, i, 118).

There is too little allusion in Shakespeare to malt itself, and especially to its warmish, evocative, indescribable odour.

MARIGOLDS

For Perdita the marigold is one of the flowers of middle summer (*The Winter's Tale*, IV, iv, 114):

> The marigold, that goes to bed wi' the sun,
> And with him rises, weeping.

For another of Shakespeare's flower-maidens, Marina in

Pericles, Prince of Tyre (IV, i, 12–20), marigolds have their place:

> No, no, I will rob Tellus of her weed,
> To strew thy green with flowers: the yellows, blues,
> The purple violets, and **marigolds**,
> Shall, as a carpet, hang upon thy grave,
> While summer-days do last. – Ay me, poor maid,
> Born in a tempest, when my mother died,
> This world to me is like a lasting storm,
> Whirring me from my friends.

In this often silly but sometimes beautiful play (Swinburne called it 'ill-fated and ill-famed') this lost princess Marina is, shortly after delivering the above speech, left in the hands of one Leonine who has been commanded to murder her on the sea-shore. But some pirates supervene and seize her, whereupon Leonine makes off saying he will come back and put her to death when she has met with a fate worse than death itself (IV, i, 100):

> Perhaps they will but please themselves upon her.
> Not carry her aboard. If she remain
> Whom they have ravish'd must by me be slain.

What else can Leonine mean by this? Marina, still strongly armed with her virginity, escapes to freedom again in the end – by way of would-be murderers, would-be ravishers, and a short term of residence in a brothel in Mytilene. An insuperable virgin!

MARJORAM

The herb marjoram – already mentioned in Perdita's list, under LAVENDER – has its name used as a password in *King*

Lear. It acts as such to what is almost the tragedy's greatest scene (IV, vi, 93–107):

LEAR: . . . Give the word.
EDGAR: Sweet **marjoram.**
LEAR: Pass.
GLOSTER: I know that voice.
LEAR: Ha, Goneril with a white beard! . . . When the rain came to wet me once, and the wind to make me chatter, when the thunder would not peace at my bidding, there I found them, there I smelt them out. Go to, they are not men of their words: they told me I was every thing; 'tis a lie, I am not ague-proof.
GLOSTER: The trick of that voice I do well remember:
Is't not the king?
                    Ay, every inch a king.

And so on, to the heights.

Descending again from the heights and from the mad Lear, why have the very names of these English herbs such charm and quaintness – marjoram, basil, lovage, lavender, chervil, tarragon?

MARYBUDS

The Oxford Dictionary declares the word marybud to be 'obsolete except in echoes of Shakespeare'. It is guessed to be probably the bud of the marigold or kingcup. But the latter word in turn is defined as the Common Buttercup *or* Marsh Marigold – all of which is more than somewhat indefinite.

Walter Pater said of the song in *Measure for Measure* that it is a lyric which 'escapes almost into the condition of music'. And the same may be said of the song in *Cymbeline* (II, iii, 20) – that it escapes almost into the condition of Schubert's setting:

> Hark, hark! the lark at heaven's gate sings,
> And Phoebus 'gins arise,

His steeds to water at those springs
On chaliced flowers that lies;
And winking **mary-buds** begin
To ope their golden eyes;
With every thing that pretty is,
My lady sweet, arise:
Arise, arise!

MEDLARS

The medlar is an odd tree-fruit which is not really edible until it looks too over-ripe to be eaten at all.

Shakespeare has only four references, and is not always able to resist the almost irresistible pun with 'meddler'.

The witty young rake Lucio, in *Measure for Measure* (IV, iii, 184), discusses the Duke of Vienna with a stranger who is really the Duke in disguise:

LUCIO: I was once before him for getting a wench with child.
DUKE: Did you such a thing?
LUCIO: Yes, marry, did I: but I was fain to forswear it, they would else have married me to the rotten **medlar**.
DUKE: Sir, your company is fairer than honest; rest you well.

Lucio has charm as well as roguery, as all who saw an early performance by Paul Scofield – at Stratford-on-Avon in 1946 – must still vividly remember.

Rosalind in *As You Like It* (III, ii, 113) discusses with Touchstone the verses written in her praise by Orlando:

ROSALIND: Peace, you dull fool! I found them on a tree.
TOUCHSTONE: Truly the tree yields bad fruit.
ROSALIND: I'll graff [graft] it with you, and then I shall graff it with a **medlar**: then it will be the earliest fruit i' the country; for you'll be rotten ere you be half-ripe, and that's the right virtue of the **medlar**.

Here there is a further quibble with 'you' and 'yew'. Or so the scholars say.

Timon with Apemantus belabours the pun with 'meddler' (*Timon of Athens*, IV, iii, 303):

APEMANTUS: There's a **medlar** for thee; eat it.
TIMON: On what I hate I feed not.
APEMANTUS: Dost hate a **medlar**?
TIMON: Ay, though it look like thee.
APEMANTUS: An thou hadst hated meddlers sooner, thou shouldst have loved thyself better now.

And Mercutio jests grossly about Romeo to his friend Benvolio (*Romeo and Juliet*, II, i, 34), and takes his turn to flog the quibble at the same time:

BENVOLIO: Come, he hath hid himself among these trees,
To be consorted with the humorous night:
Blind is his love, and best befits the dark.
MERCUTIO: If love be blind, love cannot hit the mark.
Now will he sit under a **medlar**-tree,
And wish his mistress were that kind of fruit
As maids call **medlars** when they laugh alone.
O Romeo, that she wear, O that she wore
An open et cetera, thou a poperin pear!
Romeo, good night . . .

MISTLETOE

The parasitic nature of a plant like the mistletoe (growing with its roots deep in the bark of an apple or poplar tree) was probably unknown to Shakespeare. The parasites he mentions in his plays are all of the human sort – cf. *Timon of Athens* in that character's cries of fury at his party guests (III, vi, 96):

Live loathed, and long,
Most smiling, smooth, detested parasites,
Courteous destroyers, affable wolves, meek bears!

Shakespeare's one mention of the plant is in the description of the evil place in the dark forest where Tamora has come with her two sons bent upon the ravishment and mutilation of Lavinia, Titus's daughter (*Titus Andronicus*, II, iii, 93):

A barren detested vale you see it is;
The trees, though summer, yet forlorn and lean,
O'ercome with moss and baleful **mistletoe**.

Peter Brook's stage direction for Laurence Olivier disclosed quite shatteringly that this neglected play is really a dire and probing inquiry into the ultimate refinements of vice and cruelty. Vile and evil in its emotions, dwelling far more upon hate than upon love, starkly and consistently unsentimental, this was seen – at long last – to be something vastly and disturbingly deeper than a mere crude Elizabethan melodrama of blood and blood-lust. It was one of the supreme theatrical experiences of the century.

MULBERRIES

There is a mulberry tree in Shakespeare's garden around the house – at High Place, Stratford – to which he retired and where he died; and to the tree is attached a label declaring that this is an offshoot of an offshoot of Shakespeare's own tree.

Anyway it is clear from the works that the poet had an affection for the gentle berry and the tree that bears it. It is one of the fruits with which Titania fed Bottom the Weaver (see under APRICOTS and HAY AND STRAW). And in the same play (*A Midsummer Night's Dream*, v, i, 149) we hear how Pyramus stabbed himself dead, with his Thisbe 'tarrying in **mulberry** shade'.

Volumnia tells her son Coriolanus (III, ii, 80) to subdue his pride and let his stout heart be 'now humble as the ripest **mulberry** that will not hold the handling'. And in the lush, creamy, delectable long poem of *Venus and Adonis* the goddess describes her shepherd bathing in a brook (lines 1099–104):

> When he beheld his shadow in the brook,
> The fishes spread on it their golden gills;
> When he was by, the birds such pleasure took,
> That some would sing, some other in their bills
> > Would bring him **mulberries** and ripe-red cherries;
> > He fed them with his sight, they him with berries.

MUSHROOMS AND TOADSTOOLS

Shakespeare's only mention of the mushroom is buried deep in one of Prospero's most majestic (but also most involved and lengthy) speeches. This begins (*The Tempest*, v, i, 33):

> Ye elves of hills, brooks, standing lakes, and groves,
> And ye, that on the sands with printless foot
> Do chase the ebbing Neptune, and do fly him
> When he comes back . . .

and concludes:

> > . . . graves at my command
> Have waked their sleepers, oped, and let 'em forth
> By my so potent art.

The first sentence of this speech runs to eighteen lines and 150 words, in which the only Prospero who has ever held us completely spellbound is John Gielgud with his 'so potent art'.

In the heart of the amazing speech is the further adjuration:

> ... and you, whose pastime
> Is to make midnight **mushrooms**, that rejoice
> To hear the solemn curfew ...

It is only what a great dramatic critic has called 'exquisite Gielgudry' which can make us forbear to ask here whether it be the mushrooms or some other elves who 'rejoice to hear the solemn curfew'. Surely the latter, and surely Shakespeare's phrasing – for all its magic – is a little at fault for once in a way?

The poet's only use of toadstool is figurative, and occurs in *Troilus and Cressida* (II, i, 20) in that sharp scene between Ajax and Thersites in the course of which the former calls the latter not only a toadstool but also a dog, a bitch-wolf's son, un-salted leaven, a porpentine, Mistress Thersites, a cobloaf, a whoreson cur, a stool for a witch, and some other choice examples of dog's abuse.

MYRTLE

The myrtle (*Myrtus Communis*) is a bush or shrub, with grey-green fragrant leaves, and bearing catkins which are 'long orange, male, and short red, female, on separate plants'. The catkins are borne in spring, before the leaves come.

The myrtle in Shakespeare occurs rather oftener in the poems than in the plays. Characteristically he says of Venus in *Venus and Adonis* (lines 865–8):

> This said, she hasteth to a **myrtle** grove,
> Musing the morn is so much overworn,

And yet she hears no tidings of her love;
She hearkens for his hounds and for his horn . . .

That same long and luscious poem is rather neatly summarized
in one of the sonnets in the apocryphal collection called *The
Passionate Pilgrim*:

Venus, with young Adonis sitting by her
Under a **myrtle** shade, begin to woo him . . .

But, notwithstanding:

As she fetchèd breath, away he skips,
And would not take her meaning nor her pleasure

The Passionate Shepherd to his Love has two mentions of myrtle,
but it is a poem now generally attributed to Christopher
Marlowe, Shakespeare's 'dead shepherd'.

In *Measure for Measure* (II, ii, 118) Isabella says of the thunderbolt that it rather –

Splits the unwedgeable and gnarled oak
Than the soft **myrtle**

And, still more strikingly, Euphronius, Antony's ambassador,
says to Caesar (*Antony and Cleopatra*, III, xii, 6):

Such as I am, I come from Antony:
I was of late as petty to his ends
As is the morn-dew on the **myrtle** leaf
To his grand sea.

NETTLES

The nettle, an ubiquitous weed, has already been noted under
BURDOCKS AND DOCKS, CHAPLETS, GARLANDS, NOSE-
GAYS, and HYSSOP.

But there are nettles elsewhere, and all over the place. They are among the stinging things that sully the bed-sheets of the madly jealous Leontes – 'Goads, thorns, **nettles**, tails of wasps' (*The Winter's Tale*, I, ii, 329). They are among the favours that King Richard II asks of the English soil: 'Yield stinging **nettles** to mine enemies' (III, ii, 18). Old Gonzalo (in *The Tempest*, II, i, 138) discusses how Prospero's island should be planted, and is discourteously interrupted by the other ship-wrecked noblemen:

> GONZALO: Had I plantation of this isle, my lord, –
> ANTONIO: He'd sow't with **nettle** seed.
> SEBASTIAN: Or docks or mallows.

And nettles crop up again in the dreadful dripping forest of that most sinister of all the plays, when Saturninus reads the missive from Tamora telling him of the murder pit (*Titus Andronicus*, II, iii, 271):

> Thou know'st our meaning. Look for thy reward
> Among the **nettles** at the elder-tree,
> Which overshades the mouth of that same pit
> Where we decreed to bury Bassianus.

NUTS

See also under ALMONDS and HAZELS AND FILBERTS. But Titania has unspecified nuts in mind when, at a loss for something fresh for Bottom to munch, she says to him:

> I have a venturous fairy that shall seek
> The squirrel's hoard, and fetch thee new **nuts**.

She gets the happy answer from her semi-equine lover:

I had rather have a handful or two of dried peas.
But I pray you, let none of your people stir me:
I have an exposition of sleep come upon me
                    (*A Midsummer Night's Dream*, IV, i, 40)

(Across the years one can recall the actor Ralph Richardson
lingering with wonderment upon his own word 'exposition').

And *Hamlet* (II, ii, 57) has his own use of the word nut-shell
in his very celebrated but still very enigmatic exclamation:
'O God, I could be bounded in a **nut-shell**, and count myself a king of infinite space, were it not that I have bad
dreams.'

NUTMEGS

This nutmeg is the hard aromatic seed obtained from the fruit
of the East Indian evergreen tree whose beautiful name is
Myristica Fragrans. It may have been costly when first introduced to England, otherwise Dumain would hardly suggest
'a gilt **nutmeg**' to Don Adriano as a suitable gift to Mars from
Hector (*Love's Labour's Lost*, V, ii, 640).

In *King Henry V* the French Dauphin's ecstatic description
of his horse is interrupted by Orleans saying: 'He's the colour
of the **nutmeg**,' and the Dauphin adds: 'And of the heat of the
ginger' (III, viii, 20).

And in *The Winter's Tale* the Clown includes in his grocery
list for the sheep-shearing feast (IV, iii, 40) not only saffron
and mace but also '**nutmegs**, seven'. In no Shakespeare edition
whatsoever has one seen the word 'seven' explained or even
questioned. But it is certainly odd enough to make us pause
and ask.

WSP–F

OAK

The oak (*Quercus Robur*) would appear to have been of all trees Shakespeare's first favourite. The most impressive of his thirty-odd references emphasize the tree's great strength and endurance.

In *Timon of Athens* (I, iii, 50) Nestor talks nobly of stormy occasions:

> when the splitting wind
> Makes flexible the knees of knotted **oaks**

In *The Tempest* (I, ii, 297) Prospero threatens Ariel with a terrible punishment, not for the first time:

> If thou more murmurest, I will rend an **oak**
> And peg thee in his knotty entrails, till
> Thou hast howled away twelve winters

In *Julius Caesar* (I, iii, 5) Casca says to Cicero in the course of an awe-inspiring thunderstorm in Rome:

> Are you not moved, when all the sway of earth
> Shakes, like a thing unfirm? O Cicero,
> I have seen tempests, when the scolding winds
> Have rived the knotty **oaks**
> But never till tonight . . . etc., etc.

In *Othello* (II, i, 7) Montano, caught in a storm in Cyprus, has a striking speech, which is usually cut in the theatre, perhaps because he is merely Montano:

> A fuller blast ne'er shook our battlements:
> If it hath ruffian'd so upon the sea,
> What ribs of **oak**, when the huge mountain melts,
> Can hold the mortise? (i.e. remain jointed)

In *King Lear* (III, ii, 5) the old king himself, still more tremendously, describes the lightning forks over the heath as 'vaunt-couriers to **oak**-cleaving thunderbolts', and asks them, transcendently, to singe his white head!

And, descending abruptly from the sublime to the ridiculous, in *The Merry Wives of Windsor* (v, i, 12) Sir John Falstaff, plagued by citizens disguised as fairies round Herne the Hunter's oak at midnight, recognizes the voice of Sir Hugh Evans, Windsor's Welsh parson, and calls out: 'Defend me from that Welsh fairy, lest he transform me to a piece of cheese!'

As for the seed of the oak tree, the acorn, there is the prettiest fancy in *A Midsummer Night's Dream* (11, i, 30) where Puck tells us that Oberon and Titania have been quarrelling so sharply over their Indian changeling

> ... that all their elves, for fear,
> Creep into acorn cups, and hide them there.

OATS

Dr Johnson in his Dictionary defined oats as being a sort of provender, 'a grain, which in England is given to horses, but in Scotland supports the people'. With this in mind Dr Johnson must have laughed aloud in the theatre when Bottom the Weaver, asked by Titania what he fancies in the way of food, replies: 'Truly, a peck of provender: I could munch your good dry **oats**' (*A Midsummer Night's Dream*, IV, i, 32).

In the mythological Masque in *The Tempest* (IV, i, 60) one goddess, Iris, hails another one thus:

> Ceres, most bounteous lady, thy rich leas
> Of wheat, rye, barley, vetches, **oats**, and pease ...

And in *King Henry IV, Part One* (11, i, 12) the two Carriers in the inn-yard at Rochester, marvellously alive though unnamed, have this interchange:

SECOND CARRIER: . . . This house is turn'd upside down since Robin Ostler died.

FIRST CARRIER: Poor fellow never joyed since the price of **oats** rose, it was the death of him.

OLIVES

The olive or olive-branch as a token of peace is extended in several places in Shakespeare. Thus Viola says to Olivia in *Twelfth Night* (I, v, 209) on her very first visit, disguised as a boy and Orsino's messenger:

I bring no overture of war, no taxation of homage: I hold the **olive** in my hand; my words are as full of peace as matter.

In *King Henry IV, Part Two* (IV, iv, 87) the Earl of Westmoreland brings peaceful news to his Sovereign:

> There is not now a rebel's sword unsheathed,
> But Peace puts forth her **olive** every where.

And in *Antony and Cleopatra* (IV, vi, 5–7) we have Octavius Caesar declaring that the whole of his world is at peace at last:

> The time of universal peace is near;
> Prove this a prosperous day, the three-nook'd world
> Shall bear the **olive** freely . . .

his strange adjective for 'world' being, presumably, a reference to the 'triplex mundus' of sea, earth, and sky, or else to the Triumvirate of which he is himself a member with Antony and the 'slight unmeritable' Lepidus.

The other notable references are to the olive tree (*Olea Sativa*) which flourishes apace in the otherwise very English

Forest of Arden. Rosalind tells Orlando where her dwelling is (*As You Like It*, III, v, 74): ''Tis at the tuft of **olives**, here hard by.' And in the next act (IV, iii, 7) Orlando's brother Oliver declares himself to be looking for 'a sheep-cote fenced about with **olive trees**'. This is very odd since the atmosphere of the play is as English as the Greenwood Tree, or as William and Audrey and Sir Oliver Martext, or as the rest of the flora and fauna (with the exception of Brother Oliver's inexplicable lioness (IV, iii, 114)).

ONIONS AND GARLIC

It is not generally noted that Bottom, besides wanting to play at least three characters in the little tragedy of *Pyramus and Thisbe*, also envied Quince his job as stage director. Witness his instructions to the whole company just before the actual performance (*A Midsummer Night's Dream*, IV, ii, 40) which is the purest Granville Barker, or Komisarjevsky, or Peter Brook, at the end of a dress rehearsal when it is hoped it will be 'all right on the night':

And, most dear actors, eat no **onions**, nor **garlic**; for we are to utter sweet breath; and I do not doubt to hear them say, it is a sweet comedy. No more words. Away, go away.   (*Exeunt*).

It turned out to be all wrong on the night. But so has many and many a first night, ever since.

The effect of the pungent odour of onions on the lachrymal ducts is Shakespeare's concern in every other reference to this bulbous vegetable (*Allium Cepa*). Enobarbus, whose favourite vegetable it might easily have been, says (*Antony and Cleopatra*, I, ii, 173): 'Indeed the tears live in an **onion** that

should water this sorrow.' And it is Enobarbus again who says
to Mark Antony (IV, ii, 36):

> Look, they weep,
> And I, too, an ass, am **onion**-eyed: for shame,
> Transform us not to women.

In the Induction to *The Taming of the Shrew* (lines 122–6) the
Lord arranges for his page, Bartholomew, to impersonate
Christopher Sly's wife and tells her how to shed tears:

> An **onion** will do for such a shift,
> Which in a napkin (being close conveyed)
> Shall in despite enforce a watery eye.

And the tedious old Lord Lafeu, at the tail-end of *All's Well
That Ends Well* (V, iii, 316) says to Parolles:

> Mine eyes smell **onions**; I shall weep anon;
> Good Tom Drum, lend me a handkercher; so,
> I thank thee . . .

But no one seems ever to have hazarded a guess as to why
Lafeu should suddenly call old Parolles 'good Tom Drum'.
Except, perhaps, that it is as good a name as any coming from
a tedious old bombinator.

ORANGES

As for orange, the fruit itself, as distinct from the colour, is
mentioned only in *Much Ado About Nothing*. There that im-
perfect young nobleman, Claudio, hands back the wrongly
suspected Hero to her father with the phrase (IV, i, 30):

> There, Leonato, take her back again:
> Give not this rotten **orange** to your friend.

And earlier on (II, i, 270) this same Count Claudio is described to his face by Beatrice:

The count is neither sad, nor sick, nor merry, nor well; but civil count, civil as an **orange**, and something of that jealous complexion

The best Beatrice one ever saw, Madge Titheradge (with Henry Ainley as Benedick), used to get a laugh at this sally, even though the audience may have been quite unaware of the quibble between 'civil' and 'Seville'. The part bristles with such difficulties. They proved too much for even so brilliant an actress as Lynn Fontanne in a New York production of the play (with Alfred Lunt as Benedick) which never reached its first night. Ellen Terry was, I am assured, the best Beatrice in stage history.

ORCHARDS

There are many more specified orchards than specified gardens in Shakespeare.

Among the comedies, *As You Like It* begins with a wrangle between Orlando and his big brother, Oliver, whose orchard is the scene. In *Much Ado About Nothing* several of the best and liveliest scenes happen in the orchard of Leonato. In *Twelfth Night* Sir Andrew is sent by Sir Toby to look for Cesario 'at the corner of the **orchard** like a bum-baily' (III, iv, 172). In *Troilus and Cressida* (III, ii) Pandarus is in his own orchard when Troilus visits him there to arrange an assignation with his Cressida.

Among the histories, Act V, Scene iii of *King Henry IV, Part Two* is one of the supreme things, a scene in Justice Shallow's orchard in Gloucestershire in which each character – particularly Shallow, Silence, and their visitor Falstaff – is intensely himself; and in which Time stands still, and an apple falls with a thud, and Pistol arrives with the news of the King's death in London.

A century earlier, in Northamptonshire, another King of England dies, this time of poison, in the orchard of Swinstead Abbey. Prince Henry, his son, asks: 'How fares your majesty?' And King John (v, vii, 40) answers:

> Poisoned – ill fare – dead, forsook, cast off:
> And none of you will bid the winter come
> To thrust his icy fingers in my maw.

Among the tragedies, the Ghost of Hamlet's father tells his son how he was murdered: 'Sleeping within my **orchard**, my custom always of the afternoon.' (I, v, 58). Antony tells the Roman mob that the assassinated Julius Caesar (III, iii, 250) has left to them, and to their heirs for ever, 'His private arbours, and new-planted **orchards**'. And it is in the orchard of the Capulets that Romeo and Juliet interchange their tender vows, one of which begins (II, ii, 107):

> Lady, by yonder blessèd moon I swear
> That tips with silver all these fruit-tree tops . . .

Clearly an orchard, though the word itself is not used.

PEAS, PEASE AND PEASCODS

We may hazard the theory that Bottom the Weaver had what today we call a complex on the subject of peas. He suggests to Titania on one occasion that it is what he would most like to eat, more even than nuts: 'I had rather have a handful or two of dried **peas**' (*A Midsummer Night's Dream*, IV, i, 36). Peaseblossom is the first favourite among his four attendant-fairies (more even than Cobweb, Moth and Mustardseed). At his first meeting he calls him 'honest gentleman', and when told that this fairy's name is Pease-blossom he says: 'I pray you, commend me to Mistress **Squash**, your mother, and to Master **Peascod**, your father' (III, i, 180). Bottom says also: 'Scratch my head, **Pease-blossom**!' (IV, i, 5).

In *Twelfth Night*, too, Malvolio describes to Olivia the appearance of Cesario (who is Viola appearing as Orsino's page): 'Not yet old enough for a man, nor young enough for a boy; as a **squash** is before 'tis a **peascod** . . . He is very well-favoured and he speaks very shrewishly; one would think his mother's milk were scarce out of him.' (I, v, 160).

Berowne says of Boyet in *Love's Labour's Lost* (V, ii, 315): 'This fellow picks up wit as pigeons **pease**' (and we note the vaguely plural form as in pease-pudding and the Scottish pease-brose).

The Second Carrier at Rochester says: '**Peas** and beans are as dank here as a dog' (*King Henry IV, Part One*, II, i, 8). And Mistress Quickly has a touching farewell to Falstaff (*King Henry IV, Part Two*, II, iv, 370): 'Well, fare thee well, I have known thee these twenty-nine years come **peascod**-time, but an honester and truer-hearted man, – well, fare thee well.' He is never again to see her so friendly – till he is on his death-bed.

The goddess Iris's mention of peas, in the masque in *The Tempest*, has already been noted under OATS.

PEACHES AND PEARS

The word peach occurs only in combination and as a colour – as *peach-coloured* – where it probably means *peach-blossom-*

coloured. Thus Pompey in *Measure for Measure*, who is servant to Mrs Overdone and therefore henchman to a bawd – to put it mildly – tells us in a prose soliloquy all about his mistress's customers. They include one Master Caper who had 'four suits of **peach-coloured** satin' (IV, iii, 11). Thus, too, Prince Hal who tells Poins he had observed his fashion in silk stockings: 'viz, these, and those that were thy **peach-coloured** ones'. (*King Henry IV, Part Two*, III, ii, 16).

The word pear, similarly, occurs only in the fruit's over-ripe or withered condition or – in one case – in a grossly in-delicate simile. Thus Falstaff in *The Merry Wives of Windsor* (IV, v, 96) imagines how the King's courtiers would laugh at him if they knew how he had been tricked and beaten: 'I warrant they would whip me with their five wits, till I was as crest-fallen as a dried **pear**.' And Parolles in *All's Well That Ends Well* (I, i, 16) makes jests on the subject of virginity to two ladies, one old and one young: 'Your virginity, your old virginity, is like one of our withered French **pears**, it looks ill, it eats dryly . . .'

Parolles is a raffish fellow, but not quite so rakishly raffish as Mercutio who utters that remark to Romeo about something being like a poperin-pear (already noted and quoted under MEDLAR). Hudson, a conscientious but late-Victorian editor, has this comment: 'Poperin was a variety of pear introduced into England from Poperingues in Flanders. . . . The word is here used [in Mercutio's remark] for the sake of a coarse quibble which it is not worth the while to explain.'

PINE AND BOX

When Shakespeare mentions the pine, whether literally or figuratively, he nowhere specifies what particular member of the order Pinaceae he has in mind.

In his fine long speech to Aumerle beginning 'Discomfortable cousin!' (III, ii, 42), King Richard II tells how the rising sun dispels the evils of darkness:

> He fires the proud tops of the eastern **pines**
> And darts his light through every guilty hole ...

(John Gielgud made the speech one of the great things, in this, one of the greatest of his parts).

In the Trial Scene in *The Merchant of Venice* (IV, i, 74–6) Antonio says to his assembled friends how futile and unavailing must be all argument with the hate-kindled Jew:

> You may as well forbid the mountain **pines**
> To wag their high tops, and to make no noise
> When they are fretten with the gusts of heaven ...

In *The Tempest* (I, ii, 280) the master Prospero reminds his servant Ariel what happened to him at the hands of the 'damned witch', Sycorax:

> She did confine thee,
> By the help of her more potent ministers,
> And in her most unmitigable rage,
> Into a cloven **pine**, within which rift
> Imprisoned, thou didst painfully remain
> A dozen years

And in the poems, Lucrece in her violated plight compares herself to a pine tree stripped of its bark (*The Rape of Lucrece*, lines 1167–8):

> Ay me! the bark pill'd from the lofty **pine**,
> His leaves will wither and his sap decay;
> So must my soul, her bark being pill'd away.

Another evergreen tree, the box (*Buxus Sempervirens*) is mentioned only once, but as part of the actual scenery. It is in the scene where Maria tells her fellow-conspirators in the garden that Malvolio is on his way, and that he will shortly pick up and read what he imagines to be a declaration of love from his mistress Olivia – the letter which is to make 'a contemplative idiot' of the steward. 'Get you all three into the **box-tree**,' says Maria at the start of the fun (*Twelfth Night*, II, v, 14). 'Malvolio's coming down this walk.'

PLANTS AND PLANTING

That plants live, and multiply and die, and that they provide countless analogies with living, multiplying and dying humanity – it is the great poet's unceasing contention.

This time we may leave the drama completely out of it, as being too vast a quarry, and quote only a song, a sonnet, and a stanza.

The song is the famous one about Orpheus in *King Henry VIII* (III, i, 6–8):

> To his music **plants** and flowers
> Ever sprung, as sun and showers
> There had made a lasting spring.

The sonnet is No. 15 beginning 'When I consider every thing that grows', and continuing:

> When I perceive that men as **plants** increase
> Cheerèd and check'd even by the self-same sky,
> Vaunt in their youthful sap, at height decrease,
> And wear their brave state out of memory ...

The stanza is one (lines 163–8) in which Venus, addressing her unheeding Adonis, makes an indisputable truism out of the many facts of life:

Torches are made to light, jewels to wear,
Dainties to taste, fresh beauty for the use,
Herbs for their smell, and sappy **plants** to bear;
Things growing to themselves are growth's abuse:
    Seeds spring from seeds, and beauty breedeth beauty;
    Thou wast begot; to get – it is thy duty.

PLUMS AND PLUM TREES

In another part of the amorous forest that is *Venus and Adonis* (lines 527–8) it is Adonis, still resisting the allurements of Venus, who gives utterance to a truism. He does so with a quite enchanting sophistry, instancing the case of the plum on its tree. He is comparing himself to the unripe plum as distinct from the ripe one, when he says:

    The mellow **plum** doth fall, the green sticks fast,
    Or, being early pluck'd, is sour to taste.

This is Adonis's 'word in edgeways' for it must be allowed that it is the goddess who does nearly all the talking in this burning long poem.

Hamlet expresses, to Polonius's face, his impatience with old unvenerable men with grey beards and wrinkled faces, 'their eyes purging thick amber and **plum-tree** gum' (II, ii, 199).

And in a very odd and unfamiliar long scene in *King Henry VI, Part Two* (II, i, 95 and 102) a Scots impostor called Saunder Simpcox has his lying exposed by Gloster before the King. He contradicts himself, and says he is lame through falling off a plum tree in his youth. Gloster remarks: 'Mass, thou lov'st **plums** well, that would venture so.'

For the passing reference to the plum in *King John* see under CHERRY.

POMEGRANATES

In *All's Well That Ends Well* (ii, iii, 250) the old Lord Lafeu gives the young braggart Parolles a lesson in good breeding, in the course of which he says to him: 'Go to, sir, you were beaten in Italy for picking a kernel out of a **pomegranate**, you are a vagabond, and no true traveller: you are more saucy with lords and honourable personages than the commission of your birth and virtue gives you heraldry. You are not worth another word, else I'd call you knave. I leave you.' In its explicitness and its subtle rhythm and precise phrasing, this is the perfection of Shakespearean prose.

In *Romeo and Juliet* (iii, v, 1–5), a much more famous passage, Juliet at a window overlooking Capulet's orchard says to her Romeo:

> Wilt thou be gone? It is not yet near day:
> It was the nightingale, and not the lark,
> That pierced the fearful hollow of thine ear;
> Nightly she sings on yon **pomegranate** tree:
> Believe me, love, it was the nightingale.

And every member of every audience – even though he or she would not know a pomegranate tree if he or she saw one – is thrilled by the whole scene that so begins, and is instinctively conscious of listening to the perfection of love poetry.

The exotic word pomegranate, moreover, has certainly no double meaning. It is simply a romantic fruit, of no great interest to the human palate, but of the greatest interest to birds because it is packed full of succulent seeds.

POTATOES

It is not so with the potato as it is with the pomegranate.

At the end of *The Merry Wives of Windsor* (v, v, 20) Falstaff enters the midnight forest disguised as Herne the Hunter. One hand holds that of Mistress Ford, and the other that of Mistress Page. Is the fat knight going to fulfil his double desire at last? He calls out in lusty exaltation: 'Let the sky rain **potatoes**; let it thunder to the tune of *Green Sleeves* . . . let there come a tempest of provocation, I will shelter me here.'

Without the prurient professors at one's elbow, one might think that Falstaff is here using the word potatoes about the weather – just as we should use 'cats and dogs'.

But in *Troilus and Cressida* (v, ii, 48) there is a scene in which the cynic Thersites (in company with the revolted Troilus) espies Cressida wantoning with Diomedes; and Thersites has the comment: 'How the devil luxury, with his fat rump and **potato-finger**, tickles these together! Fry, lechery, fry!' Here the meaning cannot have an innocent front, and must be as guilty as anything can be in this most *permissive* of all plays.

One scholar, Henry Hudson, does not shirk the implication here when he defines 'luxury', though he shields himself behind a much older and unnamed authority: 'Luxury, or lasciviousness, is said to have a "potato finger", because the potato was thought to "strengthen the bodie, and procure bodily lust". See *The Merry Wives*, v, v, 20.'

Potatoes, in a word, are – or used to be – regarded as aphrodisiacal. And old Falstaff knew it as well.

PRIMROSES

No two characters in the whole of Shakespeare could be less alike than Ophelia and the drunken Porter in Macbeth's castle. Yet both use the word primrose as an adjective describing the more irresponsible and reckless sort of highroad through life to ultimate doom. With the Porter it is 'the **primrose** way to the everlasting bonfire' (*Macbeth*, II, iii, 20). With Ophelia, still sane, and counselling her brother at parting, it is 'the **primrose** path of dalliance' (*Hamlet*, I, iii, 50).

Elsewhere, and mainly used as a noun, the blossom is a symbol of paleness and chaste charm. Arviragus throws upon the tomb of fair Fidele 'the flower that's like thy face, pale **primrose**' (*Cymbeline*, IV, ii, 222). Hermia and her 'sweet playfellow', Lysander, 'upon faint **primrose** beds were wont to lie' (*A Midsummer Night's Dream*, I, i, 215). And Perdita in *The Winter's Tale* utters about the primrose three lines in all (IV, iv, 122) which may be questionable as botany but are unquestionable as poetry:

> . . . pale **primroses**,
> That die unmarried, ere they can behold
> Bright Phoebus in his strength (a malady
> Most incident to maids) . . .

PRUNES

One must record, upon close inquiry into the matter, that Shakespearean prunes are quite as suspect as Shakespearean potatoes (q.v.). Only the Clown in *The Winter's Tale* (IV, iii, 48) would seem to be referring to the actual fruit, the dried plum. This is in his list of groceries for the sheep-shearing festival which concludes with 'four pounds of **prunes,** and as many of raisins o' the sun'.

It is significant that every other reference to prunes would appear to have a debased double-meaning and generally happens in a disorderly place. The 'dish of stewed **prunes'** – such as that dwelt upon in *Measure for Measure* (II, i repeatedly) – was just another name for a posse of prostitutes, since the dish was one much favoured by that particular class of person. Pompey tells this long and much-interrupted story of Mistress Elbow and her longing for stewed prunes, and draws into his narration the foolish gentleman called Froth who had been 'cracking the stones of the foresaid **prunes'** – all this narration has as many involutions of meaning as we may care to imagine. As the story apparently has no end, Angelo interrupts it like an impatient drama critic (II, i, 131):

> This will last out a night in Russia
> When nights are longest there: I'll take my leave ...

In another disorderly house – or at least the tavern in Eastcheap – Falstaff tells his hostess: 'There's no more faith in thee than in a stewed **prune.'** (*King Henry IV, Part One*, III, iii, 112). And in *Part Two* (II, iv, 140) Doll Tearsheet in a voluble rage tells Pistol to his face that he 'lives upon mouldy stewed **prunes** and dried cakes'.

And only Slender in *The Merry Wives* (I, ii, 260) may *not* be quibbling about prunes when he addresses Anne Page as follows (*veneys* being thrusts or bouts at fencing):

I bruised my shin th'other day with playing at sword and dagger with a master of fence (three veneys for a dish of stewed **prunes**), and, by my troth, I cannot abide the smell of hot meat since. Why do your dogs bark so? be there bears i' the town?

This would rather seem to suggest that by 'a dish of stewed

WSP–G

prunes' Slender means genuine prunes, and that he finds them to be a non-apéritif, a non-whetter of the appetite for meat. But even this is dubious and uncertain. The rest of the little scene is well worth reading, nevertheless, for that marvellously topical and vivid reference to bear-baiting, giving as it does some indication of all that that pastime meant to the Elizabethans.

PRUNING and GRAFTING

Without even a mention of the word pruning the Gardener in *King Richard II* (III, iv, 63) masterfully describes the whole point of the process in exactly ten words:

> ... superfluous branches
> We lop away, that bearing boughs may live.

Orlando calls Old Adam a tree beyond pruning, in *As You Like It* (II, iii, 63)

> Poor old man, thou **prun'st** a rotten tree,
> That cannot so much as a blossom yield,
> In lieu of all thy pains and husbandry.

And there are other and lesser references to pruning, which must be almost as old as the Garden of Eden.

But grafting was so new a process that Shakespeare's usage fluctuates between the two forms *graff* and *graft* (and the Oxford Dictionary not very happily or helpfully comments that 'the nature of the *t* is uncertain').

In the scene already quoted, Richard II's Queen rebukes her Gardener for comparing – in a speech she overhears – his garden to the state of England under her husband's rule:

> Gardener, for telling me these news of woe,
> Pray God the plants thou **graft'st** may never grow.

Shallow (in *King Henry IV, Part Two*, v, iii, 3) invites Falstaff into his west-country orchard: 'We will eat a last year's pippin of my own **graffing**, with a dish of carraways, and so forth.' (See, too, under MEDLAR).

And there are figurative mentions of graff and graft in other plays, too numerous to mention. The most striking and least familiar of all is in a poem not a play. It is a musing of the raped Lucrece (lines 1058–64), speaking of her own fate and future, and addressing her absent husband:

> Well, well, dear Collatine, thou shalt not know
> The stainèd taste of violated troth;
> I will not wrong thy true affection so,
> To flatter thee with an infringèd oath;
> This bastard **graff** shall never come to growth;
> He shall not boast who did thy stock pollute
> That thou are doting father of his fruit.

PURPLES

Most of the scholars and editors completely ignore three lines in *Hamlet* (IV, vii, 168) in the course of Gertrude's description of the manner in which the mad Ophelia drowned herself. They concern the 'fantastic garlands' she had made to wear when she perished:

> Of crow-flowers, nettles, daisies, and long **purples**
> That liberal shepherds give a grosser name,
> But our cold maids do dead men's fingers call them.

One would hazard the guess that the purple is the cuckoo-pint or wild arum 'whose tiny green flowers are densely packed in a stout spike projecting upwards' (to quote a popular guide to wild flowers in Britain).

Here the curious reader may like to be reminded of the

remark of Thersites about the potato-finger. (See under POTATOES). Anyhow, both the purple and the potato-finger are manifestly phallic.

· QUINCES AND DATES

Here again two fruits are conjoined because Shakespeare himself conjoined them. The occasion is Capulet's all-night supper-party before Juliet is supposed to marry the County Paris; and the scene (IV, iv) begins with Lady Capulet saying to the Nurse: 'Hold, take these keys and fetch more spices, nurse.' To which the Nurse replies: 'They call for **dates** and **quinces** in the pastry.'

The date by itself, and as a fruit, recurs at least twice. It is mentioned obscurely in *All's Well That Ends Well* (I, i, 155) where Parolles has one of his more cryptic observations: 'Your **date** is better in your pie and your porridge than in your cheek.' Again, and still more obscurely, in *Troilus and Cressida* (I, ii, 255) where Cressida has an unelucidated reply to Pandarus who has been stating all the qualities that best become a man: 'Ay, a minced man; and then to be baked with no **date** in the pie, for then the man's **date** is out.' A furtive Elizabethan quibble may be suspected here, or at least some low forgotten slang.

The quince, on the other hand, does not recur – excepting, of course, as the surname of Peter Quince, the carpenter (*A Midsummer Night's Dream*), the bluff, hearty, intensely human leader, director, producer, conductor, and prompter of the Athenian Thespians.

RHUBARB

This word 'rhubarb' denotes something more than the busy murmur of a stage mob, Roman or otherwise. It also bobs up – Shakespeare's one and only use of it – in *Macbeth* (v, iv, 55) – as a purgative medicine or means of getting rid of waste-matter (in this case the English army led by Siward). Macbeth, near the end of his tether, says to his doctor:

> What **rhubarb**, senna, or what purgative drug,
> Would scour these English hence? Hear'st thou of them?

But of the actual fruit, the common rhubarb, the plant of the genus Rheum, there is no mention whatever in Shakespeare. The gastronomers – like Edward Bunyard and André Simon, already quoted – also treat it with silent contempt, though the latter admits the existence of an Old English 'wine' made from its juice, and has a final dismissive and delightfully characteristic comment on this homely beverage: 'It needs a little lemon and a great deal of much else to have any flavour and to be acceptable.' (What a delicate command of English in a French-born connoisseur!)

ROSES

Of the countless references to the rose in Shakespeare one can only fashion here an 'odorous chaplet' of the rarest and least familiar – necessarily a purely personal choice:
(1) Laertes' exclamation (*Hamlet*, iv, v, 155) on seeing that his sister Ophelia has lost her reason:

> O **rose** of May!

(2) The bilious Don John (*Much Ado About Nothing*, I, iii, 22) on the subject of his bluff brother, Don Pedro:

> I had rather be a canker in a hedge than a **rose** in his grace.

(3) Sir James Tyrrel on the two little Princes he has murdered (*King Richard III*, IV, iii, 12):

> Their lips were four red **roses** on a stalk,
> Which in their summer beauty kissed each other.

(4) Othello just before he smothers his Desdemona (V, ii, 13)

> ... When I have plucked the **rose**,
> I cannot give it vital growth again,
> It needs must wither: I'll smell it on the tree.

(5) Friar Laurence warning Juliet of the effect of his potion (*Romeo and Juliet*, IV, i, 100):

> The **roses** in thy lips and cheeks shall fade
> To paly ashes; thy eyes' windows fall,
> Like death, when he shuts up the day of life.

(6) Berowne in *Love's Labour's Lost* (I, i, 105) expresses his spry philosophy:

> At Christmas I no more desire a **rose**
> Than wish a snow in May's new-fangled shows.

(7) Titania describes the upset of the seasons (*A Midsummer Night's Dream*, II, i, 107):

> ... hoary-headed frosts
> Fall in the fresh lap of the crimson **rose**

(8) The Earl of Somerset warns his enemy how to pick his emblem in that spacious play, *King Henry VI*, which may be said to cover the whole history of the Wars of the Roses (*Part One*, II, iv, 48):

Prick not your finger as you pluck it off,
Lest bleeding you do paint the white **rose** red,
And fall on my side so against your will.

(9) A comment of Venus in the inexhaustible poem (*Venus and Adonis*, line 574) about her insatiable love:

What though the **rose** have prickles, yet 'tis plucked.

(10) The opening of the 95th Sonnet:

How sweet and lovely dost thou make the shame
Which, like a canker in the fragrant **rose**,
Doth spot the beauty of thy budding name!

But one returns to the very first and the shortest of these references as being the loveliest of all. These four words are the test of any satisfactory Laertes – making in themselves a tiny poem of sheer sensibility. Across many years – away back in 1928 – one clearly recollects the expressive utterance given to them by Eric Portman in his youth:

O **rose** of May,
Dear maid, kind sister, sweet Ophelia!

His Ophelia was the unforgotten, unforgettable, Jean Forbes-Robertson.

ROSEMARY AND RUE

One herb follows the other in alphabetical order, and it is happily to our purpose that Shakespeare's flower-maiden Perdita should entwine the two in her greeting to some distinguished visitors (*The Winter's Tale*, IV, iv, 73):

... Reverend sirs,
For you there's **rosemary** and **rue**; these keep
Seeming and savour all the winter long;

Grace and remembrance be to you both,
And welcome to our shearing!

They are both, again, among Ophelia's offering of
emblematic herbs. She hands rosemary to her brother (iv, v,
75): 'There's **rosemary**, that's for remembrance – pray you,
love, remember.' And a line or two later she hands rue to
Queen Gertrude: 'There's **rue** for you, and here's some for
me, we may call it herb of grace o' Sundays. – O, you must
wear your **rue** with a difference.' (How memorably did the
late Martita Hunt – best of Gertrudes – break down with
weeping at this point!)

In *Romeo and Juliet* (iv, v, 80) Friar Laurence tells Capulet,
who is helpless with grief, what to do with his apparently dead
daughter:

Dry up your tears, and stick your **rosemary**
On this fair corpse, and, as the custom is,
In all her best array bear her to church.

In *King Lear* (ii, iii, 16) the naked Edgar disguises himself as a
wandering beggarman by piercing his arms with 'pins,
wooden pricks, nails, sprigs of **rosemary**'.

In *Pericles* the wandering and lost Marina finds herself
immured in a brothel in Mitylene, deeply against her will. In
the background the Bawd's servant exclaims: 'She makes our
profession as it were to stink afore the face of the gods.' The
old Bawd (himself or herself – the sex is unspecified) caustically
reproves Marina for her tenacious virtue: 'Marry, come up,
my dish of chastity with **rosemary** and bays.' (iv, vi, 147).

And we have rue reappearing at the end of the garden scene
in *King Richard II* (iii, iv, 104) where the old Gardener, in
spite of the Queen having just set a curse upon him, very
touchingly says:

Here did she fall a tear; here in this place

I'll set a bank of **rue**, sour herb of grace:
Rue, even for ruth, here shortly shall be seen,
In the remembrance of a weeping queen.

RYE

The Banished Duke's two page-boys (*As You Like It*, v, iv)
deliver their duet 'It Was a Lover and his Lass', and we are told
in the second stanza that it was 'between the acres of the **rye**'
that 'these pretty country folks would lie'. Their only reward
at the end is a severe notice from that implacable music-critic
Touchstone: 'I count it but time lost to hear such a foolish
song. God be wi' you, and God mend your voices!' (v, iv, 36).
But the song at least serves to remind us that a field of rye was
a suitable place for 'coming through' – long, long before
Burns's lass 'draiglet a' her petticoatie' in so doing.

Both of the other allusions to rye occur in *The Tempest*. For
one, see under OATS. For the other let the reader read –
preferably aloud – the marvellous opening lines of the
goddess Iris in the masque conjured up by Prospero (IV, i,
128–38):

You nymphs called Naiads of the windring brooks,
With your sedged crowns, and ever harmless looks,
Leave your crisp channels, and on this green land
Answer your summons; Juno does command;
Come, temperate nymphs, and help to celebrate
A contract of true love; be not too late. –
You sunburn'd sicklemen, of August weary,
Come hither from the furrow, and be merry,
Make holiday; your **rye-straw** hats put on,
And these fresh nymphs encounter every one
In country footing.

Transcendent verbal autumnal beauty! Yet in 350 years it would not seem to have occurred to any director of *The Tempest* that Miranda might easily 'double' the part of Iris (usually given to some inexpressive beginner). Miranda herself is a notoriously unrewarding part since she has very little to do except dally keenly with young Ferdinand and suppress yawns at her old father's long autobiographical narrations. Will the next Granville Barker look to this possibility of giving her something better to do?

SAFFRON

This preparation from the Autumn Crocus (*Crocus Sativus*) must be one of the yellowest substances in cookery, if not in nature. In England its place has largely been taken by curry, in the last century or so. But the new working poor-or-rich who take their holidays in the Mediterranean have of late been known to ask for it at their grocers when they fancy themselves in the making of such dishes *chez eux* as paella and the like, to which saffron gives the necessary colouring and flavour to the rice.

The few references to saffron faces or objects are all, let it be granted, somewhat recondite, and rather dim and dull despite the colour.

When in *The Comedy of Errors* (IV, iv, 60) Antipholus of Ephesus, berating his wife, Adriana, refers to her 'companion with the **saffron** face', it is hard to know – or care – whether or not he is referring to the schoolmaster Pinch who is in the same scene.

When the Clown in *The Winter's Tale* (IV, iii, 48) says that he 'must have **saffron** to colour the warden pies' we note and remember that 'warden' is an old word for a cooking pear (nowadays coloured with cochineal instead of saffron as of old).

When old Lafeu in *All's Well* (IV, v, 2-3) tells the Countess of Rousillon that her son Bertram has been 'misled with a snipt-taffeta fellow there, whose villainous **saffron** would have made all the unbaked and doughy youth of a nation in his colour', we wince once again at that tedious old bumbler's tautological abstruseness.

When in the mythological masque in *The Tempest* (IV, i, 78) Ceres hails Iris

> Who, with thy **saffron** wings, upon my flowers
> Diffusest honey-drops, refreshing showers

we may even have a disloyal thought that here Shakespeare may be harking forward some twenty years or so to another masque with a mythological flavour called *Comus*.

SAMPHIRE

Edgar in *King Lear* (IV, vi, 11-15) describes to his blinded father, Gloster, the dizzy view from a lofty cliff-top which Gloster is planning to jump from:

> Come on, sir; here's the place: stand still. How fearful
> And dizzy 'tis to cast one's eyes so low!
> The crows and choughs that wing the midway air
> Show scarce so gross as beetles: half way down
> Hangs one that gathers **samphire**, dreadful trade!

One editor, Hudson, has the note: 'In Shakespeare's time the cliffs of Dover were noted for the production of this plant. It was made into a pickle and eaten with relish.' He goes on to quote a history of the town of Waterford in Ireland, dated 1774: 'Samphire grows in plenty on most of the sea-cliffs in this country. It is terrible to see how people gather it, hanging by a rope several fathom from the top of the impending rocks, as it were in the air.'

But all these several writers (including Shakespeare) appear not to know that samphire grows also in salt marshes where it is easily accessible. As an odd-looking semi-seaweed it can be bought cheaply, for example, in the fish markets of Grimsby, in Lincolnshire, where it was eaten with gusto – or could be, twenty years ago, and doubtless still is.

SCENTS, PERFUMES, ODOURS

Carry him gently to my fairest chamber,
And hang it round with all my wanton pictures:
Balm his foul head in warm distillèd waters,
And burn sweet wood to make the lodging sweet.
> (The Lord in the Induction in
> *The Taming of the Shrew*, I, 44–7)

That strain again! it had a dying fall:
O, it came o'er my ear like the sweet south,
That breathes upon a bank of violets,
Stealing, and giving odour!
> (Orsino in *Twelfth Night*, I, i, 4–7)

To throw a perfume on the violet . . .
Is wasteful and ridiculous excess.
> (Duke of Salisbury in *King John*, IV, ii, 12)

For Hamlet, and the trifling of his favour,
Hold it a fashion, and a toy in blood,
A violet in the youth of primy nature,
Forward, not permanent, sweet, not lasting,
The perfume and suppliance of a minute;
No more.   (Laertes to Ophelia in *Hamlet*, I, iii, 6–10)

Then will I raise aloft the milk-white rose,
With whose sweet smell the air shall be perfum'd,
And in my standard bear the arms of York,
To grapple with the house of Lancaster
    (Duke of York in *King Henry VI, Part Two*, I, i, 252–5)

The fields are fragrant, and the woods are green
    (Titus in *Titus Andronicus*, II, ii, 2)

An odorous chaplet of sweet summer buds
    (Titania in *A Midsummer Night's Dream*, II, i, 110)

QUINCE: Speak, Pyramus. Thisby, stand forth.
BOTTOM: Thisby, the flowers of odious savours sweet –
QUINCE: Odours, odorous
BOTTOM: – odours, savours sweet:
  So hath thy breath, my dearest Thisby, dear.
    (*A Midsummer Night's Dream*, III, i, 75–9)

Hence! I am qualmish at the smell of leek.
    (Pistol to Fluellen in *King Henry V*, v, i, 20)

Lilies that fester smell far worse than weeds.
    (line 14 in *Sonnet No. 94*)

STRAW

The marvellously evocative entrance-line for the prisoner
Barnadine in *Measure for Measure* has already been commented
upon (see under HAY AND STRAW).

  But straw, squalid straw, to cover the stone flooring of a
rough cell or sty, is also introduced, three times at least, in
King Lear. First when the old King, at the very edge of his
madness, says to his Fool (III, ii, 67):

My wits begin to turn –
Come on, my boy: how dost, my boy? art cold?
I'm cold myself. – Where is this **straw**, my fellow?
The art of our necessities is strange,
That can make vile things precious. Come, your hovel. –

Again when Kent espies the fugitive Edgar covered in straw
in the same hovel and calls out: 'What art thou that does
grumble there i' the **straw**? Come forth.' And yet again when
Cordelia has recovered her royal father, and nurses him, and
has her piercingly piteous comment (IV, vii, 36–9):

Mine enemy's dog,
Though he had bit me, should have stood that night
Against my fire; and wast thou fain, poor father,
To hovel thee with swine and rogues forlorn,
In short and musty **straw**? Alack, alack!

One thinks of the three great Lears of modern times, and
names them in ascending order of merit – Olivier, Gielgud,
Scofield.

In almost every other allusion in the plays the word straw is
used as a mere symbol of triviality and worthlessness. But
there is a very striking use of the rare adjective strawy in
Troilus and Cressida (V, v, 26) in Nestor's description of the
ubiquitous valour of Hector in the field:

How here he fights . . . Then is he yonder,
And there the **strawy** Greeks, ripe for his edge,
Fall down before him, like the mower's swath.

STRAWBERRIES

The incidental mention of the strawberry in *King Henry V*
(I, i, 60) occurs in a mere piece of sententiousness uttered by the

Bishop of Ely about the wildness of the new King before his recent Coronation:

> The **strawberry** grows underneath the nettle,
> And wholesome berries thrive and ripen best
> Neighbour'd by fruit of baser quality;
> And so the prince obscur'd his contemplation
> Under the veil of wildness . . .

And as for the casual mention of strawberries in *Othello* (III, iii, 439), it is as a mere decoration on the fateful handkerchief, though it occurs in a passage which is the very essence of red-hot, alarming drama:

> IAGO: Have you not sometimes seen a handkerchief
> Spotted with **strawberries** in your wife's hand?
> OTHELLO: I gave her such a one, 'twas my first gift.
> IAGO: I know not that, but such a handkerchief
> (I am sure it was your wife's) did I today
> See Cassio wipe his beard with.

But in *King Richard III* (III, iv, 36) it is the actual luscious fruit which is commanded, sent for, brought, and enjoyed. Gloster ingeniously thinks up this device that he may have a conference – short, dangerous, and secret – with Buckingham apropos the swift beheading of Hastings:

> GLOSTER: My Lord of Ely!
> ELY: My lord?
> GLOSTER: When I was last in Holborn,
>   I saw good **strawberries** in your garden there
>   I do beseech you send for some of them.

The Bishop of Ely returns to find Hastings alone: 'Where is my lord protector? I have sent for these **strawberries**.' He had sent, doubtless, to Ely Place, at the east end of Holborn. It is still there, with its church of St Etheldrede which is certainly

older than the fifteenth century. It still has remnants of a
garden, though, no less certainly, no strawberries. One seems
to remember – possibly in his film version of the play – the
relish and speed with which Olivier's unsurpassed Richard
devoured his strawberries while waiting for his next gift to be
brought to him – the head of Hastings.*

THISTLES

The Scottish national emblem makes a few appearances in
Shakespeare, but none whatever in *Macbeth*. Still more surprisingly it is not even mentioned by the only other Scottish
character outside *Macbeth*, Captain Jamy in *King Henry V*, a
play which has so much mention of the national emblem of
Wales. In the same play, though, the Duke of Burgundy
mentions 'rough **thistles**' among the weeds with which his
land is overgrown in time of war. (See under BURDOCKS
AND DOCKS).

The thistle crops up again in the most fairy-like *bonne bouche*
thought up by Bottom the Weaver when in thrall to Titania
(*A Midsummer Night's Dream*, IV, i, 10):

Mounsieur Cobweb, good mounsieur, get you your weapons in your
hand, and kill me a red-hipped humble-bee on the top of a **thistle**;
and, good mounsieur, bring me the honey-bag. Do not fret yourself
too much in the action, mounsieur; and, good mounsieur, have a care
the honey-bag break not; I would be loth to have you overflown
with a honey-bag, signior.

That is delightful. Less delightful altogether is the only othre

---

* Sir Laurence himself corrects us at this point. The Richard III who
brought off this 'business' in England (first devised by the American
actor, Edwin Booth) was that of Donald Wolfit.

instance of a thistle in the whole of Shakespeare – in the little scene between the four ladies in *Much Ado About Nothing* (III, iv, 65) – Beatrice and Hero, Margaret and Ursula:

MARGARET: Doth not my wit become me rarely?
BEATRICE: It is not seen enough; you should wear it in your cap. – By my troth, I am sick.
MARGARET: Get you some of this distilled Carduus Benedictus, and lay it to your heart; it is the only thing for a qualm.
HERO: There thou prickest her with a **thistle**.
BEATRICE: Benedictus! why Benedictus? You have some moral in this Benedictus.
MARGARET: Moral! no, by my troth, I have no moral meaning; I meant, plain holy-**thistle**.

This little scene is usually cut in the theatre, and deserves to be. Its effect – or the effect of this page at least – depends on the audience knowing that *carduus* is the Latin for thistle. No audience ever does. Beatrice's answer to Margaret's first question ought to be 'No!' Her behaviour is unbecoming, and her wit is nil. She is also murkily involved in Don John's nefarious plot that all but ruins Hero.

THORNS

Most of the thorns in the plays are symbolical or metaphorical, and not botanical or sharp.

But one of the Lord's 'wanton pictures' which Christopher Sly is expected to revel in is thus described in the Induction to *The Taming of the Shrew* (Scene ii, 57–60):

> Daphne roaming through a **thorny** wood,
> Scratching her legs, that one shall swear she bleeds,
> And at that sight shall sad Apollo weep,
> So workmanly the blood and tears are drawn.

WSP–H

It is, too, an unspecified bush of thorn which, in *A Midsummer Night's Dream*, one of the 'hempen homespuns' playing Moon carries in one hand, with a lantern in the other. He says so, categorically and with justifiable cold anger, to quieten his chattering audience at the actual performance (v, i, 248):

All that I have to say, is to tell you, that the lanthorn is the moon, I the man i' the moon, this **thorn-bush** my **thorn-bush**, and this dog my dog.

Repeatedly in the Sonnets (notably Nos. 35, 54, 99) the poet declares the thorns to be the only faults in the perfect rose that is his love.

THYME

See under HYSSOP, where Iago's very important and Machiavellianly subtle speech beginning: 'Virtue? A fig!' is quoted at length, as it should be studied at length. The words 'weed up **thyme**' in one line are of much less moment or significance than almost any other line in the speech. It is really a soliloquy illuminating the speaker's own character, and Roderigo to whom it is addressed quite palpably makes nothing of it. Any first-rate Iago must protest at the deletion of so much as a syllable of this, one of the key-speeches of the part. In the theatre, as often as not, it is abridged and mangled.

Much better known and much simpler is Oberon's reference to thyme (*A Midsummer Night's Dream*, II, i, 250):

> I know a bank where the wild **thyme** blows,
> Where oxlips and the nodding violet grows ...
> There sleeps Titania, sometime of the night,
> Lull'd in these flowers, with dances and delight ...

All this has much less to do with chop logic than with moon magic. Puck has just delivered to the speaker the love-philtre brought from the far ends of the earth. And Oberon tells us what he is going to do with it:

> And with the juice of this I'll streak her eyes,
> And make her full of hateful fantasies.

TREES IN GENERAL

Again one can but give ten of the many instances.

Gloster in *King Richard III* (i, ii, 163) can provide a touch of poetry when it suits his fell purpose. He is speaking of the dreadful past to the Lady Anne, and telling how –

> . . . all the standers-by had wet their cheeks
> Like **trees** bedash'd with rain . . .

Lorenzo in *The Merchant of Venice* (v, i, 2) tells Jessica of romantic happenings ages long ago on just such a moonlit night as they are now enjoying:

> When the sweet wind did gently kiss the **trees**,
> And they did make no noise.

Rosalind tells Orlando (*As You Like It*, iii, ii, 276) to commit no more nuisance in the Forest of Arden: 'Mar no more **trees** with writing love-songs in their barks.'

Biron in *Love's Labour's Lost* (iv, iii, 324) speaks ineffably beautiful things largely to himself:

> For valour, is not Love a Hercules,
> Still climbing **trees** in the Hesperides?

The monarch in *King Henry VI* tells Gloster of the many nasty things that happened on the day he (Gloster) was born:

'Dogs howled, and hideous tempest shook down **trees**.' (*Part Three*, v, vi, 46).

Macbeth tells his guilty Lady of the accursed and inescapable consequences of murder (III, iv, 123):

> It will have blood they say: blood will have blood:
> Stones have been known to move, and **trees** to speak.

Octavius Caesar reminds himself before Lepidus how bark had been part of Antony's fare in rough soldiering days (*Antony and Cleopatra*, I, iv, 65):

> Yea, like the stag, when snow the pasture sheets
> The barks of **trees** thou browsedst ...

One of the songs in *As You Like It* is exquisite from its opening lines which are 'Under the greenwood **tree**, Who loves to lie with me'.

The song in *King Henry VIII* contrives to be both magical and mythological from the very start:

> Orpheus with his lute made **trees**,
> And the mountain tops that freeze,
> Bow themselves when he did sing ...

And, finally, Posthumus Leonatus (in *Cymbeline*, v, v, 264) pays his long-lost wife Imogen an ineffably beautiful compliment when at long last they come face to face again, and she embraces him, and he says:

> Hang there like fruit, my soul, till the **tree** die!

It is a line one has never heard spoken with anything like the rapturous bliss it surely deserves.

VETCHES

Thy rich leas
Of wheat, rye, barley, **vetches**, oats, and pease

The gramineous list of the goddess Iris in *The Tempest* has already been quoted and commented upon, notably under BARLEY and OATS.

The vetch belongs to the same vegetable family as the pea (a name which the old music hall, with its positively Shakespearean partiality for a pun, thought no end of a joke!). There is the bush vetch, the tufted vetch, the yellow milk-vetch. There is, likewise, the meadow pea, the marsh pea, the sea pea, and the everlasting pea.

VINES

Shakespeare's – and John Fletcher's? – play of *King Henry VIII* concludes with Thomas Cranmer, Archbishop of Canterbury, addressing the Princess Elizabeth, a babe-in-arms (later to be Queen Elizabeth). In this noble speech the author makes the vine a symbol of earthly bliss for her workaday subjects (v, v, 32):

Good grows with her:
In her days every man shall eat in safety,
Under his own **vine**, what he plants; and sing
The merry songs of peace to all his neighbours.

This, whoever wrote it, could hardly be better said.

Less noble, definitely, is the mention of the vine in the drinking song in *Antony and Cleopatra* (II, vii, 115). There is no earthly reason why we should expect nobility in a drinking song. But one might, at least, look for a better rhyme at the beginning:

> Come, thou monarch of the **vine**,
> Plumpy Bacchus with pink eyne!
> In thy fats our cares be drown'd,
> With thy grapes our hairs be crown'd:
> Cup us till the world go round,
> Cup us till the world go round!

This drinking song, in fact, could hardly be worse. It has not even the inebriated inconsequence of the one in *Othello* with the refrain 'And let me the canakin clink!'

VIOLETS

See also under CUCKOO-BUDS, DAISIES, and SCENTS, PERFUMES, ODOURS.

Three further descriptions of the violet are much too fine to be omitted, even though there have been so many, here and there.

Perdita's famous lines in *The Winter's Tale* (IV, iv, 120) cannot possibly be taken as read, not only because of their fleeting mention in thirteen words of two goddesses (two, no less!), but also for the exquisite placing of the uncannily apt adjective 'dim':

> ... **violets** dim,
> But sweeter than the lids of Juno's eyes,
> Or Cytherea's breath ...

Laertes' impulsive and grief-stricken words over the open and waiting grave of Ophelia are almost as perfect and almost as familiar (*Hamlet*, V, i, 240):

Lay her i' the earth,
And from her fair and unpolluted flesh,
May **violets** spring!

But quite unfamiliar and seldom quoted – and in every way as choice – must be the description by Belisarius of his 'two princely boys' in *Cymbeline* (IV, ii, 172):

They are as gentle
As zephyrs, blowing below the **violet**,
Not wagging his sweet head . . .

Violets dim!

WALNUTS

The walnut is seldom met with in Shakespeare. It is, in fact, only the shell of its proper self. The kernel is totally absent. So, too, is the tree.

Petruchio in *The Taming of the Shrew* (IV, iii, 65) violently criticizes the man-milliner and his idea of a hat for Kate:

HABERDASHER: Here is the cap your worship did bespeak.
PETRUCHIO: Why this was moulded on a porringer,
  A velvet dish; fie, fie! 'tis lewd and filthy,
  Why, 'tis a cockle or a **walnut-shell**,
  A knack, a toy, a trip, a baby's cap . . .

And the madly jealous Ford in *The Merry Wives of Windsor* (IV, ii, 150) looking in vain for Falstaff in the buck-basket describes himself in the third person, and with considerable self-knowledge: 'As jealous as Ford, that searched a hollow **walnut** for his wife's leman.' Falstaff who is called most things in his stormy course is nowhere else called a leman or paramour. He is called many worse things in what remains of this play –

a fat knight, a hodge-pudding, a bag of flax, a puffed man, and 'old, cold, withered, and of intolerable entrails'.

WEEDS AND WEEDING

KING: How well he's read, to reason against reading!
DUMAIN: Proceeded well, to stop all good proceeding!
LONGAVILLE: He **weeds** the corn, and still lets grow the **weeding**.
BIRON: The spring is near, when green geese are a-breeding.
DUMAIN: How follows that?
BIRON: Fit in his place and time.
DUMAIN: In reason nothing
BIRON: Something, then, in rhyme.

This snatch of cross-talk – from *Love's Labour's Lost* (I, i, 96–104) – to many of us might seem in reason nothing, and nothing much in rhyme. Yet it might fairly be called the quintessence of a very early play almost every line of which requires an explanatory note. It is the delight of the scholarly. But its euphuism makes it 'caviare to the general'.

In another play, *King Richard II*, there are two widely-apart references which both bring in an odd analogy between weeds and caterpillars (the latter word meaning, as always in Shakespeare, not butterfly grubs, but royal favourites or yes-men). In the first of these (II, iii, 166) Bolingbroke refers to Bushey, Bagot and Co. as:

> The caterpillars of the commonwealth,
> Which I have sworn to **weed** and pluck away.

In the other (III, iv, 46) that eloquent political commentator, the Gardener's apprentice, describes the state of England:

> . . . the whole land
> Is full of **weeds,** her fairest flowers choked up,

> Her fruit-trees all unpruned, her hedges ruined,
> Her knots disordered, and her wholesome herbs
> Swarming with caterpillars.

(By 'knots' here is meant the knot-garden, an example of which can be seen to this day, in beautiful trim, at New Place, Stratford-on-Avon, the house in which Shakespeare died.)

But the most striking symbolic use of the word 'weed' occurs, surely, in *Othello* when the Moor hears his wife say: 'I hope my noble lord esteems me honest', and answers her (IV, ii, 67):

> O, ay; as summer flies are in the shambles,
> That quicken even with blowing. O thou **weed**,
> Who art so lovely fair and smell'st so sweet
> That the sense aches at thee, would thou
> hadst ne'er been born.

The word 'weed' in this passage has always been given great emphasis by the best Othellos in one's experience from Godfrey Tearle down to Olivier, the actors drawing attention to the strange and singular power of such a word in such a context.

In the rightly popular New Temple Edition, that usually sound and reliable scholar, M. R. Ridley, slips and errs badly here by introducing the startling adjective 'black' into the passage. He also alters the lineation and punctuation, on no authority that one can discover. So that it reads:

> O thou *black weed*, why art so lovely fair?
> Thou smell'st so sweet that the sense aches at thee;
> Would thou hadst ne'er been born!

Could any Othello, however insane with jealousy, call his poor little white wife 'black' in any circumstance? Assuredly Desdemona was to Othello a weed unqualified.

WHEAT AND STUBBLE

See also under BARLEY and VETCHES.

Of the golden autumnal condition of wheat as grain – and as we best know it – there is hardly any mention at all. Its spring-time appearance is charmingly caught – *A Midsummer Night's Dream* (I, i, 185) – in Helena's 'When **wheat** is green, when hawthorn-buds appear'.

It changes colour in a snatch of conversation between Justice Shallow and his servant Davy – *King Henry IV, Part Two* (V, i, 14):

DAVY: ... And, again, sir, shall we sow the headland with **wheat**?
SHALLOW: With **red wheat**, Davy.

This is somewhat mysterious, as the discussion is principally about what Falstaff is to be given to eat at supper.

And it changes colour still more mysteriously when Edgar, feigning madness – *King Lear* (III, iv, 118) – tells his father Gloster about the foul fiend who leads him astray: 'This is the foul fiend Flibertigibett: he begins at curfew, and walks till the first cock; he gives the web and the pin, squinies the eye, and makes the hare-lip, mildews the **white wheat**, and hurts the poor creature of earth.'

White wheat? One does not pretend to understand. But then neither – to judge from their almost complete silence on this particular subject – does any editor, scholar, authority, or commentator.

It is almost a relief to get away from these various mysterious grades of wheat, and come to a healthy mention of stubble – in *King Henry IV, Part One* (I, iii, 35) – in Hotspur's breezy scornful tirade about an un-soldierlike soldier:

Came there a certain lord, neat and trimly dressed,
Fresh as a bridegroom, and his chin new-reaped
Showed like a **stubble-land** at harvest-home;
He was perfumèd like a milliner ...

WILLOWS AND SYCAMORES

One thinks first of Desdemona and her 'song of **willow**', as she calls it, in *Othello* (IV, iii, 40). (If one be more opera-minded than Shakespeare-minded we call the song 'Salce', and the work itself *Otello* rather than *Othello*, and its creator Verdi-Boito rather than Shakespeare. There *are* such people in the world.)

It is somehow subtly right that Viola, in a very famous speech, should talk of making a willow cabin at Olivia's gate (*Twelfth Night*, I, v, 268). No other wood would sound at all appropriate. And there is another sort of melancholy magic in the first of Gertrude's lines describing the scene of Ophelia's drowning (*Hamlet*, IV, vii, 167):

There is a **willow** grows aslant a brook,
That shows his hoar leaves in the glassy stream ...

The sycamore has a strong kinship with the maple and the mulberry, the fig and the plane. It is not, like the willow, a particularly morose tree. Boyet in *Love's Labour's Lost* (V, ii, 89) seeks for half an hour's nap 'under the cool shade of a **sycamore**'. Benvolio tells Romeo's mother that he had, very early that morning (*Romeo and Juliet*, I, i, 116) espied her son on the outskirts of Verona:

Underneath the grove of **sycamore**
That westward rooteth from the city's side ...

But it is only in Desdemona's song afore-mentioned that the

sycamore shows an affinity in sadness with the willow. The two trees are conjoined for once:

> The pour soul sat sighing by a **sycamore** tree,
> Sing all a green **willow**
> Her hand on her bosom, her head on her knee,
> Sing **willow, willow, willow** ...

YEW

The yew is a sad tree in Shakespeare, and we reflect that it seems to thrive best in cemeteries, and always did.

The County Paris stumbling through the churchyard to find Juliet's tomb in the monument of the Capulets has two mentions of yew-trees (*Romeo and Juliet*, v, iii).

Whoever is supposed to be delivering Feste's song, 'Come Away, Death' in *Twelfth Night* (II, iv, 55) has the line:

> My shroud of white, stuck all with **yew**,
> O, prepare it!

Yew-twigs turn up, inevitably, among the ingredients of the hell-broth in the Witches' cauldron in *Macbeth* (IV, i, 27):

> Gall of goat, and slips of **yew**,
> Sliver'd in the moon's eclipse ...

In the vile forest in *Titus Andronicus* (II, iii, 105) the Queen of the Goths, Tamora, tells her two sons how her enemies have threatened her:

> No sooner had they told this hellish tale
> But straight they told me they would bind me here
> Unto the body of a dismal **yew**,
> And leave me to this miserable death.

INDEX OF QUOTATIONS